Enacting Power

Enacting Power

The Criminalization of Obeah in the Anglophone Caribbean 1760–2011

Jerome S. Handler
and Kenneth M. Bilby

University of the West Indies Press
Jamaica • Barbados • Trinidad and Tobago

University of the West Indies Press
7A Gibraltar Hall Road   Mona
Kingston 7   Jamaica

www.uwipress.com

© 2012 by Jerome S. Handler and Kenneth M. Bilby

All rights reserved. Published 2012

A catalogue record of this book is available
from the National Library of Jamaica.

ISBN: 978-976-640-315-7

Cover illustration: An obeah woman at work, Paramaribo, Suriname, c.1831, from Pierre Jacques Benoit, *Voyage à Surinam* (Bruxelles, Belgium 1839), plate 12, fig. 36). Courtesy of the John Carter Brown Library.

Cover and book design by Robert Harris.

Set in Adobe Garamond 11/14.5 x 27

Printed in the United States of America.

To

Kamau Brathwaite:

Poet, Scholar, Caribbean Son

Contents

Acknowledgments / *ix*

Introduction / *xi*

1   Divining and Defining Obeah / *1*

2   Anti-Obeah Provisions in the Laws: A Comparative Overview / *16*

       Images of Obeah: Practitioners at Work in Suriname, Trinidad, and Jamaica / *29*

3   Patterns in Governance and Vagrancy Laws: Framing the Development of Anti-Obeah Legislation / *39*

4   The Territories and Their Laws / *45*

       Jamaica / *45*

       Barbados / *53*

       Trinidad and Tobago / *57*

       British Guiana/Guyana / *60*

       The Bahamas / *66*

       Leeward Islands Federation / *68*

Antigua and Barbuda / *70*

Anguilla / *73*

St. Kitts (St. Christopher) and Nevis / *75*

British Virgin Islands / *77*

Montserrat / *79*

Dominica / *81*

Grenada / *85*

St. Lucia / *88*

St. Vincent and the Grenadines / *92*

British Honduras/Belize / *95*

Turks and Caicos / *97*

Cayman Islands / *99*

Conclusion / *102*

Notes / *109*

Note on Sources / *133*

References / *135*

Index / *167*

Acknowledgments

A NUMBER OF COLLEAGUES AND friends provided considerable assistance in identifying, locating, and acquiring research materials: Kent Olson and Amy Wharton (University of Virginia Law Library), Diana Paton (University of Newcastle), Guy Grannum (National Archives [Public Record Office], London), Pamela Barnes Craig (Library of Congress Law Library), and Velma Newton (University of the West Indies Law Library, Cave Hill, Barbados). Khian Lamey, at the time a third-year student at the University of the West Indies Law School (Cave Hill), gave indispensable research assistance during July 2009 in assessing the status of contemporary West Indian laws. Vika Kalesnikava and Stephanie Bergman, graduate students at the University of Virginia and the College of William and Mary, respectively, helped in gathering current information on obeah from online copies of Anglophone Caribbean newspapers.

Other friends and colleagues affiliated with a number of institutions in several countries helped in various ways, from sharing research materials and providing ethnographic information to reading and commenting on section drafts: Hugh Alexander, Randy Browne, Sandra Browne, Trevor Burnard, Marcia Burrowes, Douglas Chambers, Paul Garrett, Barry Gaspar, Katharine Gerbner, Kean Gibson, George Gmelch, Sharon Bohn Gmelch, Jack P. Greene, Ben Guichard, Jay Haviser, Kelly Hayes, Barry Higman, Cynthia Hoehler-Fatton, Lennox Honychurch, JoAnn Jacoby, Cornelia King, Wim Klooster, Jeffrey Mantz, Woodville Marshall, Susan McKinnon, Don Mitchell, J. H. Nketia, Andrew Pilgrim, Justin Shaffner, Hazel Simmons-McDonald, Alvin Thompson, Leslie Tobias-Olsen, and Pedro Welch. David

Richardson did the map of the Caribbean (figure 1) and Mark Hauser was the perfect host, providing congenial hospitality to Handler during a brief field stay in Dominica in the summer of 2011. Handler is particularly grateful to the Virginia Foundation for the Humanities and its president, Robert Vaughan, for continuing moral and material support.

Finally, we give thanks to Kamau Brathwaite, who provided a special kind of inspiration; a "seer" as much as a man of words, he long ago saw through the colonial distortions that are responsible for obeah's bad name and helped to set us on the path that led to this book.

Introduction

> No word of African origin which has survived in the New World has taken on such grim meaning as has the word *obia* in many of the islands of the Caribbean. (Herskovits and Herskovits 1934:307)

WELL OVER TWO AND A half centuries after something called *obeah* was first explicitly criminalized in Jamaica in 1760, a variety of beliefs and practices labeled by this term continue to play a role—sometimes a prominent one—in contemporary West Indian cultures. To varying degrees, depending on the society and the social group, individuals known as obeah practitioners continue to be sought for their services, even though in the popular mind and in governmental and official circles obeah is generally viewed negatively and as a harmful, if not evil, practice. There is, in short, a "continuing popular and official hostility" to obeah in the Anglophone Caribbean (Paton 2009:1).

Negative views and stereotypes of obeah and obeah practitioners, particularly among the elite groups that made the laws and those who supported them, have a long history, and during the period of slavery virtually all territories of the British Caribbean had legislation criminalizing obeah. After emancipation, when slave laws were nullified, anti-obeah legislation was reintroduced. These laws were modified over the years, and penalties for conviction became less severe than during the slavery era. Recent times have seen changes in the laws concerning obeah, reflecting shifting societal attitudes, political positions, and efforts to discard the negative cultural and social legacies of the

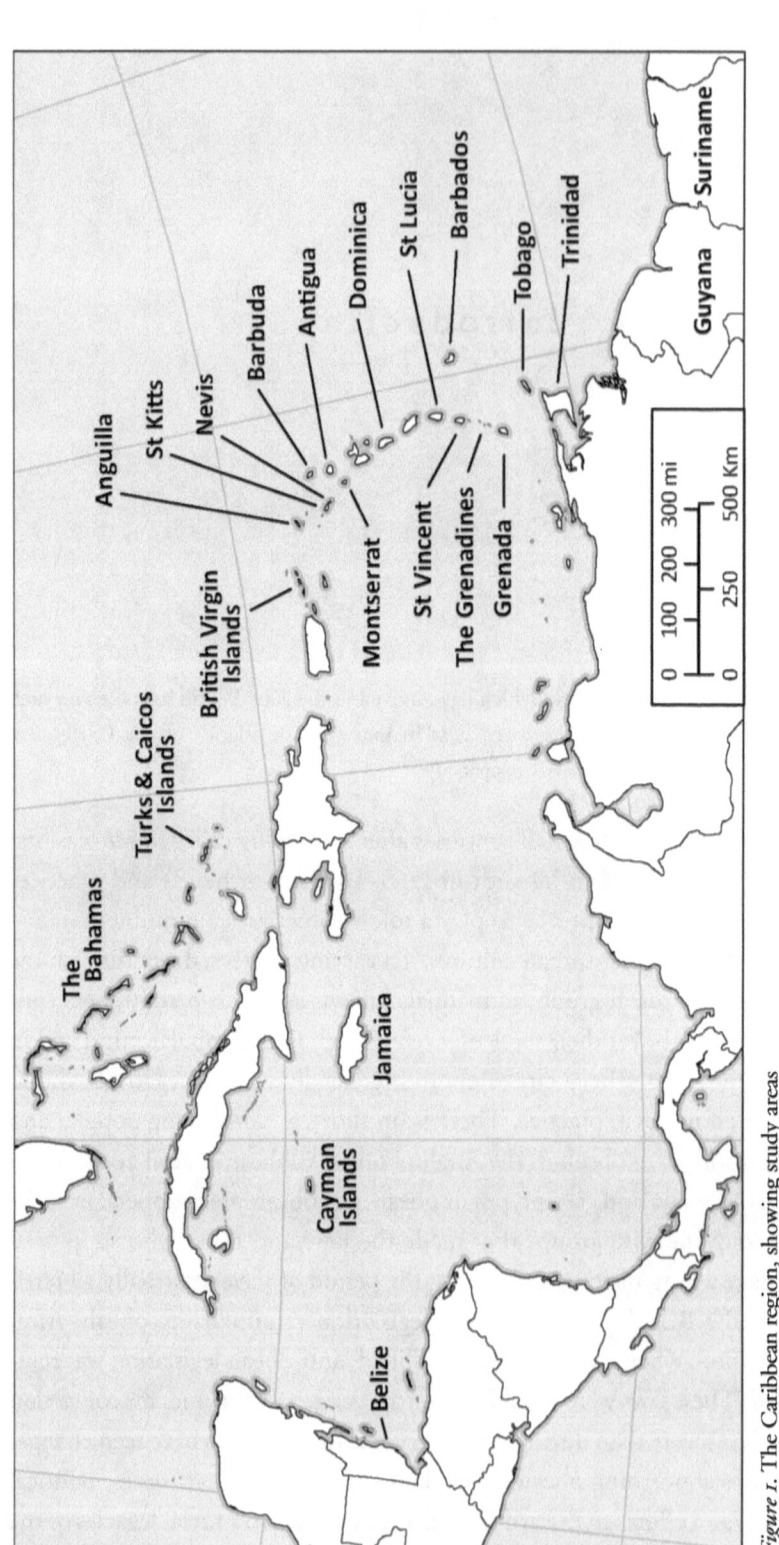

Figure 1. The Caribbean region, showing study areas

slave and colonial past. However, despite these recent ameliorative trends, virtually all of the legal systems of the former British West Indies continue to criminalize obeah. As of 2011, when our research into current laws ceased, only four countries had stricken anti-obeah language from their legal codes: Anguilla (1980), Barbados (1998), Trinidad and Tobago (2000), and St. Lucia (2004). Thus, some two and a half centuries after it was first outlawed in Jamaica, something called obeah is still legally prohibited in most of the Anglophone Caribbean, including both independent countries and current dependencies of Great Britain, although prosecutions have become increasingly rare.[1]

References to laws against obeah are occasionally found in the Caribbean scholarly literature and popular writings, including newspapers—particularly with regard to better-known territories such as Jamaica—but, generally speaking, information on these laws, their contents, and their history in particular jurisdictions remains limited (notable exceptions include Moore 1995:142–147; Moore and Johnson 2004:27–33; and Paton 2009). There exists no central source that attempts to pull together in one place all or most of the anti-obeah legislation that has been enacted over the years in Britain's former Caribbean colonies and their modern successors. Anti-obeah laws that have been mentioned and partially analyzed in secondary sources and the scholarly literature represent but a small fraction of the anti-obeah legislation proposed and ratified over the centuries, and nowhere in the existing literature on obeah is there a systematic treatment of such laws and their development. With some exceptions (e.g., Paton 2009), little comparative work has been done on the subject, and scholars who address anti-obeah legislation are often unaware of the wider regional context in which this legislation evolved. The present work attempts to address this lacuna in Caribbean scholarship. It is the only work that provides a systematic overview of anti-obeah legislation in the region from the period of slavery through the post-emancipation period and colonial times and up to the present day (as of this writing, March 2012), when virtually all territories of the former British West Indies enjoy independent statehood.

Divining and Defining Obeah

ONE OF THE REMARKABLE THINGS about obeah is the difficulty of defining the term. Not only is there much disagreement about its meaning in the present but it is also clear that its meaning has varied considerably over time and space, as has the way it has been perceived in official and popular thinking. This variability, as we understand it, is largely the product of a historical struggle between contending cultural realities—dominant and subordinate—in the context of colonization and the building of slave societies. It is difficult to determine exactly what obeah was (or is), precisely because enslaved populations in the Caribbean had their own ideas about it, while those who ruled those slave plantation societies had certain other ideas; the ideas of those who occupied these distinct social realms were often quite different.

Colonial administrators and residential elites (both locally born and foreign) developed their understandings as part of a process of establishing cultural hierarchies in the interest of social control. Through this process, a variety of African-derived cultural phenomena that were largely unfamiliar to them, but that over time became perceived as threatening, were targeted for public action. One way of exercising more effective control over those African-derived beliefs and practices was to reduce them to a finite set of properties that could be more clearly grasped (partly through analogies to European cultural concepts)—in short, to define them in the terms of the ruling class—and then systematically to devalue and stigmatize (indeed, criminalize) them. The law provided the ruling class with a formidable weapon in this struggle over meaning and morality. Through legislation, ostensible characteristics and properties of a poorly understood variety of cultural ideas and practices could be represented as established "facts," and the ideas and practices themselves could then be turned into actionable offenses. Indeed, we argue that anti-obeah legislation, particularly starting in the post-slavery years of the nineteenth century, played a central role in creating public (mis)understandings of obeah across the Caribbean region.

If this is so, then it is all the more remarkable that these laws present so vague a picture of what obeah might actually be. Apparently, attempting to define obeah clearly and make it prosecutable by law was not nearly as straightforward as those who held power in these settings would have the public believe. But the lack of rigor that from the earliest days typified legal definitions of obeah was not necessarily a liability from the perspective of ruling elites. Indeed, when viewing anti-obeah legislation as a whole, one becomes aware that the imprecision that characterizes almost all of the laws could only have served to increase the effectiveness of such legislation as a means of cultural domination and social control. In effect, by failing to define obeah in a precise or consistent manner, the anti-obeah laws helped to construct a nebulous yet heavily value-laden symbolic representation of African religiosity as a whole. From the beginning, this symbolic construction was invested with preconceptions about the nature of Africans that formed part of the ideological arsenal of European colonialism. Partly through the force of law, obeah became an emblem of all that was held to be wrong about Africans' understandings of the cosmos—understandings that were repeatedly denigrated with terms such as *savage*, *depraved*, or *debased*. Over time, as concepts from other parts of the world (including Europe) crept into certain variants of what was understood to be obeah, this symbolic umbrella was extended to cover and impeach not just spiritual concepts perceived as African-derived but also "black" and "lower-class" forms of belief in general (usually categorized as superstition). The larger the sample of anti-obeah legislation examined, the clearer this totalizing effect becomes, as the following pages demonstrate.

The legislative arena was clearly not the only one in which historical struggles over the meaning and value of obeah took place. It is obvious that, especially in the post-slavery years, missionary activities and the entire apparatus of religious instruction played a decisive role in spreading and entrenching anti-obeah feeling across the British Caribbean. And other purveyors of public culture, ranging from state-supported educational institutions to the mass media, have also contributed. Recent trends in scholarship show an increasing critical sensitivity to the various ways in which such forces and institutions have shaped and distorted understandings of obeah over time (e.g., Dobbin 1986; Murphy 1994:226; Moore 1995:142–147; Moore and Johnson 2004:51–136; Stewart 2005; Murray 2007; Brown 2008:144–152; Paton 2009; Murrell 2010:226–245; Olmos and Paravisini-Gebert 2011:158; Zips 2011:35, 145; Paton and Forde 2012). But anti-obeah legislation undoubtedly looms large among the factors that have helped to create the complex and often contradictory and confusing mélange of ideas characterizing discourse about obeah today. For this reason we hope to demonstrate that the largely untapped body of legal data that resides in the archives deserves closer attention.

Another critically important source in attempting to unravel the meaning of obeah over time—one that is largely beyond the scope of the present work—is the ethnographic record based on field research. What do those who consider themselves obeah practitioners and "users" in various parts of the Caribbean actually think and believe? What are their understandings of obeah and how do they value it? Still in its infancy (for examples, see Moore 1953:125–131; Hogg 1964; Beck 1976; Dobbin 1986; Gibson 2001:16–53; Price 2008), this is one of the most promising areas of research in the quest to reconstruct, interpret, and reevaluate the significance of obeah for those on the other side of the aforementioned cultural struggle: the enslaved and those of their descendants who remain in the lower social strata. Perspectives grounded in ethnography might help to offset the one-sided views purveyed by those historians, cultural anthropologists, literary scholars, and so forth who depend entirely on the written or documentary record for their primary source information. Such writers, we believe, are often captured by their sources and, as a result, tend to perpetuate images of obeah that stress and exaggerate its antisocial or negative dimensions. But, when read between the lines, even the primary written sources on which such scholars depend, as well as the anti-obeah laws themselves, provide evidence that helps us reinterpret the meaning and significance of obeah in the past, as we show below in our analysis of certain components of the legislation in question.

In view of the foregoing, we do not provide any hard-and-fast definitions of obeah. However, we offer below a few operative assumptions that might help to put the overview of legislation that follows in a broader context, based on some of our own recent work and that of others who reexamine obeah from new perspectives. The term *obeah* (which is confined almost entirely to the Anglophone Caribbean[1]) appears never to have referred to an organized religion. Rather, it has long been used as a catchall term, understood to be derived from an African language (see below), to refer to a wide variety of spiritual powers. We believe the term was first used in an all-embracing, totally negative sense by whites/Europeans, probably in an early English colony such as Barbados or St. Christopher (St. Kitts), where it started being applied to a very diverse range of African spiritual practices and ideas. It is also likely that whites played an important, if not primary, role in diffusing the term to various other parts of the British Caribbean—partly through anti-obeah legislation, although the term diffused long before there was any specific legislation against it—where it was ultimately adopted as a general term by African-descended populations as well (Handler and Bilby 2001:93).

Today the term *obeah*, we maintain, applies to "a wide variety and range of beliefs and practices related to the control or channeling of supernatural/spiritual forces" (Bilby and Handler 2004:154). These beliefs and practices do not form, nor have they ever formed, a unified, coherent system; in fact, as Diana Paton (2009:1–2) has observed and as we elaborate below, it was "colonial law-making and law-enforcing [that] made a crucial contribution . . . to producing obeah as a singular unitary phenomenon." Nonetheless, despite the many differences among obeah practitioners, there are certain commonalities shared by most, such as the recitation or casting of spells and the manipulation of material objects that have been endowed with spiritual qualities. We contend that the supernatural or spiritual force (or forces) that the obeah practitioner attempts to control or guide, often on behalf of a paying client, is essentially neutral; it was neither bad nor good but "could be used either way," as the historian Philip Curtin (1955:29) wrote many years ago in his pioneering study of Jamaica. Although obeah practitioners could wield their powers in either positive or negative ways, the evidence suggests that, in practice, obeah has more often been directed toward socially or personally beneficial goals such as bringing good fortune, diagnosing illness and healing, finding lost or stolen goods, protecting from harm, and so forth. Yet because these powers were sometimes used malevolently—what Chireau (2003:31) has called "supernatural harming"—to hurt enemies (including, during the period of slavery, white slave owners) and were at times associated with social tensions in slave communities, the negative or harmful dimensions of some of the spiritual beliefs and practices that came to be known as obeah stood out for Europeans, and they were heavily emphasized in the early anti-obeah laws of the British Caribbean. (It should be stressed, however, that reports in official documents, contemporary histories and commentaries, newspaper articles, and so forth that implicate obeah in misfortunes should be treated with caution. Mere reports that obeah was being used to harm someone do not necessarily mean that the accusations had a basis in reality.[2]) These same anti-obeah laws, however, also point indirectly to the fact that many West Indians attached positive values to obeah, since they reveal in certain passages that obeah practitioners were often sought for help with everyday problems. Indeed, even the highly negative characterizations of eighteenth-century writers (e.g., Edwards 1793:82–92), as well as the early laws criminalizing obeah, often contain historical evidence showing that obeah was frequently directed toward socially beneficial goals.[3]

In addition, we contend, the positive social value originally attached to obeah by enslaved West Indians (and still attached to it by many of their descendants) was most likely embodied in the word's original meaning. While virtually all authorities agree that the term itself ultimately derives from some African language or languages, its specific linguistic roots continue to be debated and may never be definitively established.[4] In a previous publication (Handler and Bilby 2001), we challenged the view widely accepted in the scholarly literature that the term ultimately derives from an African word (usually said to be from the Asante-Twi language spoken on the Gold Coast) with meanings such as "witchcraft," "sorcery," or negative, antisocial magic. Instead we argued that it is more likely to have been derived from a West African term with positive or neutral referents such as *practitioner*, *healer*, or *herbalist*—or even *doctor*. A number of such terms, phonologically similar to *obeah*, exist in

Igbo, Ibibio, and related languages spoken in the Niger delta–Bight of Biafra region of southeastern Nigeria.[5]

It bears repeating that, while obeah clearly had positive connotations for many of the enslaved, it was also believed that the powers denoted by the term could be used to harm enemies or those perceived as enemies, a belief that was repeatedly mentioned by early critics who wrote about it and was heavily emphasized in the slave laws that criminalized obeah. We know that resident whites in the West Indies condemned, despised, and feared obeah and its practitioners. But we also know that the enslaved themselves sometimes feared or held in awe those identified as obeah practitioners. In this sense, colonial legislators were not entirely mistaken in their perceptions of some of the phenomena they placed under the rubric of obeah, but more than likely they *were* wrong about the larger part of what the enslaved themselves considered to be obeah, and their misperceptions had a lasting impact on everyone who was subject to the laws they created.

Moreover, as we suggested above, it is important to keep in mind that an accusation of harmful obeah practices did not mean that in fact such practices were actually occurring. The suspicions frequently encountered in the literature on obeah reflect cultural perceptions related to the explanation of accidents, ill luck, sickness, and the like, and critics of obeah, of whatever time period, frequently accept such accusations at face value. Scholars dependent on the sources generated by such critics often fall into the trap of exaggerating the negative or antisocial dimensions of obeah. While it is clear that many of the enslaved and their descendants dissented from and resisted hegemonic ideas about obeah imposed from above, it is equally clear that the prejudicial views held by those in power profoundly informed attitudes toward obeah among all social strata, and they continue to shape public opinion in the West Indies up to the present day.

Aside from the highly negative views of obeah that often appear in popular writings, the scholarly literature in fields such as anthropology, history, and literary criticism frequently contains misunderstandings and naïve assumptions. Even in academic studies, obeah has often been defined as or equated reductively with witchcraft, sorcery, or some other type of evil magic, with little or no consideration given to its well-documented positive side. For example, in his influential *Sociology of Slavery*, Orlando Patterson (1967:188) wrote that "obeah was essentially a type of sorcery which largely involved harming others at the request of clients." For the widely respected cultural geographer David Watts (1987:545 n. 8), in his monumental *The West Indies*, "obeah was a type of sorcery or witchcraft, which may be broadly equated with West African 'bad medicine.'" David Lowenthal (1972:116), in his now classic cultural geography of the West Indies, gives a definition that briefly but assuredly states: "obeah manipulates evil spirits through black magic." Albert Raboteau (1978:34), in his frequently quoted study of North America, *Slave Religion*, defines obeah as the "use of magic for evil," and, for Philip Morgan (1998:620), in his masterful and highly regarded study of slave culture in the eighteenth-century Chesapeake and Carolinas, "sorcery is the deliberate attempt by an individual to harm others by secretive means. . . . The most common term [among enslaved persons in North America] for sorcery was obi or obia." In fact, one-sided understandings of obeah as "harmful witchcraft" or "sorcery" remain common in written depictions, regardless of intended audience.[6]

A brief digression is in order here to clarify our usage of a few key terms that have been variously defined in the scholarly literature. In its broadest sense, the term *magic* can be used to describe ways of understanding and directly influencing the material world or events, often through impersonal supernatural intermediaries or spiritual forces. By "impersonal" forces we mean those that are not conceptualized as identifiable, clearly personified entities— for example, nature spirits, deities, loas (*lwas*), and the like.[7] According to our definition, a large proportion of the beliefs and practices associated with what is called obeah comprise a form of magic, although the term is also sometimes associated with the manipulation of spirits of the dead and various kinds of divinities. Magic is closely related to the idea that certain objectives cannot be achieved by human action alone and that the material world can be influenced or directed by the manipulation of these impersonal forces through, for example, spells, rituals, and the use of objects that have been endowed with spiritual power. Most magic is oriented toward social good, such as bringing good fortune, protecting against harm, and curing illness, but magic also has its negative or destructive side and can be used for antisocial purposes such as harming others. (It must be stressed that a malevolent spiritual action against a slave master, for example, would have been considered a benevolent act from the perspective of many in the enslaved community.) The belief system of enslaved West Indians—and many of their descendants—involved these dimensions of magic. Because many enslaved West Indians, like many Africans in Africa, profoundly believed that supernatural forces, when guided or influenced by human agents through the manipulation of spiritually charged objects, could cause misfortune, the belief in evil magic was a major factor in their lives.

As anthropologists use the terms, both *witchcraft* and *sorcery* connote evil, or "bad" magic. Social anthropologists, particularly those working in African societies, have traditionally made a distinction between these terms or categories of magic, building on the classic study by E. E. Evans-Pritchard (1937) among the Azande/Zande of East Central Africa. Briefly, in sorcery, magic is consciously and knowingly performed to injure others. Sorcerers acquire their magical knowledge through learning; theoretically, their techniques can be carried out by anyone with the requisite knowledge and skill. It is important to emphasize that, in sorcery, as in socially beneficial or "good" magic, there is actual performance such as rituals, recitation of spells, and, particularly, the use and manipulation of material objects or substances. The negative powers West Indian legislators often ascribed to obeah practitioners, which they identified as witchcraft, could more appropriately be labeled as sorcery under this definition.

In contrast to the sorcerer, the power of the witch is usually, although not always, inborn or inherited. This power to exert evil cannot be learned; it resides within the individual and is directed against others for malevolent purposes. It is frequently believed that, as the anthropologists John Middleton and Edward Winter (1963:3) wrote many years ago, "the witch need merely wish to harm his victim and his witchcraft then does this, or it may be enough for him to merely feel annoyance or jealousy against someone for the power to set itself in operation without his being aware of the fact that it has done so." Witchcraft, then, is a psychic or mental act, even if unconscious, whose believers affirm that the harmful power of the witch is unleashed merely through the activation of certain negative thoughts. The distinction between these categories or terms, however, is often not clear-cut in observable practice or actual behavior; for this reason anthropologists do not universally accept this distinction, and many avoid it (e.g., Gluckman 1955; Turner 1964; Mair 1969; Geschiere 1997; Kapferer 2002).

For this reason, we eschew further discussion of witchcraft versus sorcery and the possible analytic utility of making a distinction between the two. For the purposes of this book, we simply use the terms interchangeably—as is sometimes the case in the anti-obeah legislation we discuss. Both terms convey notions of evil or malevolence, and, among other social functions, witchcraft or sorcery beliefs offer explanations for why misfortune occurs and why, for example, certain individuals succumb to bad luck, sickness, and even death. Beliefs and practices surrounding witchcraft and sorcery were profound in the African societies from which the enslaved were taken to the New World, and they continue to be important elements in modern African societies (e.g., Geschiere 1997; Kapferer 2002; Sanders 2003).

With regard to scholarly representations of obeah, many of the misconceptions that have entered the literature appear to have their roots in a handful of early attempts at scholarship on the topic, particularly the writings of Rev. Joseph J. Williams (and to some extent Hesketh Bell [1889]). An anthropologist and Jesuit priest, Williams advanced the idea that obeah was a discrete, coherent tradition that could be traced specifically to the Ashanti (Asante) people of the Gold Coast, many of whom had been transported to Jamaica as slaves, and that it was a direct continuation of a system of negative witchcraft or sorcery that was a fundamental component of religious life among this West African people. In an early book, *Voodoos and Obeahs*, Williams (1932:120) maintained "the Jamaica term Obeah is unquestionably derived from the Ashanti word Obayifo, which according to Captain [R. S.] Rattray signifies 'a wizard, or more generally a witch.'"[8] The etymology of the term thus "established," Williams (1934:209) later asserted, "Obeah, as the continuation of Ashanti witchcraft, is professedly a projection of spiritual power with the harm of an individual as an objective. Practically, its end is attained through fear, supplemented if needs be by secret poisoning."

Williams also believed that a related Jamaican religious phenomenon known as myal or "myalism," depicted in a portion of the colonial-era literature as a form of spiritual practice opposed to obeah, represented a more or less direct retention from Ashanti religion. According to him, myalism "was the old tribal religion of the Ashanti . . . with some modifications due to conditions and circumstances." "In Ashanti," he maintained, "the Okomfo [benevolent priest] openly combated the Obayifo [malevolent witch] as a matter of principle, and he had the whole force of Ashanti religious traditions and public sentiment to support him." But in Jamaica, Williams (1932:145–146) argued, since "native religious assemblies were proscribed by law" and this "greatly hampered the Okomfo [myal man] in his sphere of influence," the "Obayifo or Obeah man, who had always worked in secret, flourished in his trade." In reducing "Ashanti religion" to this simplistic good-versus-evil scheme and drawing parallels with an ostensible dichotomy between obeah and myal in Jamaica, Williams sought to strengthen his argument that obeah was part of a coherent African religious system brought virtually intact to Jamaica. Like the Asante-Twi etymology that he presented as "unquestionable," this served to reinforce (or, in Williams's view, "prove") the idea that obeah was by definition a form of pernicious witchcraft—one that had existed previously in an ethnically specific religious context in Africa and had survived in the "native religion" of Jamaica virtually unchanged.

The question of myal merits discussion here, since this term, like *obeah*, has been the source of much confusion, and some of this confusion has contributed to misunderstandings of obeah. Indeed, misrepresentations of myal appear to have made a substantial contribution to hegemonic constructions of obeah as harmful witchcraft. Like obeah, myal has been defined in the scholarly and historical literature only vaguely and in various, sometimes confused, ways, all of which relate to African-identified spiritual power. References in Jamaican sources from the slavery era are sparse, but during this early period myal was generally represented as being closely associated with obeah and connected with dances or other gatherings in which obeah was practiced (e.g., Long 1774:416–418; Jamaica 1789b:214; Lewis 1969:354). By the mid-nineteenth century something called myal was frequently mentioned in writings by missionaries in association with gatherings and practices that blended elements of Christian belief with African-derived religious practices, some of which were used to combat allegedly negative forms of obeah. Despite these varied representations of myal in the eighteenth and nineteenth centuries, those Jamaican laws that mention myal remain consistent in their condemnation of it, alongside obeah, as an ostensibly harmful African-derived belief or practice.

Owing partly to the writings of missionaries who reported on new, syncretic developments in Afro-Jamaican Christianity during the nineteenth century (see Waddell 1863; Chevannes 1971; Schuler 1979, 1980), which they sometimes labeled "myalism," and partly to the writings of Joseph Williams discussed above, myal has typically been represented in most scholarly works that mention it as a benevolent, or positive, African-derived form of religious practice opposed to obeah. This representation, we believe, is partly responsible for the entrenchment of hegemonic constructions that define obeah as an inherently evil form of witchcraft, since it posits the existence of an inherently "good" or benevolent form of African-derived spiritual practice to which obeah has traditionally been opposed.

However, based on Bilby's ethnographic research in several parts of rural Jamaica from the 1970s through the 1990s as well as a careful reading of the primary historical sources, we reject the dichotomization of obeah and myal, which we believe resulted from the misunderstandings of missionaries and other European writers who had limited knowledge of the spiritual practices they were describing. In those widely separated rural parts of Jamaica where practitioners of living religions continue to use the word *myal* today, it virtually always carries a specific sense: "the state of spirit possession" or "manifestation of a spirit operating in a human being." Nowhere do living practitioners of surviving older forms of Afro-Jamaican religion, so far as we know, see myal as being something inherently opposed to obeah; on the contrary, the kind of spirit possession known as myal is commonly seen as a way to learn about and access obeah (in the sense of power over spirits, which can be used for either good or evil). This and other evidence gathered by Bilby (as yet unpublished) suggests that, contrary to standard interpretations that have been widely reproduced in the literature on Caribbean religion and culture (but that appear to be diminishing in their influence on current scholarship), obeah and myal were never inherently opposed; rather, they have long formed complementary parts—one concerned primarily with spiritual power of various kinds, the other with spirit possession—of a single Afro-Creole cultural system in Jamaica. In her recent book on African religious experience in Jamaica, which includes an in-depth reexamination and critique of the conventional obeah–myal dichotomy, theologian Dianne Stewart (2005:33–68) comes close to the position we are advocating here. (For an early critique of Williams's dichotomization of obeah and myal, see Hogg [1964:68–73]; this dichotomy is also questioned in Besson [2002:31].)[9]

Returning to the discussion of Joseph Williams's contribution, his two books focusing on obeah (1932, 1934) were among the earliest studies of the phenomenon, and their influence, though not always apparent to later readers, was significant and lasting. Patterson (1967:185), who accepted Williams's basic assumptions about Asante-Twi origins, continues to be widely cited by scholars. Historian Robert Stewart (1992:136–137) maintains that Williams's speculations on the origins and essential nature of obeah have "remained substantially unchallenged," concluding that the more general arguments put forward in his two books on the topic are "plausible." (Authors of more recent works that reproduce aspects of the Asante-Twi origin theory include Murrell 2010:230–231 and Olmos and Paravisini-Gebert 2011:155–156).[10]

It is difficult, however, to reconcile Williams's speculations about the origins of obeah in harmful "Ashanti witchcraft," and the proposed etymology on which they are based, with what is known of obeah (or obia, as it is usually spelled) in Suriname (formerly Dutch Guiana). More than eighty years ago Melville Herskovits, who had recently returned from fieldwork in Suriname, noted the discrepancy between much of what had been written about obeah in the West Indies and his own findings. In his 1930 review of Martha Beckwith's classic ethnography of rural Jamaican life, *Black Roadways* (first published in 1929), Herskovits (1930:337) observed that "in the literature on the West Indies, 'obeah' is synonymous with evil magic, and Miss Beckwith tacitly accepts this interpretation. On the basis of the Suriname data, to say nothing of some of Miss Beckwith's own statements, this interpretation does not stand. If we take the case among the Bush-Negroes [Surinamese Maroons] . . . we find that obia is a healing principle."

Our findings concur with those of Herskovits. As we have pointed out in several publications (Handler and Bilby 2001:94; Bilby and Handler 2004:154–155, 173 n. 3), Surinamese Maroon understandings of obia are entirely positive—a fact that has been reported not just by Herskovits but by virtually every other ethnographer who has worked among these Maroon peoples. For example, the Aluku (Boni) Maroons, among whom Bilby has carried out extensive fieldwork, use the term *obia* to refer to a range of supernatural phenomena—including healing power, spiritual protection, divination, and possessing gods or spirits—all of which have positive connotations (Bilby n.d.). Negative power used to cause harm (that is, sorcery) is rarely if ever referred to as obia but rather is normally denoted by another term, *wisi* (or, among Saramaka Maroons, *sibá*).

There is some evidence that, from an early date in other parts of the Caribbean, the word *obeah* had similarly positive meanings and connotations, particularly for the enslaved, rather than being used normally to denote harmful witchcraft or sorcery. We have suggested in previous pages that the ultimate origin of the term in an African language could be translated into English in several ways, including "healer" or "doctor," and in fact, as we discuss below, some slave laws even referred to obeah practitioners as doctors. Recent work by Katharine Gerbner on eighteenth-century Moravian missionaries in Jamaica has uncovered an intriguing document that clearly suggests that—at least in the particular place and time to which this document belongs—the term was endowed with a sense that was primarily, if not entirely, positive.

The document in question was produced by Zacharias George Caries, an English-speaking German Moravian missionary who arrived in Jamaica in late 1754 and began his work at the Bogue sugar plantation in the parish of St. Elizabeth. In a letter written in German a few months after his arrival, Caries reported his success in attracting slaves to his services. "More and more of them come to the Meeting," he wrote, "so that we will soon have to enlarge our hall. They call me Obea, which supposedly means Seer, or one who is able to see things in the future. They like me a lot and I like them" (Gerbner 2010). Whether or not Caries correctly understood how much the plantation's slaves liked him, his comment provides a unique insight into how some of the enslaved in Jamaica at that time perceived those who were understood to be "obea" practitioners. Gerbner (2010) points out that the people Caries was attempting to convert viewed him as a "spiritual practitioner" who had entered into their lives by performing ritual activities, such as baptisms, and by officiating at rites, such as funerals, that we suggest had great importance in the Afro-Creole culture then forming on plantations. In addition, Caries served as a mediator or advocate in their disputes with plantation overseers and attorneys, as well as acting as "an arbiter of disputes between slaves." According to Gerbner, it came as a surprise to the enslaved that these services were performed without a fee being charged, since obeah people as "spiritual practitioners" normally charged for their work. Gerbner's research suggests that further and more focused work with untapped archival sources from this period or earlier will lend additional force to the growing body of scholarship calling into question commonly held views about what obeah originally meant to enslaved populations not only in Jamaica but also in other parts of the region.[11]

Similar cracks in the stereotypical image of obeah as malevolent witchcraft are revealed in the broader literature on the Caribbean. To take but one of a great many possible examples, the late Douglas Taylor (1945:510–511, 527) reported close to seventy years ago that the Caribs of Dominica (today usually known by their own name, Kalinago), whose culture had been heavily influenced by the Afro-Creole culture of the island, distinguished between *kémbwa* or *obia* on the one hand and *piáy* on the other. The first two terms were used synonymously "to designate all kinds of sorcery [i.e., magic] while the latter is limited to the making and working of black magic." "Magical practices," Taylor writes, that are directed toward beneficial ends for an individual—for example, ensuring fertility, protecting an agricultural field or its produce against theft, "or to influence the attitude of a person or persons in a particular circumstance (especially that of judge or jury during a trial)"—are referred to as obeah "but not piáy."[12]

While the positive understandings of obeah held by the Maroons of Suriname and traditionally by the Caribs/Kalinago of Dominica may represent "minority" views, they are, in fact, not entirely foreign to people elsewhere in the Caribbean. Not just in Jamaica but also in many other parts of the region, as we have seen, ideas about obeah are often contradictory. The same powers and practitioners that are often "officially" seen as inherently evil and harmful are also widely understood to be amenable to positive ends, and in practice they are frequently tapped with socially or personally beneficial goals in mind. This positive dimension of obeah, though seldom explicitly acknowledged in public and often vehemently denied by the "guardians of morality" (e.g., clerical authorities), is tacitly accepted by many across the region, as reflected from time to time in newspaper reports and popular culture—for instance, in the lyrics of popular music (Bilby 2012).

Indeed, as discussed below, this positive dimension is discernible even in anti-obeah legislation both past and present. Among the things we can infer from this legislation is that in lumping together a diverse array of Afro-Caribbean religious or spiritual practices and ideas, labeling them with a single term, and imposing imperfect, vague, and highly prejudicial understandings of this term on the populace at large—not to mention making anything associated with the term potentially punishable by law—legislators made a major contribution to the cultural and psychic dissonance that characterizes discourse about obeah (and Afro-Caribbean religious expressions more generally) in much of today's Anglophone Caribbean.

Anti-Obeah Provisions in the Laws

A Comparative Overview

STARTING IN JAMAICA IN 1760 and continuing to the present, scores of laws criminalizing obeah have been enacted in the seventeen jurisdictions of the Anglophone Caribbean. These include laws concerned solely with obeah—so-called "obeah acts" or "obeah ordinances"—as well as anti-obeah provisions in sections of penal codes, criminal codes, police acts, vagrancy acts, and summary jurisdiction acts. The anti-obeah laws of the Anglophone Caribbean, despite their differences, have a number of common characteristics in how they are structured, their underlying premises, and the major issues they address. In the following discussion we outline some of what we consider to be the more relevant topics and general themes touched on in these laws. (Individual territories and the historical development of their laws are discussed in more detail in chapter 4.)

Laws that specifically included the term *obeah* in their titles emerged during the period of slavery, first in Jamaica in 1760 and then in Barbados in 1806 (although an 1800 Trinidadian slave governance law mentioned the term in its text). By the end of the slave period (1834–38), virtually all territories of the British Caribbean had criminalized obeah. After emancipation, with the nullification of slave laws, anti-obeah legislation in one form or another was gradually reintroduced in all of the territories. The first specifically anti-obeah provisions to appear in this new context were enacted in six British West Indian jurisdictions between 1838 and 1840, but within forty to fifty years all of the territories had criminalized obeah. Sometimes anti-obeah provisions were contained in vagrancy laws intended to address a variety of social issues (discussed further in chapters 3 and 4) or in sections of criminal codes or penal codes; at other times such provisions formed the basis of special "obeah acts" or ordinances directed solely against obeah.

In most cases, anti-obeah laws follow a format that is standard for acts in general in British law (e.g., Walker 1980:16–17). First comes a brief preamble giving the reasons for the law (which usually includes an attack on obeah as a fraudulent and evil practice), followed by the substance of the law, consisting of itemization of the types of activities that are condemned, then a discussion of the judicial procedures for trying suspected cases, and finally specification of the sanctions or penalties against those convicted.

Legal Definitions of Obeah

The difficulty modern scholars experience in trying to define obeah mirrors the lack of precision characterizing all of the laws we have examined. Although the term *obeah* is mentioned any number of times in this body of legislation, only a few laws actually attempt to define it. Even then the definitions are usually vague and imprecise, not to mention highly ethnocentric and prejudicial. Without clearly pinpointing or defining what constitutes obeah, every West Indian law criminalizing it nonetheless condemns obeah as a social evil based on fraudulent motives. The laws either state explicitly or imply by their wording that obeah practitioners are themselves aware that their claims to "supernatural power or knowledge" are false and duplicitous (cf. Paton 2009:7) and that they are only concerned about their own pecuniary interests. Trinidad's 1901 ordinance, for example, states merely that "obeah signifies every pretended assumption of supernatural power or knowledge for fraudulent or illicit purposes or for gain, or the injury of any person"; essentially the same definition, with only minor differences in wording, is found, for example, in the laws of British Guiana (1918), the Bahamas (1927), St. Lucia (1887), and St. Vincent (1988). The 1904 Obeah Acts of the Leeward Islands and Dominica are particularly vague, merely stating tautologically that obeah, for the purposes of the law, simply "means obeah as ordinarily understood and practiced," while St. Lucia's 1872 "obeah ordinance" defines obeah as the "practice of witchcraft, palmistry or any occult art as well as what is commonly termed Kembois or obeah."

Many laws also emphasized that obeah was used "for the purpose of frightening any person," and in most territories, starting in the nineteenth century (and in many cases continuing until the present), the word *intimidate* is linked in the laws with obeah. At times the fears referenced by legislators are couched explicitly in European-derived concepts, as revealed in several slave laws that castigate the practitioner for "pretending to have communication with the devil and other evil spirits." This phrase, first appearing in Jamaica in 1761 (and also present in several later Jamaican laws of 1789, 1809, 1826, and 1831), also occurs, albeit only once, in the laws of British Honduras (1791), Barbados (1806), Antigua (1809), and Grenada (1825). The phrase is absent in the laws of other islands and disappeared in post-emancipation legal codes. More commonly, slave laws equate obeah with witchcraft—the most common term—or sorcery, although neither term is defined; sometimes (in the laws of a number of jurisdictions) witchcraft is simply used synonymously with obeah. Both terms continued to be used at times throughout the nineteenth century and remain in present-day laws. However, in post-emancipation times, as Diana Paton (2009:2) has quite rightly observed, "the legal construction of obeah shifted from being primarily about witchcraft to being primarily about fraud." By the late nineteenth century, changes in the wording of the laws show that fraud, not witchcraft or sorcery, had become the centerpiece in anti-obeah legislation.

The Obeah Practitioner

Over time, representations of the obeah practitioner in legislation became increasingly uniform. By the middle of the nineteenth century and throughout the twentieth century, when West Indian laws went so far as to characterize the obeah practitioner, they emphasized fraud and deception, often repeating verbatim or closely paraphrasing the wording of England's 1824 Vagrancy Act (see chapter 3). In that act, offenses associated with the definition of a "rogue and vagabond" include "pretending or professing to tell fortunes, or using any subtle craft, means or device, by palmistry or otherwise, to deceive and impose." In post-emancipation nineteenth- and twentieth-century West Indian laws, the word *obeah* is usually inserted immediately after the word *palmistry* where it appears in England's Vagrancy Act. In addition, in their nineteenth-century vagrancy acts, some of which remained in force in one form or another well into the twentieth century, several jurisdictions—for example, Trinidad (1838) and British Guiana (1895)—merely repeated the 1824 English act's phrase " to deceive or [and] impose." Others inserted the phrase "superstitious means" before "to deceive or [and] impose"—for example, Jamaica's 1840 Vagrancy Act, which includes the wording "pretending or professing to tell fortunes, or using or pretending to use, any subtle craft or device, by palmistry or any such like superstitious means, to deceive or impose." The same wording occurs in various laws of Barbados, the Bahamas, St. Kitts, Nevis, Anguilla, Dominica, St. Vincent, and Belize.

In general throughout the West Indies, the vagrancy acts, special obeah acts or ordinances, and anti-obeah sections in other laws such as criminal or penal codes were very similar in their wording. Key phrases or terms from the 1824 English act, such as "subtle craft," "tell fortunes," "means or device," "palmistry," and "deceive and [or] impose," are found throughout the anti-obeah laws. In some cases these terms and phrases have persisted well into the twentieth century and, indeed, to the present day. This similarity in wording, Paton (2009:5) has observed, "resulted both from deliberate copying by one colony of the laws of others and from imperial pressure toward consistency across Britain's Caribbean colonies."

Instruments of Obeah

Some laws refer to "instruments of obeah" or indicate the material items allegedly used by practitioners; however, these "instruments" are usually not specified or are only vaguely (and sometimes tautologically) defined. For example, the 1898 Jamaica Obeah Act defines an instrument of obeah simply as "anything used or intended to be used" in the practice of obeah. Identical or virtually identical wording occurs from time to time in the laws of various territories, including Dominica (1904), the Leeward Islands Federation (1904), Montserrat (1983), Grenada (1897), St. Lucia (1905), St. Vincent (1988), Antigua (1904), and the Cayman Islands (1975). Sometimes these vague definitions and phrasings are combined with slightly more specific descriptions. For example, the 1927 Bahamian penal code defines an instrument of obeah as "any philtre, vial, blood, bone, image, or other article or thing, which . . . is used or intended to be used in the practice of obeah." Similar wording is found in the 1872 St. Lucia Obeah Ordinance. As far as can be ascertained, only the laws of the Bahamas (1927 to present) and St. Lucia (1872 to 2004) mention an "image," probably referring to some sort of likeness of a person such as a doll or drawing. An earlier St. Vincent slave law (1803) singles out anyone who uses "instruments" that include "any charm, ceremony, cards, sieve, bible and key" (see chapter 4, n. 53). The 1918 British Guiana ordinance is unique among anti-obeah laws in that it includes the only known reference to "any human skull or part thereof or other portion of the human body or any other article . . . being used in the practice of obeah or witchcraft." An 1800 Trinidad slave law mentions "an amulet, a fetische [sic] or the customary attributes and ingredients of the profession."

The most detailed itemization of "instruments of obeah" can be found in Jamaican anti-obeah legislation, starting in 1760 and continuing through a series of later laws enacted during the slave period. Specified items include "any blood, feathers, parrots beaks, dogs teeth, alligators teeth, broken bottles, grave dirt, rum, egg-shells" (these items are also listed in Grenada's 1825 Consolidated Slave Act).[1] In Jamaica's 1809, 1816, and 1831 slave laws, the earlier list is reduced to only parrots' beaks, dogs' teeth, and alligators' teeth, but "pounded glass" and "poisonous drugs" have been added. None of the "instruments" mentioned in Jamaica's slave laws are mentioned in the island's post-emancipation laws.[2]

This was also the case with poison. Poison was and is not an intrinsic feature of obeah—some obeah practitioners were accused of employing poison while others were not—and it appears that people who did not consider themselves obeah practitioners also used poison. Poison was first explicitly associated with obeah, as one of a number of reputed "instruments," in a 1788 Dominican slave law.[3] Later it appeared in legislation in Jamaica (1792), followed by Barbados (1806), Antigua (1809), St. Vincent (1821), and Grenada (1825). Our information on British West Indian slave laws is not exhaustive, and a few other laws may also have linked poison with obeah. In Antigua, for example, during the first decades of the nineteenth century, obeah practitioners were considered adept in their knowledge of "plants which yield poison" (Flannigan 1844:51), but poison does not seem to have been mentioned in the island's anti-obeah laws. In any case, references to poison do not occur in the post-emancipation laws of Dominica, Jamaica, or other territories.

No matter how imprecise or vague the definitions of "instruments of obeah" in the laws, in several jurisdictions in the post-emancipation nineteenth century, and in some cases continuing to the present, it was presumed that a person found to have such an "instrument" on his person or in his home was an obeah practitioner. If anyone was discovered carrying a concealed "instrument of obeah" into court or other judicial proceedings against an accused obeah practitioner, this could be deemed sufficient evidence of an offense under the anti-obeah provisions of some colonies such as the Bahamas, Grenada, and St. Vincent. In general, however, given the vagueness of definitions in most laws—and the wide array of objects that practitioners are reported to use or have used—prosecution of obeah practitioners on the basis of possession of "instruments of obeah" is difficult. Keith Patchett (1970:24), former dean of the Law School at the University of the West Indies (Barbados), aptly summed up the problem as follows: "Since in practice almost any instrument can be claimed by those who seek to benefit by it, to possess occult or supernatural power, the task of determining which instruments found in the possession of someone who practices obeah are actually used in such practice is not always an easy one."

Penalties for Practicing Obeah

Not only the wording of anti-obeah laws but also the punishments or sanctions against those convicted of practicing obeah were broadly similar throughout the West Indies, although penalties varied somewhat from territory to territory and changed over time. Slave laws contained severe penalties for conviction—the minimum was usually execution. The laws did not specify how execution was to be carried out, although hanging was probably the most common method. Mutilation of the corpse and decapitation were probably reserved for very serious cases allegedly involving, for example, inciting or leading a revolt, physical assaults on whites, or murder (for descriptions of how the bodies of executed slaves were treated, see, for example, Paton 2001; Brown 2008; cf. Handler 1982, 1997).

Some laws gave judges the option of "transportation" or "banishment" of the convicted individual from the territory. Transportation was a major form of punishment for "serious crimes" in eighteenth-century England (Paton 2001:937). In the context of the West Indies this meant, in effect, being sold into slavery elsewhere and thus the breaking of local family and other social ties, relationships of fundamental importance to many enslaved persons.[4] With minor variations depending on the territory and the year the legislation was enacted, transportation was specified as a penalty for obeah convictions in the slave laws of Jamaica, Barbados, Grenada, British Honduras, Dominica, and St. Vincent.

Only Trinidad in 1800 left the sentence entirely vague—specifying only "inflict proper punishment"—although in other jurisdictions, in addition to execution, another vaguely stated option was sometimes "such other punishment as the court decides." Several laws in Dominica allowed the judiciary to choose "banishment and flogging on the bare breech" (the only West Indian law to specify "breech"). By 1831 Dominica had made the sentence completely optional, stating that the person convicted "shall suffer such punishment as the court in its discretion shall award." Despite variations among territories, the slave laws contained penalties that were relatively uniform and stable over time, far more so than the penalties specified in laws enacted after emancipation and in modern times.[5]

With the end of slavery, the death penalty and transportation or banishment were eliminated, and penalties gradually became less harsh. The most common penalties during the greater part of the post-emancipation period were jailing, with or without hard labor (the most frequent type), and whipping or flogging; the latter was imposed much less frequently and occurred primarily in Jamaica, although also occasionally in other areas, such as British

Guiana, Trinidad, St. Lucia, Dominica, and St. Vincent. These punishments were also sometimes combined with fines, primarily in laws enacted in the twentieth century.[6] The frequency with which the punishments appeared in the laws varied by time period and by jurisdiction. Different penalties could also be combined; for example, convictions sometimes led not only to imprisonment with hard labor but also to whipping. Penalties became more severe with repeat offenses, and second and third convictions meant higher fines and longer jail sentences. (Some of the many combinations and variations in penalties for obeah convictions are discussed further in chapter 4, with reference to individual territories.)

In the present-day Anglophone Caribbean, the remaining laws against obeah are infrequently enforced, and in those places where the practice is still criminalized, penalties for conviction vary. In Jamaica, conviction can result in up to one year of imprisonment, with or without hard labor, or—in addition to or in lieu of prison—whipping. Jamaica stands alone in continuing to include hard labor and whipping in its laws. The other territories impose as a minimum a jail sentence, sometimes in combination with a fine or, as the case may be, in lieu of a fine. For example, conviction in Antigua, St. Kitts and Nevis, St. Vincent, and Guyana can bring a jail sentence of up to one year. In Dominica an offender can be imprisoned for one year or be fined, and in Montserrat and the Virgin Islands, sentencing options include one year in jail, a fine, or both jail and a fine. In Belize the punishment provided by law is up to six months in jail plus a fine, while in the Bahamas and Grenada it is three months in jail.

Penalties for Consulting Obeah Practitioners

By the mid- to late nineteenth century, and continuing in some cases to the present, most jurisdictions, with the apparent exception of the Bahamas, Barbados, Belize, Grenada, and Trinidad and Tobago, at one time or another made it illegal to consult obeah practitioners. The penalties varied, but they usually involved at the minimum a jail sentence or a fine; sometimes they included both, and in some instances hard labor was added to these. The 1904 Obeah Act of the Leeward Islands Federation imposed a penalty of a fine or one year in jail, and this remained in force until the dissolution of the Federation in 1957. The same penalties were in effect in the various colonies of the Federation, and in some cases they remain in force. In St. Vincent the penalty since 1988 has been one year in prison. The sentence in St. Lucia from 1872 to 1920 was up to six months in jail; after 1920 this was reduced to three months, but a fine was added. In 2004, anti-obeah provisions were finally dropped from the island's laws. In an 1855 British Guiana act, conviction for consulting an obeah practitioner was punished with imprisonment for up to one year, with or without hard labor, and this sentence remained in effect until 1973, when it was reduced to six months—where it remains at present.

Jamaica's laws between 1857 and 1898 distinguished between the different motives for consultations. Paid consultations with the intent of bringing harm to someone else's person or property brought a prison term of up to three months. However, if the consultation was "to bring about some event" not injurious to others through "the supposed supernatural agency of obeah or myalism," the convicted individual could be fined or imprisoned for thirty days if unable to pay the fine. Jamaica's Obeah Act of 1898, which is substantially still in effect today, included a number of modifications to the 1857 law. Consulting an obeah practitioner "or any person pretending to possess supernatural power . . . for any fraudulent or unlawful purpose" could now result in prison with hard labor for up to six months and a flogging in addition to—or in lieu of—imprisonment (females could not be flogged). A person who consulted an obeah practitioner "for the purpose of effecting any object, or bringing about any event by the use of occult means or any supernatural power or knowledge" and who paid for such services, was liable to a fine or to imprisonment, with or without hard labor, for up to one year. In brief, jail sentences, like fines, varied, ranging from a minimum of three months to, more commonly, up to six months or a year.

Penalties for Writing, Printing, and Distributing Obeah-Related Materials

A final component of many laws—one that did not emerge until the late nineteenth century but remains in effect today in several parts of the region—relates to the production and distribution of written materials promoting obeah. In what was apparently the first stipulation of its kind, Jamaica's 1898 Obeah Act imposed a fine for writing, publishing, selling, or distributing any printed matter that promoted "the superstition of obeah." Most other jurisdictions (except perhaps for Barbados, Belize, and Trinidad and Tobago) followed with similar restrictions, sometimes with identical wording. The penalty for conviction varied but usually involved a fine (the amount varied and was changed over the years, usually to conform with changes in currencies and their values), a prison sentence if the fine could not be paid, or sometimes both.

In the laws of Jamaica, St. Kitts and Nevis, and Dominica since the late nineteenth and early twentieth century, the sentence for the offense of consulting an obeah practitioner (which remains on the books as a crime to this day) has been a fine or up to six months in jail, as was the case in the Leeward Islands Federation from 1904 to 1957. In Grenada since 1908 and Guyana since 1958 (or possibly earlier), the penalty has been up to three months in jail. In St. Lucia from 1905 to 2004, it was a jail term of up to six months. In the British Virgin Islands and Montserrat since 1904, the penalty has been a fine or jail for up to one year or both. Finally, the sentence in St. Vincent since 1988 has been one year in jail.

Positive Social Functions of Obeah Reflected in the Laws

Finally let us consider what we, as historical/social anthropologists, find to be one of the most interesting dimensions of law in general and anti-obeah laws in particular: namely, what can be gleaned from legal documents about important aspects of the behavior, values, and ideas of the people against whom such laws are directed. The slave laws enacted by colonial authorities and local white elites emphasized what they perceived to be the deleterious influence of obeah among the enslaved. The writers of these laws asserted that obeah practitioners had considerable power and influence in their communities. According to the laws, these practitioners claimed "any supernatural power in order to affect the health or lives of others" and extorted money or goods "under false pretences." Most important, they were also able to use their ostensible powers to encourage slaves to escape their masters, hide fugitives or Maroons, or incite them to rebel or revolt. Obeah practitioners, it was claimed, could also convince the enslaved that they would be protected from harm while under the influence of a spell or some other spiritually charged protective device.

Although obeah laws enacted during the post-emancipation era no longer mention revolts or escape, they continued—in highly ethnocentric terms—to stress the negative and antisocial influences that ruling elites associated with obeah and its practitioners. Yet even while doing so, the laws also inadvertently or implicitly pointed to a number of common social issues or personal concerns that prompted clients to seek help from obeah men and women. That is, alongside their condemnation of certain activities or behaviors, the laws also suggest the kinds of problems that typically led people to seek help from and patronize obeah practitioners.

One of the most common practices condemned in the laws is "fortune telling" or "pretending or professing to tell fortunes"—in effect, divination, the practice of foretelling future events or discovering hidden knowledge by supernatural means. While the word *divination* appears in only two slave laws (one from St. Vincent in 1803, the other from Barbados in 1826), *fortune-telling* or some variation of this phrase is quite common. From the perspective of enslaved Africans and their descendants, whose cultures were heavily influenced by African traditions and belief systems, divination played a fundamental role in everyday life.[7] In many parts of Africa, today as in the past, divination (often involving forms of "fortune telling" that employ a wide variety of techniques) allows people to control chance and minimize ambiguity in their lives so that important decisions can be made under favorable circumstances. It also permits the finding of lost or stolen objects (and the identification of thieves)—a practice commonly attributed to obeah practitioners in West Indian laws—as well as the uncovering of hidden or special knowledge, such as the causes of illness or other types of misfortune. Diagnosis of disease is crucial to divination in Africa, where the diviner's immediate objective is most often to ascertain the cause of the illness and then prescribe appropriate healing rituals and treatment.[8]

Although West Indian laws commonly depict obeah practitioners as having a supposed ability to "inflict any disease" or otherwise cause injury, at the same time they reveal that practitioners were often consulted to "restore any person to health" or "to cure injuries or diseases"; that is, practitioners were said to be able to cure as well as cause "disease or sickness, pain or infirmity." For this reason, a few slave laws reflect usage in the slave communities themselves and actually refer to obeah practitioners as "doctors." In St. Vincent in 1803 they were referred to as "obeah men or obeah doctors"; in an 1800 Trinidad slave law, "spell-doctor"; and in the 1788 slave code of Dominica, "Doctor Men." A Nevis slave law enacted between 1818 and 1823 refers to those who practice "confu, or obeah doctor" (see chapter 4, n. 35). All such terms, however, were dropped in subsequent slave laws and, probably because the term *doctor* gave too much respectability to obeah practitioners, did not reappear after emancipation.9 Nonetheless, even after this more nuanced language disappeared from legal documents, the laws continued to provide evidence that medical help was a major reason why obeah practitioners were consulted. In short, in the words of a St. Lucia law, the obeah man or woman could, "by any supernatural devices . . . cure or impart as the case may be, disease, love, or any other good or evil affectation," as well as "tell fortunes or future or past events or discover lost or stolen property, or in any way . . . benefit or injure another, either in person or property." A similar range of characteristics is associated with many African diviners.

In general, the more substantive portions of anti-obeah laws suggest that early West Indians sought the help of obeah practitioners for many of the same reasons that their descendants do today. This said, there is no denying that obeah is widely invoked today in the West Indies to explain evil happenings or bad luck, although the frequency with which it is invoked as an explanatory device for misfortune varies from society to society (cf. chapter 1, n. 2). Nonetheless, despite the negative views of obeah expressed by many contemporary West Indians and the fact that obeah is still criminalized in most territories, practitioners continue to be sought out—to varying degrees in different societies—for help with a wide range of life's problems. The services contemporary obeah practitioners typically provide include, for example, cures for ailments or disease, protection from harm, good luck in everyday affairs (e.g., school exams or finding and keeping a job), and help with achieving pregnancy, discovering lost objects, and ameliorating social relationships (e.g., stopping an errant husband from cheating on his wife, or holding on to a lover).

Contemporary newspaper reports about obeah practitioners often center on these or similar themes. Although such reports are especially common in Jamaica, they are hardly unique to that island. In Barbados, for example, recent newspaper articles have reported on women who consulted an obeah man "for problems of the heart": they wanted "to get their men to stop cheating or to get them to love them more or to carry away other women's men" (Bradshaw 2005). A woman was reported to have paid visits to an obeah woman in Bridgetown, from whom she bought "various love potions" in order to entice a man away from his wife (*Nation News* 2006); and a young mother, trying to ensure that her daughter successfully passed an exam to get into a top school, "visited a popular obeah woman who gave her daughter a special necklace to wear" (*Nation News* 2009).[10] Recent examples from Jamaica also reflect the positive value attached to obeah practitioners and the beneficial services they claim to be able to provide. A prominent obeah man in the parish of Manchester boasted of his skills to a newspaper reporter as follows: "You name it man. Anything you want done for you I will do it. If you want a visa I have something for that. If you woman leave you I can get her back for you. If you have a court case I will deal with that too" (*Jamaica Gleaner* 2007). Another newspaper report noted how "Obeah men in sections of the island are boasting of an increase in profits from thugs visiting them to stay out of jail . . . the increase for the aid of obeah comes in the wake of intense pressure on members of the underworld by police in recent times" (*Jamaica Star* 2010). Such examples could be multiplied by recent newspaper accounts elsewhere in the Caribbean.

Close to forty years ago, Kamau Brathwaite (1974:74–75) published an essay that challenged conventional scholarly perspectives of the time. He stressed:

> the principle of obeah is . . . like medical principles everywhere, the process of healing/protection through seeking out the source or explanation of the cause . . . of the disease or fear. This was debased by slave master/missionary/prospero into an assumption, inherited by most of us, that obeah deals in evil. In this way, not only has African science been discredited, but Afro-Caribbean religion has been negatively fragmented and almost . . . publicly destroyed.

The history of anti-obeah legislation in the West Indies and the texts of the laws themselves amply support Brathwaite's perspective on this widely misunderstood dimension of West Indian society and culture.

Images of Obeah

*Practitioners at Work in
Suriname, Trinidad, and Jamaica*

Figure 2. An obeah woman at work, Paramaribo, Suriname, c.1831 (from Benoit 1839: plate xvii, fig. 36). Courtesy, the John Carter Brown Library.

PIERRE JACQUES BENOIT (1782–1854), a Belgian artist, visited Suriname around 1831; internal evidence in his illustrated book indicates he probably stayed for "many months" (De Groot 1968:292–296). The 100 lithographs he published are derived from drawings he made during his visit, including time in Paramaribo, the capital, as well as trips into the interior visiting Maroons and Amerindians.[1] The lithographs are usually accompanied by textual descriptions of the scenes he graphically recorded. Although the description of the scene shown in figure 2 (Benoit 1839:25–26) is relatively brief and sparse in ethnographic detail, it nonetheless represents a rather unique firsthand account of a practitioner of one kind of obeah at an early date. She is engaged in a characteristic activity (i.e., healing), although we do not know to what extent her particular practices and the layout and furnishings of her house typified those of Suriname healers in general at this time.

Although Benoit does not mention the term *obeah* or explicitly refer to her as an "obeah woman," the practices he describes come under the rubric of what is known as obeah (or obia) in Suriname today and most likely would have been qualified as such by spiritual practitioners during the period of his writing. It appears from Benoit's description that these practices are related to the particular Afro-Surinamese religious complex today known as *Papa* or *Vodu*, variants of which are found among both the coastal Creole population and the Maroon peoples of the interior, such as the Saramaka and Ndyuka. Papa, which is but one of a number of distinct Afro-Surinamese religious traditions, centers on the veneration of the spirits or gods (known as *papa gadu*) believed to inhabit the bodies of boa constrictors (known as *papa sineki*). When they possess mediums, these divinities are sometimes referred to as *papa obia*; the spiritual power emanating from them, which can be tapped for healing and other positive purposes, is also called *papa obia*. (For more on the Papa, or Vodu, religious tradition in the Guianas, see Hurault 1961; Wooding 1981; Stephen 1986.) Other Afro-Surinamese religious traditions, such as Kumanti (Kromanti) and Ampuku, use the term *obia* in similar or identical ways. Indeed, of the terms referencing African-identified spiritual beliefs and practices in Suriname, obia is one of those applied most broadly.

For most of its colonial history, Suriname was a Dutch colony and not a part of the British West Indies. Nonetheless, because Suriname began as an English plantation colony and was connected through migration with other English colonies in the Caribbean, such as Barbados and St. Kitts, during the seventeenth century and because the term *obia* remains prominent in Suriname today, we believe that Benoit's illustration of one kind of obeah practice in Suriname serves as a suitable representation for the purposes of the present book.

Benoit's description of the scene, as translated from the French, follows:[2]

> For a long time I had wanted to know one of the women who we would call a sibyl in Europe, but in this country they call *Mama Snekie*, Mother of Serpents, or *Water Mama*.[3] These women are regarded as oracles by the Negroes who made me concerned that, as a White, it would be very difficult for me to see a Mama Snekie. A Negress who I knew and to whom I expressed this wish, promised to speak to one of her acquaintances about my interest. A month later, she told me that she was going to consult the *Water Mama* about the plight of her sick child. Having renewed my promise to remunerate her as well as to reassure her that I would disclose nothing of such a visit, she arranged a meeting along the *Platte Brug*[4] for the following day at seven-o-clock in the evening.
>
> The next day, as soon as she saw me she left her companions and moved towards the top of the *Sarameca-Straat*.[5] I followed her. At the end of the street, she took several little winding paths, crossed a hedge, and went towards a very dense grove of trees. After she had pushed aside some large leaves from a banana tree, I noticed a very low cabin that had been hidden by the leaves.
>
> My guide knocked on the little door. When it opened I saw an old and emaciated Negress whose face, neck, and chest were tattooed.[6] Her head was covered with a long white cotton sheet, whose two ends went down her back. A white skirt fell from about her loins to halfway down her legs; the rest of her body was naked. The woman was hardly visible but for a weak light shining from a lamp she held in her hand. She presented the living image of one of these furies, so beautifully described by the ancient poets.
>
> After I responded by making affirmative signs to questions that I did not understand, I was admitted into the sanctuary, that is to say into the first room. In a corner, a wool blanket was spread on the earthen floor, there were two to three calabashes and several Indian jugs on a small wooden table; tree trunks served as chairs. This was how the first room was furnished.
>
> After she had exchanged a few words with my guide, the sibyl took her lamp and went through a little door in the back of the front room which led into the next room.
>
> When I had first arrived, I thought I had noticed something black crouched in the corner of the first room. But when the Water Mama left the room, I could hear much more distinctly someone sighing, *Tata, Tata. helpie wie*[7] (God help me).

But a bright light shining through the cracks of the wooden planks that separated the rooms suddenly distracted me from this strange noise. The little door opened, and we were admitted into a kind of sanctuary that was only lit by a lamp burning spirit or *voorloop* ["une lampe dans laquelle brûlait de l'esprit ou voorlop"].[8] A big earthen pot filled with water was on the floor under this lamp. The pot contained several little garter snakes ["petites couleuvres"] that all Africans have the art of taming.[9]. The wall was covered with stuffed snakes and with crudely modeled little clay idols of men and animals.

After having struck herself several times with a tree branch ["une branche"], and after having made some convulsive, writhing motions, the sibyl took a stick ["un bâton"[10]] and stirred the water in the pot several times (Fig. 36), while addressing a little clay figure next to her.

My guide, seemingly more dead than alive, stood erect in front of the Mama Snekie who addressed several words to her. In her fright, my guide did not respond except by nodding her head and raising her eyes to the ceiling. She otherwise stayed immobile, like a statue.

The sorceresses poured water from the pot into the calabash and then made the Negress drink. She made her drink again and then gave her herbs to be administered to her child. All finished, we departed and I left my offering in the sibyl's hands. *Tankie, masra* (thank you, master), she responded to me.

As we went through the first room, I again saw the black mass which I had earlier heard breathing painful sighs. She was standing and I supposed from her tattoos that she was a priestess, the sibyl's companion.

We left by the same way we had come. The Negress told me that now her child would not die. I gave her my present, and I promised that I would never show a white person the house of the sorceress—which would have been very difficult for me to do anyway. The cannon shot separated us; because she was a slave, she was obliged to return to her quarters.[11] As for me, I returned to my lodging to record the scene that I had just witnessed.

Sibyls, as well as men that perform the same work and are called *Quasi*[12], are sometimes summoned to discover Negroes who use poison and steal or to be consulted in cases of illness.

After describing his visit to the Water Mama, Benoit (1839:26–27) then recounts a few incidents that had been related to him but that he had not observed. These incidents involved calling in a "Quasi" for several problems, including identifying a thief, curing a white man who had been allegedly poisoned, and discovering some lost objects. Benoit is highly skeptical, if not critical, of these procedures, but nowhere does he suggest these practices were associated with malevolence.

Figure 3. An obeah man at work, Trinidad, early nineteenth century (from Bridgens 1836: plate 21). Courtesy, Library of Congress.

THIS IMAGE OF AN OBEAH MAN was originally published by Richard Bridgens (1836: plate 21) in his *West India Scenery*.[13] A sculptor, designer, and architect, Bridgens was born in England in 1785, but in 1825 he moved to Trinidad where his wife had inherited a sugar plantation. Although he occasionally returned to England, he ultimately lived in Trinidad for seven years and died in Port of Spain in 1846.[14]

In this image, an obeah practitioner, referred to as a "dadie," is addressing a characteristic issue, widely reflected in anti-obeah laws throughout the British Caribbean, that is, discovering an alleged thief or someone who had committed some other crime within the enslaved community. At the time the original drawing was made, between 1825, when Bridgens arrived in Trinidad, and 1836, when his book was published, these activities would have been illegal in Trinidad. We have no information, however, whether the procedures described by Bridgens existed elsewhere in Trinidad when he made the drawing or in earlier or later periods; moreover, we cannot say whether what he describes can be generalized beyond the specific, unidentified, plantation reported here and we do not know whether terms such as *Doo di Doo bush* and *dadie* were common.[15]

Bridgens captioned this image "Negro superstition, the Doo di Doo bush, or which is the thief" and describes this scene, "which passed under the eye of the author," as follows:

> This is a kind of ordeal in use among the Negroes, for extorting a confession of guilt from persons suspected of theft or other crime. The officiating person is generally some Negro, whose success on previous occasions has procured him the superstitious veneration of his tribe. The ceremony is conducted with much solemnity. The injured party communicates his suspicions to the Dadie (as the reputed sorcerer is called), who appoints a time for the trial. A refusal of the suspected person to accept the challenge is considered an admission of guilt. If he abides the trial it is conducted as follows: the Dadie twists a band out of the branches of a common shrub, at intervals sprinkling salt on it, and accompanying the operation with some rude form of incantation in his own language. Thus formed, it is passed round the neck of the supposed culprit, who is then called upon to clear himself by oath of the imputed crime. The Negroes are led to believe that if they perjure themselves on this occasion, the band would remain immovably twisted round the neck, and, by gradually tightening itself, ring from the party an acknowledgment of his guilt. This effect is produced by a dexterous turn of the hand by the operator when from circumstances he

has reason to suspect that the accusation is true. The numerous confessions obtains this mere anticipation of what is so much dreaded, added to those extorted by this last stroke of art, confer on the Dadie all the dignity of magic powers.

It is clear that the ordeal described by Bridgens is based on African oath-taking practices, although determining the specific African origins of this particular instance, were it possible, would require further research. Similar practices were described in various other parts of the Caribbean during the slavery period, and related oath-taking procedures relying on divination continue to be followed by contemporary Maroons in the Guianas (and to a lesser extent, those in Jamaica) even today (see Bilby 1997 for a few examples). Among the Aluku and other present-day Guianese Maroons, divination of this kind—indeed, divination in general—is referred to as *obia*, this being one of the term's primary meanings (Bilby n.d.).

Figure 4. *Jamaican Spiritual Balm-Yard* (detail), painting by Sylvester Woods, c.2003. Collection of Wayne Cox; courtesy, Sylvester Woods and Wayne Cox.

BALM-YARD IS A COMMON JAMAICAN term for a place where traditional spiritual techniques, including obeah, are used for healing. Martha Beckwith (1969:131–132), for example, in the 1920s noted that "obeah practitioners may act as doctors to cure the sick. Either they may visit the patient in his home, or they may keep what is called a balm-yard, where the patient is brought to be cured" (cf. Cassidy and Le Page 1967:22).

Sylvester Woods (who died c.2007) was a self-taught Jamaican artist from Port Maria, St. Mary parish, whose paintings have been exhibited at the National Gallery of Jamaica and a number of galleries in the United States. Known for his depictions of traditional Jamaican spiritual contexts and themes, Woods himself dabbled in obeah as a young man and at one point considered studying to become an obeah man.

In an interview with Kenneth Bilby (January 11, 2004), Woods elaborated on this painting (to which he gave the title *Jamaican Spiritual Balm-Yard*), as follows (paraphrased here from Bilby's notes): The scene depicted is a healing ceremony, presided over by an obeah man (in a robe, holding candles). The skull on the table belongs to the dead man whose duppy (spirit) the healer uses to carry out his work. The skeleton in a policeman's uniform represents this duppy, which has been sent by the obeah man to get rid of another, evil duppy that has been afflicting the patient currently being attended to (seated at the table); the duppy controlled by the obeah man chases the afflicting duppy out one of the windows. Several other patients sit on a bench behind the healer awaiting their turn. Next to the other window, another duppy is seen hovering over one of these patients, trying to harm him (preparing to give him a spirit "blow" or "lick" with a stick or club). This evil duppy will soon also be vanquished by the healer and the duppy working for him.

While skulls and other human bones often carry fearful associations in Jamaica and other parts of the Caribbean, summoning up stereotypes of harmful "black magic," they can be used, as this painting clearly shows, for healing and other positive purposes. However, it should be stressed that the evidence suggests that only a small proportion of what is known as obeah today makes use of human bones.

Patterns in Governance and Vagrancy Laws

Framing the Development of Anti-Obeah Legislation

THIS BRIEF CHAPTER SERVES AS a prelude to chapter 4, offering some basic information on the history of governance and legislative processes in the British West Indies and English vagrancy law as these affected the development of anti-obeah legislation. It is intended to provide a larger interpretive framework to assist in understanding the mass of factual materials presented in chapter 4, which consists of an extensive survey of anti-obeah legislation across the Anglophone Caribbean over more than two centuries. Collected from a wide array of sources, this survey contains detailed summaries of the vast majority of anti-obeah laws and makes the actual contents of this legislation readily accessible to a scholarly and broader readership for the first time. In the present chapter we briefly discuss the legislative bodies that enacted the laws, as well as England's 1824 Vagrancy Act, which greatly influenced anti-obeah legislation in the post-slavery period. In chapter 4, we discuss the laws themselves. Our discussion is broken down into a number of discrete sections, each devoted to a particular West Indian jurisdiction. For each territory a summary of relevant local legislation is presented in chronological order. We believe this method of presentation opens the way to new insights and promises to enhance our understanding of larger patterns in the development of anti-obeah legislation and how obeah was perceived by the ruling elites. For example, by viewing these diverse materials from across the region and from different periods of time back to back, one can begin to see the degree to which legislators from different territories drew upon a common pool of sources for their understandings, frequently borrowing ideas and language from one another. At the same time, one is struck by the arbitrariness of some of the local variations that made their way into the laws of particular jurisdictions. (Time and resource limitations have prevented us from probing the reasons for these variations. For example, we have not delved into legislative proceedings, such as minutes of Houses of Assembly, that might offer clues. But we believe we have provided the materials for future researchers.)

Another noticeable pattern is a gradual reduction in the harshness of punishments during the post-emancipation era. However, in certain territories there are also curious reversals of this trend from time to time, with sudden increases in penalties that call out for explanation. Yet another trend that becomes apparent when viewing these materials in close succession is a shift over time from representations of obeah practice as an actual or ostensible use of supernatural or spiritual power, directed toward particular ends, to language portraying it as an inherently and consciously fraudulent economic activity.

Who Made the Laws: The Old Representative System and Crown Colony Rule[1]

The constitutional history of the British colonies in the Caribbean—what is today the Anglophone Caribbean—is quite complicated and, especially during the earliest years, not entirely uniform. However, by the 1660s all territories had a similar form of internal governance, with a royal governor appointed by the Crown to represent its interests. The old representative system (ORS) is essential to understanding constitutional history and legislative enactments in many former British West Indian colonies. Under this system, the governor theoretically controlled both the executive branch of government and the judiciary; he had the power of veto over all bills passed by the legislature, and bills required his assent for passage.

The legislature was composed of two houses. The upper house, or Council, included members who were usually prominent merchants or planters (all of whom were slaveholders) and were nominated by the governor or representatives of the Crown in London. The lower house was the House of Assembly. Its members were elected by male "freeholders" who represented their local unit of governance—usually the parish—on the basis of a narrow franchise that was contingent on property and, during the earlier periods, usually race and religion as well (non-whites and non-Christians were excluded from the electorate). Membership in the lower house was invariably composed of the most prominent and wealthy landowners and slaveholders. Although the governor was theoretically the supreme legislative authority, the lower house in actual fact exerted a powerful influence in the shaping of local legal systems. In effect, it was the local white elites, through their representative institutions, who dominated local governance from the earliest days of settlement and colonization (Greene 2010). There were "minor variations" in this system of governance among colonies and at different periods of time, but "there was nevertheless a remarkable uniformity of constitutional usage in them all" (Wrong 1969:37). The old representative system predominated throughout the seventeenth and eighteenth centuries.

By the early nineteenth century Britain had instituted a new form of government, Crown colony rule, which superseded representative governance; it was first imposed on the new British colonies of Trinidad and St. Lucia, but after 1838 it was applied in various ways to older colonies. The Crown colony model, Barry Higman (2011:191–192) has written,

> was designed to put control firmly in the hands of governors and the newly emerged Colonial Office in London. Rather than an assembly made up of rich white men elected by their equals, the governor of a crown colony needed only the support of a Council, the members of which he nominated and most of whom were officials appointed ex officio. The governor, in turn, was under the thumb of the Colonial Office.

Over the course of the nineteenth century, with the exception of Barbados and the Bahamas, the Crown colony replaced the old representative system.

By the end of the nineteenth century there were essentially "two contrasting types" of colonies in the British Caribbean: Crown colonies and "partially self-governing colonies." In both types a Crown-appointed governor and executive council constituted the executive branch of government. In the Crown colonies, whose autonomy varied in individual cases, the legislative branch consisted of a legislative council with members who were usually appointed. The "partially self-governing colonies" had some elected representation, although this was limited; the legislative branch was typically composed of both an assembly and a council (Higman 2011:210; cf. Wrong 1969:71 n. 1).

Whatever the specifics of the governance system in any given British West Indian territory at a particular moment in its history, all legislation, including that directed against obeah, was enacted by colonial authorities and plantocratic and merchant interests. In other words, the laws were created by a white elite, with a few individual exceptions from the "colored class" among the Crown colonies, whose lifestyle and politico-economic interests were far removed from those of the mass of the population—those for whom anti-obeah and comparable social control laws were essentially intended. With the introduction of universal adult suffrage in the British West Indies, starting in the mid-1940s in Barbados and Jamaica and in other colonies in the early to mid-1950s, legislative authority increasingly came into the hands of representatives of the majority, most of whom were descended from the former slave population. Nonetheless, despite a new, more democratic era, the imprint of an oppressive colonial past defined by slavocracy and the abuses of the post-emancipation era continued to be discernible in certain components of local legislation, as exemplified by the fact that obeah has continued to be criminalized—albeit in a mitigated form—in most territories to the present day. Current legislation and prevailing attitudes to obeah, we maintain, represent a lingering echo of the slave and colonial past that resounds in the present.

Vagrancy Acts

After the abolition of slavery in 1834–38, the slave codes were nullified, but the legal sanctions against obeah, rather than being removed, were incorporated into a series of vagrancy acts that were introduced over the course of the nineteenth century. In this way, the negative views and legal opinions of those who had enacted the older laws were given new life in the post-emancipation era. Vagrancy laws have an ancient history in English law, and over the centuries they have periodically been changed and amended. In 1824 a new vagrancy act came into force in England. This act was intended to address a variety of social issues associated primarily, if not entirely, with the working class and the poor. This piece of English legislation served as a model for the post-emancipation vagrancy acts in the British West Indies, some of which have endured in one form or another until the present day.

As C. G. Hall (1997:338, 353), a British lawyer and former member of the law faculty at the University of the West Indies (Barbados), explains, the West Indian vagrancy laws "were a direct response [by local white elites and colonial authorities] to the real, supposed and potential problems posed by emancipation"; these laws "merely borrowed the jargon" of England's 1824 law by incorporating a number of its features, including its phraseology. Clause IV of the 1824 act is the one most immediately relevant to anti-obeah provisions in West Indian vagrancy acts. The clause included some fourteen offenses that defined a "rogue and vagabond," punishable on the first offense with a jail sentence of up to three months with hard labor. Heading the list of "rogues and vagabonds" were those "pretending or professing to tell fortunes, or using any subtle craft, means or device, by palmistry or otherwise, to deceive and impose on any of His Majesty's subjects" (Raithby 1824:781).[2] West Indian vagrancy laws incorporated this phrase, sometimes with minor variations in wording, but with the word *obeah*, as will be shown below, inserted after *palmistry*.

Unlike the slave laws that preceded them, West Indian vagrancy laws were not phrased in explicitly racial terms, but they were clearly directed against the new class of emancipated slaves. These acts, in the words of Rose-Marie Belle Antoine, a Trinidadian lawyer and member of the law faculty at the University of the West Indies (Barbados), "continued to reflect the unequal structure of the ex-slave, colonial society [and] were used deliberately to reinforce this structure." Although the acts were used as "instruments of social control" in both England and the West Indies, they had a special significance in the latter, where they were specifically intended to maintain "the pre-emancipation status quo as far as possible." Despite the similarity of the West Indian vagrancy laws "in content and form to English vagrancy laws . . . their focus and objectives were exceedingly different"; in the West Indies these laws functioned "to subjugate sociological, cultural and legal identity and the very sense of dignity, personhood and statehood . . . in the black masses" (Antoine 2008:21–23). In brief, the principle of control that was fundamental to West Indian societies during the slavery era persisted in somewhat altered forms in the "free societies" constructed after emancipation, as local white elites and their colonial supporters, unwilling to relinquish their dominant position, continued to rely on time-tested means to keep the mass of the population under their control. Not only the vagrancy acts but also the specific obeah acts, as well as anti-obeah provisions in other laws, must be understood in this context.

The Territories and Their Laws

IN ORDER TO GIVE A GENERAL idea of the local legal and political contexts within which anti-obeah legislation developed, we precede each territorial discussion with a brief overview of the territory's legislative and political history.[1]

Jamaica

Political and Governmental History

England seized Jamaica from the Spanish in 1655. By 1663 the old representative system had been established, but in 1866, in the wake of the Morant Bay Rebellion, Crown colony government and direct rule by the Crown replaced it. Jamaica's Crown colony status continued until 1944, when universal adult suffrage was introduced and there was a shift toward internal self-government. In 1958 the island became a member of the Federation of the West Indies (full internal self-government was obtained in 1959), but it withdrew in 1962 when it gained full independence from Britain.

Anti-Obeah Laws

In December 1760 Jamaica enacted the earliest law in the British West Indies to include a provision explicitly directed against obeah. This piece of legislation was introduced in response to a major slave revolt in 1760 known as Tacky's Rebellion, in which obeah men were alleged to have played a major role by convincing participants that they could be made "invulnerable" to British weapons (Long 1774:451–452; Jamaica 1789b). Titled "An Act to Remedy the Evils Arising from Irregular Assemblies of Slaves," the law went into effect on January 1, 1761, and was intended to regulate several areas of slave life.² The question of obeah was raised as an important concern in the law's preamble, which pointed to the presence on "many estates and plantations" of "obeah men and obeah women by whose influence over the minds of their fellow slaves . . . many and great dangers have arisen destructive of the peace and welfare of this island."

Clause 10 specifically addresses "the practice of obeah." Characterizing obeah as a "wicked art" and accusing obeah men and women of "pretending to have communication with the devil and other evil spirits"—a phrase later employed in other Jamaican slave laws, as well as in the laws of British Honduras (1791), Barbados (1806), Antigua (1809), and Grenada (1825)—the law applied to "any Negro or other slave, who shall pretend to any supernatural power, and be detected in making use of any blood, feathers, parrots beaks, dogs teeth, alligators teeth, broken bottles, grave dirt, rum, egg-shells or any other materials relative to the practice of obeah or witchcraft, in order to delude and impose on the minds of others." (This itemization of material objects allegedly used in obeah practices was reproduced in later Jamaican laws enacted during the slave period; outside of Jamaica, Grenada is the only colony to have adopted the same wording, in its 1825 Slave Consolidation Act, discussed below). Conviction could result in execution or transportation from the island (Jamaica 1771:52–57; Jamaica 1792:27).

The 1760 act was slightly modified in December 1761, but the obeah clause remained the same (Jamaica 1771:63; Jamaica 1792:26–27). In December 1781 a number of separate earlier laws regulating the enslaved population (including the 1760 law) were repealed, and a new consolidated slave law was enacted. The 1781 law merely repeated in its entirety the obeah clause of the 1760 law

(Jamaica 1786:277, clause 49). The 1781 law expired in 1784 (Jamaica 1789a:v) and was replaced by the consolidated slave law of December 1788, which went into effect on January 1, 1789, and was designated as the "present Code Noir" of Jamaica (Jamaica 1789a).[3] In the sections dealing specifically with obeah, there were some minor changes in wording and sentencing from earlier laws. In clause 40 the phrase "pretending to have communication with the devil and other evil spirits" was retained, and the law still asserted that obeah people could influence the "weak and superstitious" into believing that they could protect them from "any evils that might otherwise happen." The penalty of death or "such other punishment as the court shall think proper" (transportation from the island is not mentioned) was still imposed on "any slave who shall pretend to any supernatural power, in order to affect the lives of others, or promote the purposes of rebellion." Although clause 41 does not mention obeah (an apparent oversight that was rectified in later laws), it includes a provision directed at "any negro or other slave" who used a "poison or poisonous drug" against someone even though "death did not result"; the penalty was execution or confinement for life with hard labor (Jamaica 1789a:10–11). The 1789 provisions remained in effect in a 1792 law, but the word *obeah* was added in connection with poison, making it illegal to use "any poisonous drug in the practice of obeah." A person convicted of this crime could, like those found guilty of other obeah infractions, be "hanged, transported, or otherwise punished, at the discretion of the court" (Jamaica 1793:156). These anti-obeah provisions remained on the books over the following years.

In December 1809 Jamaica enacted a lengthy Consolidated Slave Act containing ninety-one clauses, of which three related to obeah.[4] Clause 37 essentially repeats the wording of the 1760 law, including the phrase "pretending to have communication with the devil and other evil spirits," and the practice of obeah was still punishable by death or transportation if "supernatural power" was used to promote rebellion or "affect or endanger the life or health of any other slave." Clause 38 addresses the use of any "poison, poisonous or noxious drug, pounded glass, or other deleterious matter in the practice of obeah"; even if no death resulted, the convicted person could be put to death (transportation was not given as an option). Finally, clause 39 includes certain elaborations on the wording used in the 1760–61 law, focusing on "any slave" who was found to possess poison, "pounded glass, parrots beaks, dogs teeth, alligators teeth, or other materials notoriously used in the practice of obeah or witchcraft, and in a state of evident preparation for carrying on such dangerous and nefarious practice"; the penalty was transportation "or such other punishment, *not extending to life*, as the court" should decide (Jamaica 1809:144–145; emphasis added).

On December 31, 1816, another lengthy consolidated slave law repealed and revised earlier laws and added many new provisions. Only two of the more than one hundred clauses of this "Act for the Subsistence, Clothing, and the Better Regulation and Government of Slaves" dealt with obeah. Clause 52 ordained that any "negro or other slave" was to "suffer death" if convicted of using "any poison, or poisonous or noxious drug, pounded glass, or other deleterious matter in the practice of obeah," even if the victim did not die. Clause 53 specified that if "any slave" were to be found with "any poisonous drugs, pounded glass, parrots' beaks, dogs' teeth, alligators' teeth, or other materials notoriously used in the practice of obeah or witchcraft," that person was liable to be transported from the island "or such other punishment, not extending to life, as the court shall think proper to direct" (Lunan 1819:124–125).

A few other laws with anti-obeah provisions were enacted during the remainder of the slave period, but they never actually went into force. For example, a major consolidated slave law passed by the Assembly and Council in December 1826 contained 139 clauses. However, only one of these, clause 84, was germane to obeah. This clause repeats some of the wording in earlier laws—for example, "communication with the devil and other evil spirits, whereby the weak and superstitious are deluded into a belief of their having full power to exempt them, whilst under their protection, from many evils"— and was similarly directed against "any slave who shall pretend to any supernatural power, in order to excite rebellion or other evil purposes, or shall use, or pretend to use, any such practices with intent or so as to affect or endanger the life or health of any other slave." The penalty for conviction was death or transportation (Jamaica 1826:169). Although it was signed by the governor, who then forwarded it to the colonial secretary for approval, the entire law was disallowed by the Crown, as were two subsequent efforts by the island's legislature to produce a comprehensive slave law.[5] Thus the 1816 act, including its anti-obeah provision, remained in force until February 1831, when

Jamaica enacted a new Consolidated Slave Law that was acceptable to the Crown.

The February 1831 law also contained 139 clauses, two of which pertained to obeah. Clause 83 essentially repeats the wording of earlier laws concerning the "wicked art of negroes, going under the appellation of obeah or myal men and women . . . pretending to have communication with the devil and other evil spirits" and their power over "the weak and superstitious" (this seems to be the earliest specific reference to myal in Jamaican laws and the only mention of the term in any British West Indian law of the slavery era). The law also repeats some of the other phrasing in earlier laws, for example, the 1809 law, which similarly mentions inciting to rebellion and intent to harm or kill and includes the same penalty of death or transportation. Clause 85 addresses the use of poison, pounded glass, and so forth to cause harm or death, but now the penalty was death or "such (other) punishment as the court shall award" (Jamaica 1831a:34–35).

In preparing for the post-emancipation period, the Jamaican legislature enacted in December 1833 a lengthy vagrancy act. This Jamaican law copied a great deal of the wording of England's 1824 Vagrancy Act. With respect to defining "rogues and vagabonds," it reproduces verbatim the following phrase from the English law: "all persons pretending to tell fortunes, or using any subtle craft, means or device by palmistry or otherwise to deceive or impose upon any of His Majesty's subjects."

To this, however, the Jamaican law adds "all persons pretending to be dealers in obeah." Conviction of being a "rogue and vagabond" carried a penalty of one to three months in jail with hard labor (Jamaica 1833; Raithby 1824:781). This was apparently the earliest mention of obeah in a British West Indian law intended to be in force during the post-slavery period, but it was disallowed.[6] Not long after this, however, in 1839 Jamaica enacted another vagrancy act that shared a number of features with vagrancy acts passed elsewhere in the British West Indies during the post-emancipation period. Dealing with "idle and disorderly persons, rogues and vagabonds, and incorrigible rogues," the law applied—as had the disallowed 1833 Vagrancy Act, with certain conditions—to those refusing to support their families although capable of working, as well as "every common prostitute wandering in the public streets or highways, or in any place of public resort, and behaving in a riotous or indecent manner" and certain types of beggars. Convicted persons were to be jailed with hard labor for up to six months. Obeah is not included or mentioned in this act (Curran 1889–90, vol. 2:54–60, 3 Victoria).7

However, in 1840, at the next session of the legislature, the 1839 act was amended to include among "rogues and vagabonds" anyone "pretending to be a dealer in obeah or myalism," as well as those "pretending or professing to tell fortunes, or using or pretending to use, any subtle craft or device, by palmistry or any such like superstitious means, to deceive or impose on any of Her Majesty's subjects." Persons convicted of being "a rogue and a vagabond" under this law could be committed to "hard labour" in the "house of correction" for up to twenty-eight days (Curran 1889–90, vol. 2:118–120, 4 Victoria). As with other laws, neither obeah nor myalism/myal was defined in the 1840 act. The 1840 Jamaican act was the first post-emancipation West Indian law to mention myalism and the only one to incorporate this term until well into the twentieth century, when it appeared in the laws of Montserrat and the British Virgin Islands.

"An Act for the More Effectual Punishment of Persons Convicted of Dealing in and Practising Obeah and Myalism" was passed in February 1856 because it was felt "expedient to increase the punishment" of persons who had been convicted of these practices under the 1840 act. This was the first time in the post-emancipation period that obeah was treated in separate legislation rather than being incorporated into a vagrancy act. The 1856 law revised some procedural features of the 1840 act and instituted new punitive measures; now convicted persons were to be placed in the "nearest prison" and sentenced to hard labor for up to three months. Alternatively, the accused could be tried in a criminal court and, if convicted, could be sent to the "general penitentiary or any other prison" for a period of up to one year with hard labor. In addition, at the discretion of the court, the convicted person could receive "corporal punishment" of up to seventy-eight whiplashes—but not more than thirty-nine lashes were to be given at one time, with a month's interval between each flogging (Curran 1889–90, vol. 3:357–358, 19 Victoria). As in the earlier laws, neither obeah nor myalism was defined.

In 1857, however, an "act to explain" the 1840 and 1856 laws "for the more effectual punishment of obeah and myalism" attempted to rectify various shortcomings in these laws, as well as to give "increased power for the punishment of the same." The 1857 law modified procedures by which suspected persons could be detected, arrested, arraigned, and sentenced and also attempted for the first time to define obeah and myalism, although it did so only in vague terms. Noting that "doubts may be entertained as to the meaning" of these two terms, the law laboriously defines "an obeah or myal man, or a dealer in obeah and myalism" as a person who

> shall for false, crafty, or unlawful purposes pretend to the possession of supernatural power, or who, by threat, promise, persuasion, or action, shall induce, or attempt to induce, any other person to believe that he can, by the exercise of any such supernatural power, bring about or effect any object, or carry out any design of his own, or of any other person, or, for the purpose of carrying out any such design or object, shall falsely, cunningly, or unlawfully make use of omens, spells, charms, incantations, or other preternatural devices.

By this law, continues the text, "the words 'obeah' and 'myalism' shall be understood to be of one and the same meaning and the like offence." And even though worded in the masculine gender, the law applied to both males and females. A convicted person could be sentenced to prison with hard labor for up to sixty days. Persons who consulted "anyone pretending to be a dealer in obeah and myalism" with the intent of bringing harm to someone else's person or property could be sentenced to prison for up to three months. If consulting an obeah or myal practitioner "to bring about some event" not injurious to others or "connected with any criminal intent, but which the said consulting party wishes to accomplish by the supposed supernatural agency of obeah or myalism," the person seeking the consultation could be fined up to forty shillings or imprisoned, with or without hard labor, for up to thirty days if the fine could not be paid (Curran 1889–90, vol. 4: 44–46, 21 Victoria).

The 1856 law against obeah and myalism was amended in 1892 to include modifications to legal procedures and the powers of the judiciary; for example, resident magistrates' courts were given the power to try obeah cases. In addition, the terms used to describe punishment were clarified, imprisonment was reduced to up to six months "without the option of a fine," flogging was reduced to "not more than thirty-nine lashes on the bare back with a cat-of-nine tails," and females were exempted from flogging; however, the main substance and wording of the earlier laws remained in force (Jamaica 1892). An

1893 law revised the punishments specified in 1856 and modified in 1892, but nothing of substance was changed in the anti-obeah definitions and provisions of earlier laws; now, however, the number of lashes was reduced to thirty-six for persons sixteen years old and above and to eighteen for those under sixteen (Jamaica 1893).

By 1893, then, several anti-obeah laws were in force in Jamaica, but a few years later these laws were repealed and consolidated in the major 1898 Obeah Act, a law that was later copied in one form or another by several other jurisdictions in the British West Indies. Assented to by the governor of Jamaica in June 1898, the "obeah law," following earlier laws, considered *obeah* and *myalism* to have "the same meaning." Neither was clearly defined. The obeah practitioner was simply categorized as "any person who, to effect any fraudulent or unlawful purpose, or for gain, or for the purpose of frightening any person, uses, or pretends to use any occult means, or pretends to possess any supernatural power or knowledge." The definition of an "instrument of obeah" was equally vague: "anything used or intended to be used" by an obeah practitioner. The prison term for conviction under the 1898 act was increased to up to one year, with or without hard labor, and one could receive a flogging in addition to or in lieu of prison. The number of lashes was reduced for those both over and under sixteen years of age, and women were exempted from flogging.

Also, anyone who "for any fraudulent or unlawful purpose" consulted an obeah practitioner or one "reputed to be an obeahman" (including anyone who had been previously convicted of "any enactment relating to obeah") could be imprisoned with hard labor for up to six months and be flogged in addition to or in lieu of imprisonment (females, however, still could not be flogged). A person who consulted an obeah practitioner "for the purpose of effecting any object, or of bringing about any event" and who paid for such services was liable to a fine of up to fifty pounds (later one hundred dollars) or to imprisonment, with or without hard labor, for up to one year. Anyone who was found to be in possession of "any instrument of obeah" was presumed to be an obeah practitioner—unless there was evidence to the contrary—and could be arrested and held liable under the act. Furthermore, anyone who wrote, published, sold, or distributed any printed matter that promoted "the superstition of obeah" was liable to a fine of up to forty dollars; if the fine could not be paid, that person could receive a jail sentence, with or without hard labor, for up to six months (Jamaica 1898).

With only minor modifications made in 1899 and 1903 (Jamaica 1899; Jamaica 1903), the 1898 law remained in force essentially unchanged throughout the twentieth century (e.g., Brown 1938:4593–4596). It was still in effect as of January 2011, nearly a half-century after Jamaica became independent, despite increasing protests against its retention. In fact, in November 2010 the island's deputy director of public prosecutions, Jeremy Taylor, called for repeal of the law. He was quoted as saying, "It cannot be shown in Jamaica where the practice of obeah is a danger to the public safety, public order and public morality or public health. . . . The retention of this law is repugnant to the spirit of the Constitution [i.e., Chapter 3, section 21, Protection of Freedom of Conscience]" (ChatyChaty 2010; cf. Pragg 1999; *Jamaica Gleaner* 2011).[8]

Barbados

Political and Governmental History

The British settled Barbados in 1627. The old representative system was in full operation by 1663 and persisted, with a slight interruption in the 1870s, until 1946–51, when universal adult suffrage was instituted as the first step toward internal self-government, which was achieved in 1961. Barbados remained a British colony until November 1966, when it became an independent nation within the British Commonwealth.

Anti-Obeah Laws

Early Barbadian slave laws did not specifically address or mention obeah. However, slaves accused of harming, injuring, or killing others through physical or supernatural devices could be tried under a 1688 slave law for committing, as Governor Combermere wrote in 1818, "such heinous and grievous crimes as obeah"—although, he noted, "the crime itself of obeah was not specified in the original [1688] law" (Combermere 1818b; cf. Hall 1764:116–117).[9] According to Combermere (1818a), whites considered obeah one of the most "heinous and grievous crimes"; it was "associated in the European mind with witchcraft," which in England had "been dealt with by a succession of Witchcraft acts" (Hall 1997:350–351).

The island's first law to explicitly mention obeah was passed in November 1806. According to the governor (Combermere 1818a), "the practice of obeah being a growing evil, it was thought necessary to pass an act for the punishment of it." The 1806 law did not define obeah or delineate its characteristics, but it did make it a capital offense if the death of a slave was caused by "any slave . . . pretending to any supernatural power, or by the practice of what is called obeah"; in addition, "any negro or other slave" convicted of preparing or administering "any poison or poisonous drug to any other slave in the practice of obeah"—even if the victim did not die—could be executed, transported from the island "for life," or receive "such other punishment" as the authorities deemed suitable. The law's preamble asserted that

> many valuable slaves have lost their lives or have otherwise been materially injured in their health by the wicked arts of certain Negro and other slaves going under the appellation of obeah men and women, pretending to have communication with the devil and other evil spirits, whereby the weak and superstitious are deluded into a belief of their having full power to exempt them, whilst under their protection, from any evils that might otherwise happen (Barbados 1806).[10]

Another anti-obeah law was passed in July 1818 because the one of 1806—which the new law repealed—had been "found ineffectual." The 1818 law was directed specifically against

> any person who shall willfully, maliciously, and unlawfully pretend to any magical or supernatural charm or power in order to promote the purposes of insurrection or rebellion of the slaves . . . or to injure and affect the life or health of any other person, or who willfully and maliciously shall use or carry on the wicked and unlawful practice of obeah.

It is significant that the word *person* was now substituted for *slave*, presumably to include free people of color (freedmen), a number of whom were former slaves and some of whom had been implicated in the island's major 1816 slave revolt (Handler 1974:85–86).[11] The penalties for practicing obeah under the new law were death or transportation (the 1806 law had mandated death alone); the use of poison against "any person (whether the said person be white or black or a person of colour)"—even if death did not result—could also bring a penalty of death or transportation or "such other punishment" as the court decided (Barbados 1818a).[12]

The judicial procedure specified in the 1818 law was slightly modified and clarified in a new anti-obeah law of May 1819, which also repealed the 1818 law (Barbados 1819). However, no substantive changes in wording were made to the 1818 law, and in the new law obeah continued to be a capital offense, although transportation was also an option.[13]

The major 1826 Slave Consolidation Act repealed all antiquated slave laws and incorporated all of the island's current slave laws into one piece of legislation (Barbados 1826). The "wicked and unlawful practice of obeah" continued to be a felony, but there were some modifications in wording and sentencing, and now the anti-obeah provisions were explicitly applied to the entire population, including any "white, free-colored, free-black person or slave." Persons convicted of using or pretending to use "any magical or supernatural charm or power" in order to encourage slaves to revolt or to "injure or affect the life or health of anyone" or who should otherwise "use and carry on the wicked and unlawful practice of obeah" could be executed without benefit of clergy or transported from the island (clause 37). Free persons or slaves who used poison or "any noxious substance" in "the practice of obeah" or who had in their possession such a substance with the intention of using it to harm or kill anyone, even though "death might not ensue," received the same sentence of death or transportation (clause 38). At one point the law features entirely new wording, now targeting "any person" who claimed to "have the power of divination," as well as anyone who practiced "fortune telling" or claimed to have "the charm or power of discovering or leading to the discovery" of lost or stolen goods. A slave convicted of this offense could be whipped (not to exceed thirty-nine lashes), jailed, "or worked in the public service" for up to a month. If the convicted individual was a "white, free-coloured, or free black person," there was instead a fine of from ten to twenty-five pounds in local currency (clause 39).[14]

The Slave Consolidation Act became invalid with the advent of general emancipation. In 1838 and 1840 Barbados, along with other jurisdictions in the British West Indies around the same time, passed the earliest of its vagrancy acts.[15] Although the 1840 law is identical in several respects to the one enacted in 1838, there are also some significant differences. With regard to obeah in particular, while the 1838 Barbados act makes no mention of it by name, the 1840 act simply adds the word *obeah* after the word *palmistry* found in the 1824 English Vagrancy Act (Hall 1997:353). Thus, in the 1840 law, *rogue* and *vagabond* now referred to, among others, "every person pretending or professing to tell fortunes, or using or pretending to use any subtle craft or device, by palmistry, obeah, or any such like superstitious means, to deceive and impose on any of Her Majesty's subjects." Obeah was not singled out for a unique penalty; along with the other infractions mentioned together with it, it now became a "vagrancy offence," with up to twenty-eight days of imprisonment with hard labor for conviction on the first offense—a significant reduction from the three-month sentence specified in 1838 (Barbados 1855:256–257; Hall 1997:358, 360).

Close to sixty years later, the Barbados legislature enacted the vagrancy act of 1897. The 1897 act incorporated most of the provisions of the 1840 act, and the obeah provision was identical. There were some procedural modifications in 1897, and the sentence for being a "rogue and vagabond" was raised to up to two pounds in local currency or imprisonment with hard labor for up to one month (Goodman and Clarke 1912:265–269; Archer and Fergusson 1944:145–146). The 1897 vagrancy act was periodically amended over the years but remained in force until the end of the twentieth century with no major substantive changes. The anti-obeah provision in particular—applying to any person who "pretends or professes to tell fortunes or uses or pretends to use any subtle craft or device, by palmistry, obeah, or any such like superstitious means, to deceive and impose on any person"—remained the same, except for changes in the amounts of fines to make them consistent with current currency (for example, by 1971 the fine could be up to $3,500 in Barbados currency). Modifications were also made in the jail terms for all offenders, not just those involved with obeah; the penalty was increased to a maximum of two years (Archer and Fergusson 1944:144–146; Barbados 1971; Barbados 1997).

The 1897 vagrancy law, as amended in 1971, was finally repealed in January 1998 with passage of what is known as the Minor Offences Act (1998). The latter incorporated certain offenses of the 1897 law—for example, "disorderly behaviour," aggressive and public solicitation by prostitutes, loitering, "obscene and profane language to intimidate a person," and lewd exposure—and imposed a fine of $2,500 or imprisonment for two years, or both (Barbados 1998). Although the Minor Offences Act, as Hall (1997:338 n. 60) points out, is "not to be called a Vagrancy Act [it] would seem to be redolent of the same odour." In any case, the 1998 law does not mention obeah; the word was simply dropped from the statute books.[16] For the first time in almost two hundred years and some three decades after Barbados became an independent member of the British Commonwealth, obeah, as such, was no longer illegal.

Trinidad and Tobago

Political and Governmental History

Before the separate islands of Trinidad and Tobago were amalgamated into a single political unit in the late 1890s, the administrative and constitutional experience of the two territories had differed greatly. In the sixteenth century the Spanish colonized Trinidad in a limited way, but in 1797 it was captured by the British and was formally ceded by Spain in 1802. Spanish law continued in force for many years, gradually being replaced by English law and locally enacted legislation. In 1848, all Spanish law was officially nullified.

Tobago was claimed by the Dutch, British, and French at varying times during the seventeenth and eighteenth centuries, but it ultimately came under British control in 1803. While Trinidad was a Crown colony for most of its colonial history, Tobago, in contrast, was governed under the old representative system until 1877, when, as for most other British Caribbean territories (except for Barbados and the Bahamas), the British government imposed Crown colony government. That form of government was virtually eliminated in the 1950s, when the twin-island territory began to move toward internal self-government; this was achieved in 1956 after universal adult suffrage was granted. Trinidad and Tobago was a member of the Federation of the West Indies during 1958–62 but gained independence in 1962. In 1976 Trinidad and Tobago proclaimed itself a republic, and today the country is known as the Republic of Trinidad and Tobago. In administrative terms, British Trinidad functioned as a separate colony until the union with Tobago in the late nineteenth century, while Tobago before the union was part of the government of the Windward Islands.

Anti-Obeah Laws

An ordinance proclaimed by the Trinidad governor in June 1800, about three years after the island became a British colony, introduced a new set of regulations governing the lives of the enslaved. Focusing primarily on the responsibilities and obligations of plantation owners or their representatives in regard to the material and labor conditions and treatment of slaves, the ordinance also contained an obeah provision. "Any Negro who shall assume the reputation of being a spell-doctor or obeah-man," article 11 specified, "and shall be found with an amulet, a fetishe [sic] or the customary attributes and ingredients of the profession" was to be taken before a local authority who could "inflict proper punishment" (not specified in the law). However, if it was ascertained that the accused had caused the death of someone ("as very frequently happens"), then the person was to be taken to jail and "prosecuted and dealt with according to law" (published in Carmichael 1961:379–383).[17]

After emancipation, an anti-obeah provision was included in Trinidad's 1838 vagrancy ordinance, passed on September 10, 1838. This seems to have been the earliest anti-obeah provision enacted in the West Indies during the post-emancipation period (followed by the Bahamas in 1839 and Jamaica, Barbados, and Dominica in 1840).[18] As in the vagrancy acts of other jurisdictions during this period, a number of offenses were associated with "idle and disorderly persons"; these were followed by offenses attributed to "rogues and vagabonds." The first offense placed in the latter category was

> pretending or professing to tell fortunes or to discover by means of any subtle art, craft or device, lost or stolen goods, or the person or persons by whom such lost or stolen goods had been taken, or professing or pretending by means of any such art, craft, or device, or by means of any tricks, device, preparation, or other such like matter or thing, to exercise any undue influence over the mind of any other person or persons; every person vending or practicing obeah, or any such like art, or using any subtle craft, palmistry, means or device, to deceive or impose on any other person or persons.

Conviction could mean jail for up to two months, with or without hard labor (Trinidad 1838, clauses 2 and 3).[19]

The Summary Convictions Ordinance of 1868 incorporated and modified provisions in the 1838 vagrancy act concerning "rogues and vagabonds," but now—under the heading "Superstitious Devices"—obeah was treated as a separate crime and not included under the offenses of "idle and disorderly persons" or "rogues and vagabonds." Stressing the fraudulent nature of obeah, as did laws in other jurisdictions, the new law defined obeah as "every pretended assumption of supernatural power or knowledge whatever for fraudulent or illicit purposes or for gain, or for the injury of any person." Employing wording similar to the earlier vagrancy act, the 1868 law was explicitly directed against those "who by the practice of obeah or by any occult means or by any assumption of supernatural power or knowledge" would intimidate; obtain goods or money; or "pretend" to discover lost or stolen goods and the person responsible for the same, to "inflict any disease" or otherwise injure a person's health, or "to restore any other person to health." The penalty was now made harsher: up to six months in prison, with or without hard labor. While in prison, a male could be whipped once (whipping could take place only "within the walls" of the jail), while a female could be kept in solitary confinement for a maximum of three days at a time and for not more than one month during the entire term of imprisonment (Garcia 1883–86:71, 80; Trinidad 1868 contains the same ordinance).

The 1868 Summary Convictions Ordinance was revised and consolidated a number of times over the years, but its anti-obeah provisions continued virtually unchanged. Although the Summary Convictions (Offences) Ordinance of 1901, for example, now defined various terms used in the ordinance, including obeah—"obeah signifies every pretended assumption of supernatural power or knowledge for fraudulent or illicit purposes or for gain, or the injury of any person"[20]—the only change in wording under the heading "Superstitious Devices" was that the phrase "corporal punishment" replaced "privately whipped" in the penalty for convicted males (Trinidad 1902–05, vol. 1:123, 130–131, vol. 6:33). With a couple of other small changes in wording, the anti-obeah provisions of 1901 were included in the Summary Convictions Offences Ordinance of May 1921 (Huggard 1925:333–334). When the 1921 ordinance was revised in 1940, there were again a couple of minor wording changes (and hard labor was deleted from the prison sentence), but the anti-obeah provisions of 1868 remained substantially unchanged (Devaux and Maingot 1941:439–440). Similarly, the revised ordinances of 1950 and 1980 also included minor changes in wording. The latter distinguishes between those over and under sixteen years of age with respect to corporal punishment, but the penalty remains the same (Maingot 1951:528; Trinidad 1980:24–25).

The 1980 Summary Offences Act, which in its sections on obeah was substantially the same as the one enacted in 1868, was amended in November 2000 with the passage of a lengthily titled law with the short title the Miscellaneous Laws Act, 2000. As a result of this act, all references to obeah were deleted from the laws of Trinidad and Tobago. However, the phrase "by any fraudulent means" replaced the earlier wording that had read "by the practice of obeah or by any occult means or by any assumption of supernatural power or knowledge." Thus, persons who engaged in any of the activities that earlier had been encompassed by obeah now could be prosecuted for fraud; obeah per se, however, was no longer an indictable offense (Trinidad 2000:1118–1120).

Guyana/British Guiana

Political and Governmental History

Colonized by the Dutch in the early seventeenth century, the three regions of Berbice, Demerara, and Essequibo were administered by the Netherlands until the mid-1790s, when they were taken over by Britain. After being temporarily restored to the Dutch, they were recaptured by the British in 1803. A complicated administrative and legal history followed. In 1814–15 the Netherlands ceded the colonies to Britain, and in 1831 they were united, officially becoming the Colony of British Guiana. Prior to this Berbice had been administered separately, while Demerara and Essequibo had been administered as the United Colony of Demerara and Essequibo. For most of its colonial history under British rule, British Guiana combined a few elements of representative government with direct rule from London. The move toward internal self-government began in 1953 with the introduction of universal adult suffrage.

Full internal self-government was achieved in 1961, and independence was finally granted in May 1966. Changing its name to Guyana, the country declared itself a republic in 1970. Today it is officially known as the Cooperative Republic of Guyana but remains a member of the Commonwealth of Nations (the former British Commonwealth).

Anti-Obeah Laws

It is unclear whether obeah specifically was criminalized in any of the slave laws that existed in the individual territories that later became part of the Colony of British Guiana.[21] In any case, the governor of Berbice issued a proclamation in 1810 (at which time anti-obeah laws already existed in about seven territories of the British West Indies) "against the practice of obeah." The proclamation was directed against "any negro or other slave" who was "found guilty of practicing obeah" or who claimed to have "supernatural powers" or to use "secret arts" to "threaten the life, health or happiness of any other slave or individual." Conviction was punishable by "death or such other punishment [as the] . . . case shall appear to require" (reproduced in Thompson 2002:149). It is unknown how long this proclamation was in effect.[22] However, nine years later another proclamation was issued by the Berbice Court of Criminal Justice against Hans, "a Negro of the Congo nation," for "carrying on a regular obiah [sic] trade," and more specifically for having been discovered on a plantation "with an obiah image and other spells" intended to help discover "poison or to remove bad things from that estate." Another slave, the documentary record indicates, had apparently sought Hans's services to obtain protection from harm. Hans was convicted and sentenced to be "severely flogged with rods" and then branded and imprisoned in chains for a year; after serving his jail sentence he was to be kept in chains and was to perform hard labor "for the benefit of the colony" for the remainder of his life (Thompson 2002:149–150).[23]

Similar proclamations may have been issued at other times during the period of slavery but, as far as we can tell, British Guiana had no specific anti-obeah legislation until after emancipation. The Colonial Office disallowed an 1838 "ordinance on vagrancy" on technical grounds, apparently because it was too heavily influenced by the "old slave codes" (Shahabuddeen 1973:74). We could not find a record of the 1838 ordinance contents (see Firth 1864:law number 16 under "disallowed acts"), but it is likely that it contained an anti-obeah provision, as did several other West Indian laws in effect around the same period.

The earliest anti-obeah legislation we could locate for the post-emancipation period was contained in an ordinance of January 1, 1855. It was enacted because, as the preamble stated, "the practice of obeah has increased to a great extent in this colony." With phrasing similar to that of laws found elsewhere in the West Indies, the British Guiana law was directed against those "practicing or pretending to practise obeah or witchcraft . . . to tell fortunes or to discover stolen goods or to deceive or impose upon any person." On first offense, the guilty person was jailed with hard labor for up to one year; males could be publicly whipped during their jail term, and females could also be placed in solitary confinement for up to one month. If convicted a second time, the jail sentence was extended to up to three years; a male could be publicly whipped up to three times, and a female was also subject to solitary confinement. The law also applied to persons who threatened "to have recourse to the practise of obeah" to extort money or intimidate anyone; the punishments were the same as above. Finally, anyone convicted of consulting an obeah practitioner was also subject to imprisonment—for up to one year with or without hard labor (British Guiana 1855; Firth 1864:527).

As in virtually all other West Indian anti-obeah laws, there was no attempt in the 1855 ordinance to define obeah, and this absence, as Brian Moore (1995:146) has pointed out, was (for those concerned about social justice) its "great weakness" because of the indiscriminate prosecutions and punishments it made possible.[24] Ordinance 21 of August 1856 delineated various offenses conventionally associated in West Indian vagrancy acts with an "idle and disorderly person" and a "rogue and vagabond"; the ordinance, however, makes no mention of obeah or related practices (British Guiana 1873:592–596). Meanwhile, the 1855 ordinance continued for several decades, but in 1877, according to Moore (1995:146), it was "decided that in the absence of a definition of obeah [in the 1855 ordinance], a person could only be convicted for receiving money under false pretences if he or she claimed to be capable of working charms and so forth." This problem was addressed by an 1877 ordinance that, although it "omitted all reference specifically to the term obeah . . . made anyone practicing witchcraft, sorcery, enchantment, conjuration, fortune-telling, palmistry, etc., aimed at deceiving, punishable under Ordinance 21 of 1856 as a rogue and a vagabond" (Moore 1995:146).

The anti-obeah provisions of the 1855 ordinance were ultimately replaced by an 1893 ordinance that went into effect in March 1894. As in other nineteenth-century legal codes, obeah was now treated under the category "Rogues and Vagabonds." This category included, among other offenses, "attempts to intimidate" others by "any kind of witchcraft, obeah, sorcery, enchantment or conjuration"; claims "to tell fortunes"; or the use of "any subtle craft, means, or device, by palmistry, cards, or otherwise, to deceive and impose upon any other person." Convicted "rogues and vagabonds" were liable to a fine of fifty dollars or three months in jail. As in other jurisdictions, an "incorrigible rogue" was a person who had previously been convicted of being a "rogue or vagabond" or who resisted when being arrested as one; such persons were liable to six months in jail "and to whipping or flogging" (British Guiana 1895:523–525).

Later revisions of the colony's laws continued the anti-obeah provisions of the 1893 ordinance (Rayner 1905:197–199), but in 1918 that ordinance was amended. The new version singled out and focused on "the practice of obeah." Obeah was now defined as "every pretended assumption of supernatural power or knowledge whatever for fraudulent or illicit purposes for gain, or for the injury of any person." In wording similar to that of the laws in other West Indian areas, the British Guiana law was directed against obeah practitioners and those who "by any occult means or by any assumption of supernatural power or knowledge, or by any pretended love philtre or medicine" attempted to "intimidate or influence any person"; defraud someone of money, property, or other valuables; discover lost or stolen goods (or the party responsible); cause illness or personal injury; or "restore any person to health." For the first time the law made medical fraud explicit. Persons who "shall procure, counsel, induce, or persuade, or endeavor to persuade" others to engage in such acts—including those who consulted obeah people, with or without payment—were also liable under the law.

A person convicted was considered "a rogue and vagabond" and could be imprisoned, with or without hard labor, for up to six months; males could also be sentenced to a "flogging" while in jail, and females could be placed in solitary confinement for up to three days at a time. Convicted persons could also be fined up to one hundred dollars in local currency. Another section of this ordinance dealt with persons discovered to have in their possession "any human skull or part thereof or other portion of the human body or any other article or thing for the purpose of being used in the practice of obeah or witchcraft"; such materials could then be "used in evidence in any case in which it may be required." (These references to a human skull and other body parts are unique among anti-obeah provisions in West Indian laws.) Those convicted of possessing "any article or thing" for use in "obeah or witchcraft" could be jailed for up to six months or fined up to five hundred dollars (MacKenzie 1923:497–498; British Guiana 1918).

The "Summary Conviction (Obeah) Ordinance," passed in March 1920, continued the 1893 and 1918 ordinances. It amended them by authorizing the post office to search any material sent through the mails that was suspected of containing "any charms or other articles of any description whatsoever to be used in witchcraft" or letters or printed matter "giving instructions in witchcraft or sorcery" (MacKenzie 1923:511–512; British Guiana 1920). In brief, the 1893 ordinance—with its amendments in 1918 and 1920 and subsequent minor revisions in wording, paragraph and section arrangement, and numbering—remained in force after Guyana's independence from Great Britain in 1966.[25]

The revised edition of the laws of Guyana published in 1973 retained earlier anti-obeah provisions as part of new legislation titled the Summary Jurisdiction (Offences) Act. Obeah was still defined as "every pretended assumption of supernatural power or knowledge whatever for fraudulent or illicit purposes or for gain, or for the injury of any person." Persons could still be convicted as "rogues and vagabonds" if they committed the violations specified in the 1918 ordinance, for example, if they were found to "pretend" to discover lost or stolen goods, inflict "disease" or "personal injury," cure or heal illness or disease, or "cause or divert affection," or, if consulting an obeah practitioner, to become a party to any such practices, whether or not payment was involved. Those convicted were liable to the same penalties of imprisonment (now for up to six months), flogging, and fines (the amount was now higher, in line with contemporary currency values). The section referring to the human skull or other human body parts remained the same, as did other sections concerning possession of materials "used in the practice of obeah or witchcraft," fortune-telling, and so on. Jail sentences for these offenses remained the same as well; only the amount of the fines was changed (Ramphal et al. 1973:54–55).

Although the new Guyanese constitution, like those of newly independent former British colonies elsewhere in the Caribbean, granted freedom of conscience and worship to all religions, there was no specific repeal of the anti-obeah provisions in earlier laws. However, in 1973 Prime Minister Forbes Burnham announced, as Kean Gibson (2001:16–19) has written, "that steps would be taken by his Government to repeal that part of the constitution that made it a specific offence to practice obeah—but the law would be there to ensure that some persons did not seek to practice obeah for capitalist gains." Although the obeah law was not actually repealed in 1973, many people believed that it had been, and Burnham's widely circulated statement, Gibson notes, "gave elite sanction to the practicing of obeah." Because of the widespread belief that obeah had been legalized, "obeah became a lucrative and competitive profession."

Guyana's Summary Jurisdiction (Offences) Act of 1973—which, as noted above, kept the anti-obeah provisions established in the late nineteenth century and retained them throughout the twentieth century—was amended in 1997 and again in 1998. In both cases the substance and wording of earlier anti-obeah provisions were not affected except that the fines were increased and made consistent with contemporary currency values and standards. However, the 1998 amendment also increased the jail sentences for several offenses: practicing obeah could now incur twelve months in prison, possessing "articles" that could be used in obeah could bring eight months, and fortune-telling, palmistry, and the like ten months; in the 1973 law the jail sentences had been, respectively, six months, six months, and three months (Guyana 1997; Guyana 1998).

The Summary Jurisdiction (Offences) Act was again amended in 2007, but none of the earlier anti-obeah provisions was altered or even mentioned in the revisions (Guyana 2007). Thus, despite what many people in Guyana and elsewhere continue to believe, the laws against obeah were still in force in Guyana as of January 1, 2008 (e.g., Guyana 2009:116), and probably remain on the books today (cf. Guyana 2010), with a conviction for practicing obeah still carrying a penalty of up to one year in jail.[26]

The Bahamas

Political and Governmental History

By the mid-seventeenth century, English settlers had colonized various islands within the archipelago of the Bahamas Islands, and the Bahamas remained a British colony for more than two centuries. Like Barbados, the Bahamas are an anomaly in terms of British Caribbean constitutional and political development. Neither territory became a Crown colony, and in both territories an oligarchy of British descent—the local white elite—remained highly influential in lawmaking throughout most of the colonial period. In the Bahamas, the old representative system was in full operation by 1728, and it remained essentially unchanged until 1959, when a shift toward internal self-government began with the granting of universal adult suffrage. Achieving full internal self-government in 1964, the Commonwealth of the Bahamas became a sovereign state and independent member of the British Commonwealth in July 1973.

Anti-Obeah Laws

It is uncertain whether anti-obeah provisions were included in eighteenth-century Bahamian slave laws (e.g., Bahamas 1789). A 1796 consolidated slave act included a clause invoking death or transportation for "any negro or other slave" convicted of using poison to kill, even if the intended victim did not die; however, unlike similar clauses elsewhere (e.g., Jamaica, Barbados, Dominica, Grenada, St. Vincent), the Bahamian law made no reference to obeah (Bahamas 1796:36). Another consolidated slave act, initially passed in 1824 (a later version went into effect a few years later), did not mention obeah either (Bahamas 1824).

The earliest anti-obeah provisions in the post-emancipation period appear in the Vagrancy Act of June 1839. This act was in fact one of the earliest post-emancipation laws in the West Indies to mention obeah. The list of "rogues and vagabonds" included those "pretending or professing to tell fortunes, or using, or pretending to use, any subtle craft or device, by palmistry, obeah, or any such like superstitious means, to deceive or impose on any of Her

Majesty's subjects, or upon any other person." Conviction could lead to jail with hard labor for up to twenty-eight days (Anderson 1850:286–288).

The 1839 Vagrancy Act was retained through subsequent revisions of the laws (e.g., Anderson 1862:659–662) and remained in effect until April 1873, when a new "Police Regulations" act incorporated its major provisions. Part IV of the Police Act was intended "for the better suppression of vagrancy, and for the punishment of idle and disorderly persons, and rogues, vagabonds, and other vagrants." A "rogue and vagabond" was still defined as in the 1839 law, and the wording relating to obeah and associated practices was also retained; the sentence for conviction remained the same (Malcolm 1901:580–582). However, sometime after 1873 the anti-obeah provisions were excised from the vagrancy acts and incorporated instead into the 1924 Bahamian penal code, which went into effect on January 1, 1927.[27]

The preamble to the 1924 penal code defined various terms employed in the code, among them *obeah* and *instrument of obeah*. The former was "any pretended assumption of supernatural power or knowledge, whatever, for fraudulent or illicit purposes, or for gain, or for the injury of any person," and the latter "any philtre, vial, blood, bone, image, or other article or thing . . . used or intended to be used in the practice of obeah"; these definitions have been retained in the current Bahamian penal code. Title XV of the penal code addressed "common offences against public order, health and morality" and included a section titled "Practising Obeah, etc." This section was directed against

> whoever practices obeah or by any occult means or by any assumption of supernatural power or knowledge intimidates or attempts to intimidate any person, or obtains or endeavors to obtain anything from any person, or pretends to discover any lost or stolen thing or the person who stole the same, or to inflict any disease, loss, damage or personal injury upon any person, or to restore any person to health.

The penalty was increased from earlier laws to "imprisonment for three months." The house of a person suspected of practicing obeah could be searched for "any article or thing used, or intended to be used, by him," and, if such an article was found, unless there was evidence to the contrary, it was presumed he was an obeah practitioner. In addition, if the accused—or anyone in the court when the accused was tried—was suspected of carrying a concealed "instrument of obeah," he could be searched without a warrant; if the "instrument" was found, the person was fined five pounds (Malcolm 1929:583–584, 707–708).[28]

The obeah section of the 1924/1927 penal code continued unaltered, except for one or two minor changes in wording, in the penal codes in force as of January 1, 1957; April 1, 1965; and, most recently, April 2002. In the last, the fine for having a concealed "instrument of obeah" in court was now twenty-five dollars, in keeping with the new currency, but the jail sentence was still three months (Bliss 1957:847–848, 973–974; Bahamas 1965:862, 863, 992; Bahamas 2000:148–149). As of January 1, 2009, the anti-obeah provisions of the Bahamian penal code had not been repealed (Bahamas 2007; Bahamas 2010a), and, as far as we can ascertain (e.g., Bahamas 2010b), obeah is still illegal in the Bahamas.

Leeward Islands Federation

Political and Governmental History

The Leeward Islands Federation, or Colony of the Leeward Islands, was formed by an act of the British Parliament in 1871 and was legally born in 1872. It consisted of Antigua, including Barbuda; Dominica; Montserrat; St. Kitts, Nevis, and Anguilla; and the Virgin Islands. The governor of the Federation resided in Antigua. Each unit had its own legislature, although the British Virgin Islands legislature abolished itself in 1902. There was also a federal legislative body composed of individuals appointed by the legislatures of each constituent unit.

Two kinds of laws were in force during most of the colonial period: those enacted by the federal legislature and those enacted by the individual colonies (the "presidential legislatures"). But where the laws of individual jurisdictions conflicted with those of the colony as a whole, the latter took precedence (Semper and Burns 1911:ix–xvi). The laws passed by the federal legislature, which applied to the whole colony, are discussed below. These remained in effect until the British government dissolved the Leeward Islands Federation in 1957, at which point each presidency (with the exception of the British Virgin Islands) became a separate colony that was incorporated into the short-lived West Indies Federation (January 1958–May 1962). Essentially, however, the Leeward Islands Federation was a Crown colony at both its central and unit levels; that is, the Crown could legislate on any matter that it considered of paramount importance.

Anti-Obeah Laws

The first law of the Leeward Islands Federation to contain anti-obeah provisions was the Small Charges Act (1891), which went into effect in 1892. It consolidated the various vagrancy acts of the Federation's individual jurisdictions, often retaining the original wording. Clause 45 was directed against "any person who pretends or professes to tell fortunes or uses any subtle craft means or device by palmistry obeah or otherwise or who pretends to cure injuries or diseases or effect any purpose by means of any charm incantation or other pretended supernatural practice"; conviction could lead to imprisonment "not exceeding six months" (Leewards 1892).

The 1904 Obeah Act, a major piece of legislation, superseded clause 45 of the 1891 law. The 1904 law pointedly did not define obeah, merely noting that the term "means obeah as ordinarily understood and practised, and includes witchcraft and working or pretending to work by spells or by professed occult or supernatural power." In explaining the 1904 act to the British colonial secretary in February 1905, Commissioner Watkins of Montserrat wrote—in a comment that could very well apply to all of the West Indies—"Though perfectly well understood by every inhabitant, obeah is difficult to define, and it is therefore best to leave it as 'obeah as ordinarily understood and practiced'" (quoted in Skinner 2005:148). "Instrument of obeah" was also vaguely defined, as in other West Indian laws, as "anything ordinarily used in the practice of obeah or intended to be so used" by one claiming "to be possessed of any occult or supernatural power." If an "instrument of obeah" was found on a person or his property (after a search by constituted authority), it was presumed that such person was "practising obeah."

Anyone convicted of "practising, or in any way concerned in the practice of obeah" could be imprisoned, with or without hard labor, for up to one year; a male could be whipped with a maximum of twenty-four strokes, with or without imprisonment. Those who consulted obeah practitioners could be fined up to fifty pounds or imprisoned for up to one year, and those who wrote, published, sold, or otherwise distributed any materials promoting "the superstition of obeah" were liable to a fine of up to fifty pounds or up to six months in jail if unable to pay the fine. The 1904 Obeah Act also applied to "any person who pretends or professes to tell fortunes, or uses any subtle craft, means or device, by palmistry . . . or pretends to cure injuries or diseases or to intimidate or effect any purpose by means of any charm, incantation or other pretended supernatural practice"; those convicted were liable to imprisonment not to exceed six months (Leewards 1928–30:627–629).[29]

In subsequent years there were occasional minor changes in wording to the 1904 act.[30] The most significant modification occurred in the 1932 Obeah (Amendment) Act, in which, in addition to small changes in wording, the General Legislative Council increased the jail sentence to up to five years, "with or without hard labour, with or without solitary confinement." If a male was convicted, he could also be whipped, in addition to or in lieu of imprisonment (Leewards 1933:1–2).

The 1904 Obeah Act remained in force without any substantial changes until the Leeward Islands Federation was dissolved in 1957. Over the years since, many of its anti-obeah provisions have remained in effect in the laws of the individual jurisdictions that had been part of the colony.

Antigua and Barbuda

Political and Governmental History

Claimed by the English in 1632, Antigua remained continuously in British hands for several centuries, with a brief hiatus in 1666–67 when it fell under the control of the French. Barbuda, which had been colonized from Antigua and claimed by the English Crown in 1685, legally became part of Antigua in 1860. In 1872 Antigua and Barbuda were joined to the Leeward Islands Federation. After the Federation was dissolved in 1957, Antigua and Barbuda were incorporated into the short-lived West Indies Federation (from 1958 to 1962). From 1967 to 1981, the islands of Antigua and Barbuda together became an associated state of Great Britain, with control over its own internal affairs. In November 1981, Antigua and Barbuda—the latter with a certain degree of internal autonomy—became an independent state within the British Commonwealth.

As was true for other territories of the Leeward Islands Federation, the old representative system existed in Antigua and Barbuda from 1663 to 1866, and Crown colony government replaced it from 1866 until the early 1950s. By 1956 internal self-government (with universal adult suffrage) had succeeded Crown colony government.

Anti-Obeah Laws

The presence of obeah practitioners among the enslaved population of Antigua was commonly acknowledged during the eighteenth century, but, as the agent for Antigua notified a British parliamentary committee in the 1780s, there was "no law in the island of Antigua which specifies the crime of practicing these arts." The "punishment" for "practicing these arts," he reported, "is left to fall under some general clause for punishing Negroes for offences that are not specifically named in the laws made for their government" (Antigua 1789).

It appears that the earliest Antiguan law containing specific anti-obeah provisions was enacted in August 1809. This law contained four clauses, three of which specifically mentioned slaves. Clause 1 mentioned only "persons" and stressed the need to "punish such persons as pretend to exercise any witchcraft, fortune-telling, or any crafty science to discover stolen goods [and the person responsible for the theft]; whereby many ignorant persons are frequently deluded and defrauded." Conviction carried a one-year jail term, during which period the convicted person was also to "stand openly" for one hour in the pillory of St. John, the island's capital. Clauses 2, 3, and 4 of the 1809 act specifically mentioned slaves. Clause 4 was essentially a paraphrase of Clause 1 and addressed the same issues of stolen or lost property, but it explicitly included "any slave or slaves" (in contrast to "persons"). Conviction under Clause 4 carried a penalty of "corporal punishment as shall be judged proper" but not to extend "to loss of life or limb." It should be stressed that attempts to discover lost or stolen property were often associated with obeah practitioners in British West Indian laws, but there was no mention of lost or stolen property in the two clauses that specifically addressed obeah in the 1809 Antigua act.

Clause 2 was enacted

> to prevent many mischiefs ... from the wicked art of Negroes going under the appellation of obeah men and women, pretending to have communication with the devil and other evil spirits, whereby the weak and superstitious are deluded into a belief of their having full power to exempt them, whilst under their protection, from any evil that might otherwise happen, or to affect them with any evils.

This wording was taken from earlier Jamaican slave laws. Under the clause, "any slave who shall pretend to any supernatural power, in order to promote the purposes of rebellion, or who shall pretend to exercise witchcraft whereby death shall ensue" was to be executed. The wording of this clause is vague, since the practice of obeah per se is not being criminalized, only the acts of promoting rebellion or causing the death of someone. In Clause 3, "any Negro, or other slave" convicted for preparing or administering poison "in the practice of obeah, or otherwise" was to be executed, even if the intended victim did not die (Antigua 1818:177–181).

We are unable to specify how long the 1809 law remained in effect, but in July 1834 Antigua's first vagrancy act was passed. It was similar in all major respects to vagrancy acts passed elsewhere in the British West Indies in its definition of a "rogue and a vagabond." Its second clause referred to, among other offenses associated with this definition, "every person pretending to be a dealer in obeah, every person pretending or professing to tell fortunes and using any subtle craft, means or device by palmistry or otherwise to deceive and impose on any of Her Majesty's subjects." Conviction could result in up to three months in jail with hard labor; no distinctions were made by sex (Antigua 1834).[31]

The 1834 act was modified in March 1851 with passage of an act "to repeal a part of the second clause" of the 1834 vagrancy act. The wording with respect to obeah remained the same, but there were some procedural modifications and key changes in terms of sanctions. Now conviction could bring a jail term of up to one year with hard labor for both males and females. In addition, a male could also receive a public whipping at the start or during the course of his sentence; a female was exempt from whipping, but during her jail term she could be placed in solitary confinement for up to one month at a time, not to exceed a total of three months (Antigua 1851). In 1857, the 1851 law was repealed with the passage of a lengthy act "for further improving the administration of criminal justice," although obeah was still criminalized. The penalty, however, was reduced to jail, with or without hard labor, for up to three months, and no distinctions were made based on gender (Antigua 1857, clauses 38 and 39).[32]

By 1872 the Leeward Islands Federation had been formed. The colony's Small Charges Act (1891) went into effect in 1892 and applied to Antigua as well as to other jurisdictions in the colony. This law included an anti-obeah provision, and the law remained in force until the major 1904 Obeah Act superseded it. The latter act was identical to the one enacted by the Federal Legislature of the Leeward Islands in the same year, and the penalties were essentially the same: for practicing obeah, imprisonment for up to twelve months; for consulting a practitioner, a fine or imprisonment for up to twelve months; and, for publishing or distributing obeah materials, a fine or jail for up to six months (Jacobs 1992:2–3). After the dissolution of the Leeward Islands Federation in 1957, the 1904 act remained in force in Antigua, although it was occasionally amended, primarily in the amounts of the fines (Jacobs 1992:1–4). In any case, most provisions of the 1904 act were still in force in Antigua as of January 1, 2010, since they had not been significantly modified by any subsequent legislation (Antigua 2010a; Antigua 2010b).[33]

Anguilla

Political and Governmental History

Colonized by English settlers from St. Christopher (better known as St. Kitts) in 1650, Anguilla functioned as a separate British colony until 1825, when it was incorporated into St. Kitts. In 1883 Nevis was joined with St. Kitts and Anguilla to form the Presidency of St. Kitts and Nevis. The Presidency became a unit of the Leeward Islands Federation (1872–1957), and from 1956 to 1962 it was also part of the short-lived West Indies Federation. When the Federation was dissolved, Anguilla, as part of St. Kitts, Nevis, and Anguilla, became an "associated state" of Great Britain, with full internal self-government. In 1967 the island "seceded" from the associated state of St. Kitts, Nevis, and Anguilla and declared itself the independent Republic of Anguilla. British forces invaded in 1969, and shortly after that the British Foreign Office started governing the territory as a "separately administered" part of the associated state, with its own governor and elected legislature. In 1982, at its citizens' own request and with the agreement of the St. Kitts and British governments, Anguilla became a British Dependent Territory (subsequently called a British Overseas Territory).

Legislative authority in Anguilla, as in all British Caribbean territories, varied over time. Until 1866 the old representative system was operative, and Anguilla enjoyed a large measure of legislative autonomy. This situation changed drastically when the British instituted Crown colony government in 1866; this lasted, with minor modification, until the early 1950s, when representative institutions were restored along with universal adult suffrage.

Up to August 4, 1971, the laws of Anguilla were coterminous with the laws of the "State of St. Christopher, Nevis, and Anguilla" (e.g., St. Kitts 1857; St. Kitts 1961–76; Lewis 1964), but after that date the Anguilla legislature made the island's own laws. In the 1970s and 1980s the legislature passed various statutes that were specifically germane to Anguilla, and provisions were dropped that had been inherited from the St. Kitts legal code.

Anti-Obeah Laws

The anti-obeah provisions in the laws of St. Christopher and Nevis and the Colony of the Leeward Islands, including the Obeah Act of 1904, applied for many years to Anguilla; they remained in force there after the dissolution of the Leeward Islands Federation in 1957. However, in November 1980, Anguilla's legislature enacted an ordinance that repealed obsolete earlier laws as well as those "not applicable to Anguilla"; the Obeah Act of 1904 was among those repealed laws (Anguilla 1985:69–70; Anguilla 1988:67). With passage of the 1980 ordinance, Anguilla became the first jurisdiction in the Anglophone Caribbean to eliminate anti-obeah provisions (those specifically mentioning the term *obeah*) from its laws.[34]

St. Kitts (St. Christopher) and Nevis

Political and Governmental History

The English established their first permanent Caribbean colony in St. Kitts in 1624; shortly thereafter the French also settled the island. At first claimed by both nations, St. Kitts was formally ceded to Britain in 1713, as was Nevis, which was settled by English colonists from St. Kitts in 1628. Both colonies remained under British rule from then on, with the exception of a brief hiatus in 1782 when they were seized by the French. The two closely linked islands have experienced several changes in administrative arrangements and constitutional status during their long colonial history. The old representative system was in effect from 1663 to 1866, when Crown colony government was imposed.

For a time, St. Kitts and Nevis were structured as individual presidencies of the Federation of the Leeward Islands (legally born in 1872), but in 1882 they were amalgamated into a single presidency within the Leeward Islands Federation, which status they continued to hold until dissolution of the Federation in 1956. Joined with Anguilla, they became part of the ill-fated West Indies Federation of 1958–62. As elsewhere in the British West Indies, universal adult suffrage was introduced in the early 1950s as the colony moved toward internal self-government—a status that was achieved in 1967, when St. Kitts and Nevis became an associated state of Britain. In September 1983, the Federation of St. Kitts and Nevis (Anguilla having seceded in 1967) became an independent nation within the British Commonwealth.

Anti-Obeah Laws

In the late 1780s, the agent for Grenada and St. Kitts reported to a British parliamentary committee investigating slavery in the colonies that "there are no laws in St. Christopher's or Grenada, nor do I believe in any of the Leeward [Antigua, Montserrat, St. Kitts, Nevis, Virgin Islands] or Ceded [Dominica, Grenada, St. Vincent, Tobago] islands, which take cognizance of obeah, or its professors" (Grenada 1789). This apparently remained the case in St. Kitts and Nevis for many years; none of the slave laws enacted in those territories between 1788 and 1828 specifically mentioned obeah (IUP 1816–18; IUP 1823–24; St. Kitts 1828; Nevis 1862).[35]

The earliest anti-obeah provisions in the laws of St. Kitts and Nevis (which also applied to Anguilla) appeared in the 1847 Vagrancy Act. This act was very similar to vagrancy acts elsewhere in the British West Indies, and its anti-obeah provisions, including penalties, were identical in phrasing to some of those in other territories—for example, Dominica in 1840, from which the St. Kitts law may in fact have been derived. "Rogues and vagabonds" included, among others, those "pretending or professing to tell fortunes, or using any subtle craft or device, by palmistry, obeah, or any such like superstitious means, to deceive and impose upon any of Her Majesty's subjects." Conviction brought jail and hard labor for up to twenty-eight days (St. Kitts 1857:203–205; cf. Dominica 1858:393–402). The 1847 act was repealed in 1876 by Act 15 of the Federal Legislature of the Leeward Islands Federation (Michelin 1922:xix). The 1891 Small Charges Act, which applied to all territories in the colony, ultimately replaced it. As elsewhere, the 1891 law was replaced in 1904 (see below).

In January 1860 the administrator, council, and assembly of Nevis passed "An Act to Make Provision for the Punishment of Persons Who May Use Delusive and Superstitious Devices, or Other Frauds, for Purposes of Deception." Emphasizing fraud, the law for some reason did not specifically mention the word *obeah*, but its wording was similar to that found in laws of other jurisdictions, being directed against those "who may impose on the credulity of the ignorant, by falsely pretending, by means of deceptive and superstitious devices, to discover offenders, to foretell future events, or to cure diseases, or ... by some secret craft or power alleged to be possessed by them, shall deceive or impose on any person whomsoever." Conviction could lead to up to three months in prison, with or without hard labor, or a fine, depending on the inclination of the "convicting Justices" (Nevis 1862:415). We do not know how long the 1860 law remained in force, but it was probably superseded by the Leeward Island Federation's Small Charges Act of 1891, which in turn was replaced by the 1904 Obeah Act.

With some minor differences in wording, the 1904 Obeah Act of St. Kitts, Nevis, and Anguilla was essentially the same as the 1904 Obeah Act passed by the Leeward Islands Federation. It was amended a few times over the years, with occasional changes in phrasing as well as modifications in the penalties, particularly fines. However, in the 1959 revised edition of the laws, published two years after the dissolution of the Leeward Islands Federation, the language of the Obeah Act of 1904 remained substantially unaltered. The previous definitions of obeah and "instrument of obeah" were retained, and offenders were still described as any person "who pretends or professes to tell fortunes, or uses any subtle craft, means or device, by palmistry . . . or pretends to cure injuries or diseases to intimidate or effect any purpose by means of any charm, incantation or other pretended supernatural practice." Those convicted could be imprisoned for up to one year (whipping and hard labor were no longer among the sanctions), and those who consulted an obeah practitioner could be fined up to $240 (the previous fine had been fifty pounds) or imprisoned for up to one year. Persons who wrote, sold, or otherwise distributed any materials promoting "the superstition of obeah" were likewise liable to a fine of up to $240 or imprisonment for up to six months if unable to pay the fine. While there was no change in the prison sentence, the new fine reflected currency changes from the earlier amount of fifty pounds (Lewis 1964:531–533).

The 1904 Obeah Act was amended once again in 1976 with the removal of certain technical provisions concerning judicial procedures. The fine of $240 for writing or distributing obeah-related materials was also changed, being increased to $500; prison sentences, however, remained the same (St. Kitts 1987:69–70, 77).[36] With these minor modifications, the 1904 Obeah Act was still in force in St. Kitts and Nevis as of January 1, 2009 (St. Kitts 2009), and, as far as can be ascertained, obeah still remains an illegal activity in these islands (e.g., St. Kitts 2010).

British Virgin Islands

Political and Governmental History

The British Virgin Islands, which today include sixteen inhabited and more than twenty uninhabited islands, were settled by the English in the mid-1660s and have remained a British possession ever since. As with the other Leeward Islands, their administrative and constitutional status has varied over the years.

The old representative system was in effect from around 1773. From 1859 until the late 1960s, the territory was a Crown colony, constituting a separate presidency within the Leeward Islands Federation. Internal self-government was achieved in 2007, and today the British Virgin Islands constitute an overseas territory of Britain, with its own governor and elected legislature.

Anti-Obeah Laws

None of the slave-period laws of the British Virgin Islands appear to have contained specific anti-obeah provisions (see, for example, IUP 1816–18; IUP 1823–24), and it is uncertain whether any laws related to obeah were enacted before the last decade of the nineteenth century. In any case, the Small Charges Act (1891) of the Leeward Islands Federation, including its anti-obeah provision, applied to the British Virgin Islands, as did the Obeah Act of 1904 that superseded it. The 1904 act was also separately incorporated into the laws of the Virgin Islands. This legislation was virtually identical to the obeah acts found in other territories of the Leeward Islands, although slight modifications were made to it over the years, primarily to bring fines into line with contemporary currency standards (Trotman et al. 1991:621–623).

The 1904 law remained in force after the Leeward Islands Federation was dissolved in 1957, and it was not repealed until 1997 (BVI 2003:40). Although the 1904 law was repealed, new anti-obeah provisions were incorporated into the criminal code of 1997.[37] Section 290 of the 1997 Virgin Islands criminal code addresses the practices of both "obeah and myalism," and, with the exception of minor changes in wording and alterations of paragraphs, it is identical to section 297 of Montserrat's 1983 penal code (BVI 1997:136–137; see also Montserrat, below). The 1997 criminal code of the British Virgin Islands took effect on September 1, 1997, and, although subsequently amended several times, it was still in force—including its anti-obeah provision—as of January 1, 2010 (BVI 2010a:13; BVI 2010b). Under this law, conviction for practicing obeah could result in jail for up to one year or a $1,000 fine, or both.[38]

Montserrat

Political and Governmental History

Colonized by English and Irish settlers from St. Kitts in 1628, Montserrat briefly came under French control on two occasions in the seventeenth and eighteenth centuries, but by 1783 it was firmly in British hands. Its administrative and constitutional status has varied over the years. The old representative system was in effect from 1663 to 1866, when the island became a Crown colony, a status that continued until the 1950s. During this period, universal adult suffrage was introduced, bringing the island closer to internal self-government. From 1872 to 1958 Montserrat was a presidency in the Leeward Islands Federation, and in 1958 it became a unit within the West Indies Federation. After the dissolution of the Federation in 1962, Montserrat became a dependent territory of Britain. It achieved internal self-government in 1989 and today is a British Overseas Territory—one of the few remaining dependent territories of the former British West Indies.

Anti-Obeah Laws

In the late 1780s, as noted above, the agent for Grenada and St. Kitts reported to a British parliamentary committee that none of the Leeward Islands, including Montserrat, had laws "which take cognizance of obeah, or its professors" (Grenada 1789). Apparently none of Montserrat's later slave laws specifically addressed obeah either (IUP 1816–18; IUP 1823–24). It seems that the colony's first actual anti-obeah provision was incorporated in the Small Charges Act passed by the Leeward Islands legislative council in 1891; this act applied to Montserrat as well as the other islands in the colony. As was also the case in other jurisdictions in the Leeward Islands Federation, the Obeah Act of 1904 superseded the 1891 act, and the version of this act that obtained in Montserrat was identical to the version in other jurisdictions of the Leeward Islands. Although slightly modified or amended over the years, the Montserrat version of the 1904 act, including its anti-obeah provisions, remained in force after the dissolution of the Leeward Islands Federation until it was finally repealed in 1983 (Lewis 1965:527–529; Montserrat 2006:83; cf. Skinner 2005:157–158).

However, anti-obeah provisions did not disappear from Montserrat's laws in 1983; rather, as in the British Virgin Islands, they were included in the island's new penal code.[39]

Although it took much of its wording from the 1904 Obeah Act, Montserrat's 1983 penal code newly introduced the concept of myalism. Section 292 included nine categories of offenders who were to be defined as "idle and disorderly persons," including anyone who "pretends to deal in obeah (as defined in section 297), myalism, duppy catching or witchcraft, or tells fortunes by palmistry or like superstitious means intending to deceive or impose on people." "Duppy catching," it should be noted, is a rare phrase in Anglophone Caribbean laws, being found only in the 1975 penal code (and subsequent codes) of the Cayman Islands; similarly, the term *myalism* turns up only in Cayman Islands, Jamaican, and British Virgin Islands laws.[40] The penalty for conviction of an individual as an "idle and disorderly person" could be three months in jail or a $250 fine or both (Montserrat 1983:120).

Section 297 of the penal code dealt entirely with "obeah and myalism." The law specifically addressed any "person practicing or dealing in obeah or myalism" or "who pretends to possess any supernatural power." Notably, the law included the presumption that such a person's motivations could only be fraudulent—that practitioners always had the intention of seeking self-advantage or gain or using "occult means" to frighten someone else. Those convicted of practicing obeah or myalism, as well as persons who consulted obeah or myalism practitioners with the intent of "bringing about any event by the use of occult means or any supernatural power or knowledge," could be fined $1,000 or jailed for not less than one year or both. The same penalties applied to anyone found with "any instrument of obeah or myalism" or anyone who wrote, published, or distributed "any pamphlet or other printed or written matter calculated to promote the superstition of obeah or myalism."

As with all other such laws, neither obeah nor myalism is defined, and "instrument of obeah or myalism" is vaguely described as "anything commonly used in or associated with the practice of obeah or myalism." Finally, anyone convicted under this law, in addition to a fine or jail sentence, is to be "subject to police supervision" for two years from the date the fine is imposed or the jail sentence completed, "whichever is the later date," and thereafter that person "shall be subject to the provisions of the Prevention of Crimes

Act" (Montserrat 1983:124–125). Based on his fieldwork in Montserrat in the mid-1990s, Skinner (2005:161) observes that "the Obeah Act continues to be invoked and revered, the practice of obeah feared and forbidden." Although the 1983 penal code was amended several times during the 1990s, its anti-obeah provisions were left intact and remain in force today. The penalties specified in section 297, it should be noted, are harsher than current penalties for obeah in any other part of the Caribbean (Montserrat 2002:116, 120–121).

Dominica

Political and Governmental History

Britain captured Dominica from the French in the 1750s, and the annexation was formalized in 1763. Dominica's constitutional and political history is similar to that of most other British West Indian territories. The old representative system was in place by 1775, and in 1865 Crown colony government replaced it. In 1833 the island, though geographically a Windward island, was incorporated into the Leeward group, then consisting of St. Kitts, Nevis, Antigua, and Montserrat. In 1872 this group became the Leeward Islands Federation or Colony of the Leeward Islands. However, in 1940 Dominica was detached from the Leeward Islands Federation and linked administratively with the Windward Islands. The island later became a unit in the Federation of the West Indies; in 1962, after the dissolution of the Federation, it became an associated state of Great Britain. Internal self-government was achieved in 1967, after a process that had started in the early 1950s with the introduction of universal adult suffrage. In November 1978 the Commonwealth of Dominica became an independent nation within the British Commonwealth.

Anti-Obeah Laws

The 1788 slave code of Dominica voiced a common view among whites in the West Indies, observing that

> it frequently happens that slaves assume the art of witchcraft, or are what is commonly called obeah or Doctor Men, and, under pretence of a gift of supernatural

powers, do influence the minds of weak and credulous slaves, and frequently stimulate them to acts of mutiny or rebellion against their masters, renters, managers, and overseers, and administer certain drugs or potions of a secret and generally a poisonous nature, as well to slaves, as to free people of every description. [This was the earliest slave law in the West Indies to explicitly link poison with obeah.]

Upon conviction of practicing obeah under this law, the slave or slaves ("he, she, or they") were to be executed or, at the discretion of the judiciary, suffer "banishment and flogging on the bare breech," the number of strokes not to exceed thirty-nine (Dominica 1789).

A comprehensive slave law, "An Act for the Encouragement, Protection and Better Government of Slaves," was passed sometime after 1788 and then renewed and "made perpetual" by an act of March 1793 (Dominica 1793). We were unable to locate a copy of the post-1788 law, but it apparently contained an anti-obeah provision, since such a provision was included both in the 1788 law and in a comprehensive slave law passed in 1818 (Dominica 1818). The lengthy preamble to clause 23 of the 1818 law borrowed some of the language of the 1788 slave code (although it dropped the term *Doctor Men*) and elaborated on the earlier law with the observation that

> instances frequently occur of slaves assuming the art of witchcraft, or pretending to supernatural powers, or professing what is commonly called by them obeah, and dealing in spells, charms and philtres, and thereby influencing the minds of weak or credulous slaves, and frequently stimulating them to actions of the highest atrocity against their masters, renters, managers and overseers, by administering drugs and potions of secret and generally of a poisonous nature, as well as to their fellow slaves or others to whom they bear evil intentions. (Dominica 1818:113)

As in the 1788 law, slaves convicted of practicing obeah "or pretending to any supernatural powers" or being in possession of "any drugs or potions" could be executed or receive other punishment, including "banishment" or "flogging on the bare breech," with up to thirty-nine lashes.

Another clause (number 28) inflicted the death penalty on "any negro or other slave" who returned to Dominica after having been convicted of "rebellion, conspiracy, or obeah" and having been transported from the island for this conviction (Dominica 1818:114). In 1821 another slave act (Dominica 1821) contained several clauses relating to obeah, all of them identical to the 1818 law. An 1826 consolidated slave act also included an anti-obeah preamble and clause that were essentially the same as in the 1818 and 1821 laws; now, however, "flogging on the bare breech" was omitted and the penalty was execution or "such other punishment" as the court would decide (Dominica 1826:542–543; Ragatz 1963:418).

In 1831 Dominica enacted what was to be its final major slave law. This act repealed the acts of 1788, 1821, and 1826, and, like those earlier laws, it contained an anti-obeah provision, albeit one that was briefer. Clause 30 was directed simply against "any slave" who "shall practise the pretended art of witchcraft or obeah by administering to any person whomsoever drugs or potion [sic] or by the use of charms, amulets or other contrivances"; the law also applied to "any free person" who might use obeah "against or upon any slave." The penalty was left open, the act stating only that the convicted offender "shall suffer such punishment as the court in its discretion shall award" (Dominica 1831).

A couple of years after the end of the apprenticeship period, in May 1840, Dominica enacted its first vagrancy act. This law contained, as did vagrancy acts elsewhere, an anti-obeah provision whose phrasing was identical or very similar to those found in other laws. The definition of a "rogue and vagabond" included anyone "pretending or professing to tell fortunes or using or pretending to use any subtle craft or device by palmistry, obeah, or any such like superstitious means to deceive and impose upon any of Her Majesty's subjects." The penalty was hard labor not to exceed twenty-eight days (Dominica 1858:395–396). A very similar law was enacted seven years later in St. Kitts; although there were some differences between the two laws, the reference to obeah and the penalty for conviction were the same (St. Kitts 1857:203–205).

The 1840 law was apparently superseded by the Leeward Islands Small Charges Act (1891),[41] which remained in effect until August 1904, when the Obeah Ordinance was enacted in Dominica. With some minor differences in wording, this was the same act that was passed in the same year in the Leeward Islands Federation, and it included the same sanctions against practicing obeah (jail for up to one year, and a male could receive a whipping as well as or in lieu of jail); consulting an obeah practitioner (a heavy fine or jail for up to one year); writing, publishing, or distributing literature "calculated to promote the superstition of obeah" (a fine or prison up to six months); or engaging in fortune-telling or palmistry or "other pretended supernatural practice" to "cure injuries or disease or to intimidate" (jail for up to six months). In addition, as in other jurisdictions, if someone was found with an "instrument of obeah" (not defined), it was presumed the person was a practitioner (Alleyne 1963:537–539).

The 1904 Obeah Act remained in force for many years, even after the dissolution of the Leeward Islands Federation in 1957, although the penalties were occasionally modified, primarily in the amount of the fines. The most recent published edition of Dominica's laws, which appeared in 1991, represents a continuation of the 1904 act (as revised in 1990) under the title "An Act for Preventing and Punishing Persons Who Pretend to Exercise or Use Any Kind of Witchcraft, Sorcery, or Other Supernatural Devices"—or in short, the Obeah Act. Little of substance was changed from the 1904 law. For example, basic terms such as "obeah" and "instrument of obeah" remain undefined; as with laws in other jurisdictions, the former "means obeah as ordinarily understood and practised," and the latter "means anything ordinarily used in the practice of obeah." There were some changes, however, in the penalties, whose jail sentences became somewhat harsher. Aside from the fines, which were adjusted to eastern Caribbean dollars to reflect new currency standards, the jail term for one convicted of practicing obeah became less flexible, consisting of one year and, for a male, a whipping (the 1904 law had specified up to one year and the option of a whipping in lieu of jail). Conviction for consulting an obeah practitioner could result in a fine or jail for twelve months (in 1904 the jail term had been up to twelve months), and engaging in practices that promised healing brought jail for six months (the 1904 law had specified "not exceeding six months"). The penalty for writing, publishing, or distributing literature promoting obeah remained the same as in the 1904 law—a fine or six months in jail if the fine was not paid—and the provision targeting possession of "any instrument of obeah" was also unchanged (Harris et al. 1991:3–6).

As of July 2011 (when Handler briefly visited Dominica), the 1904 law (with the revisions in penalties enacted in 1990) was still on Dominica's statute books, and the practice of obeah continues to be an illegal activity subject to, for example, one year in jail plus a whipping if the convicted person is a male. The penalty is one year in jail or a $3,000 fine if the offense is consulting an obeah practitioner and a $3,000 fine or six months in jail if one is convicted of writing or publishing literature on the subject (Dominica 2008; Dominica 2009:43; Dominica 2011). As elsewhere in the West Indies, however, the law is rarely enforced, and, according to a prominent Dominican lawyer, there have been no prosecutions over the past ten to fifteen years.[42]

Grenada

Political and Governmental History

Settled by the French in the mid-seventeenth century, Grenada remained under French control until it was ceded to Britain in 1763; in 1779 it was retaken by France but was then restored to Britain in 1783. Under British rule, the old representative system was in effect from 1766 until 1875, when it was replaced by Crown colony government. Following the period of Crown colony rule, the island became a unit of the short-lived Federation of the West Indies (1958–62). Universal adult suffrage was established in the early 1950s, leading to internal self-government in 1967. Full independence from Britain was granted in February 1974.

Anti-Obeah Laws

None of Grenada's slave laws seem to have singled out obeah for special attention until passage of the island's Consolidated Slave Act in 1825 (Grenada 1830; cf. Grenada 1789; Grenada 1808; IUP 1816–18:24–25).[43] Clause 35 of the 1825 law was specifically directed against obeah and depended heavily on earlier laws enacted in Jamaica, although it included certain small modifications. "It is absolutely necessary," the preamble reads,

> to use all practical efforts to prevent the many mischiefs that may hereafter arise from the wicked persons going under the appellation of obeah Men and Women, and pretending to have communication with the Devil and other Evil Spirits, whereby the weak and superstitious are deluded into belief of their having full power to exempt them, whilst under their protection, from many evils that may happen.

The law applied to persons, "whether Free or Slaves," who "use any art or mystery" that could "affect the life or health of any slave or other person"—specifically through the use of poisons or "pounded glass or other deleterious matter"—whether or not death resulted. The law also applied to those found in possession of "poisonous drugs, pounded glass, parrots' beaks, dogs' teeth, alligators' teeth or other materials" used in the "practice of obeah or witchcraft"—the same itemization of material objects found in earlier Jamaican laws. In addition, the law applied to persons who attended "any meeting" that involved "administering unlawful oaths, . . . drinking human blood mixed with rum, grave dirt, or otherwise." Those convicted were to be executed or transported from the island or to receive "such other punishment as the court decides." Clause 36 mandated that anyone with knowledge of the activities specified in clause 35 who did not report this information to the authorities could be fined or imprisoned or both, if free, or given a "public whipping" if enslaved (Grenada 1830:332).[44]

As with slave laws throughout the British West Indies, the 1825 act was rendered invalid by emancipation. In the following years, Grenada passed a criminal code as well as police and vagrancy acts, but nothing in these newer laws appears to have been related directly or indirectly to obeah (see, for example, Grenada 1852). In fact it was not until September 1874 that a new law, consolidating "offences punishable on summary convictions," included a section that criminalized practices such as palmistry, reading cards, or "any subtle craft or occult science"; the latter category included, for example, to "tell fortunes," find "lost or stolen goods," and cure (or inflict) sickness. A conviction could lead to a fine of up to fifty pounds in local currency or jail, with or without hard labor, for up to one year; a male could also be whipped while in jail (Grenada 1875:586–587). It should be pointed out that the term *obeah* is conspicuously absent from this law; however, it seems clear that persons accused of practicing obeah could have been indicted under it.

In 1897 a new criminal code (which probably came into force in early 1898) was produced, this time with anti-obeah provisions, some explicit, others implicit. Section 101 specified, without mentioning obeah, that persons convicted of fraudulent practices, such as receiving monetary or other compensation for "using any kind of witchcraft, sorcery, enchantment, or conjuration, or art of telling fortunes," were to be imprisoned for three months. Section

149 targeted "idle and disorderly persons," including those who "pretend or profess to tell fortunes"; those convicted were liable to a month in jail. Although not mentioned by name, the practice of obeah was implied in both sections. In contrast, obeah was explicitly referenced in sections 158–160 of the 1897 criminal code. Under the heading "Practising Obeah," a three-month jail sentence (reduced from the one year of the 1874 law, and with whipping eliminated as well) was to be administered to "whoever practices obeah or by any occult means or by any assumption of supernatural power" should intimidate anyone, "pretend" to find lost or stolen objects (as well as discover the thief), or cause or cure illness. The law authorized a search of any person suspected of possessing "any article or thing" for use in obeah; if such an article was found, it was presumed that, with no evidence to the contrary, the person was an obeah practitioner. Finally, a fine of five pounds was to be levied if, during an obeah trial, the defendant or any of the witnesses were found to be carrying a concealed "instrument of obeah." As in other West Indian laws, such an "instrument" was never defined (Grenada 1897:742–743, 755, 756–757).[45]

The anti-obeah provisions of this section of the 1897 criminal code (under the heading "Practising Obeah, etc.") remained substantially unchanged for many years, with occasional slight modifications in wording and renumbering of chapters in later published compilations of Grenada's laws. In 1908 an ordinance was added that made it illegal to import, publish, or sell any written matter that "has a tendency to propagate or encourage a belief in the efficacy of obeah"; violators could incur up to three months in jail (Tudor 1911:1807–1808). The anti-obeah provisions of 1897 (as amended in 1908) were still in force at the end of December 1934, and they were reproduced, essentially unchanged, in the criminal code of 1958, sections 98 and 147 (Reece 1935:619–620; Malone 1962:765–766). By 1958, although the jail penalties remained the same, the fine for being found with "an instrument of obeah" during court proceedings had been changed to twenty-four dollars in local currency. In addition, under the heading "Stealing," the 1958 law mandated three months in jail for persons convicted of various fraudulent or illegal activities, which included offering or accepting compensation "for or on pretence of using any kind of witchcraft, sorcery, enchantment, or conjuration, or art of telling fortunes."[46]

Although the Family Court Act of 1994 modified a section of the 1958 criminal code (Grenada 1995: 229–240), there were no changes to the anti-obeah provisions. As of January 1, 2010, they were still in force (e.g., Grenada 2010a:14; Grenada 2010b).[47]

St. Lucia

Political and Governmental History

For much of the seventeenth and eighteenth centuries, Britain and France fought for control of St. Lucia. Possession of the island alternated between them fourteen times until 1803, when France ceded St. Lucia to Britain. The island eventually became a Crown colony, a status it held until the 1950s, when universal adult suffrage put the colony on the road to internal self-government. After being part of the West Indies Federation (1958–62), St. Lucia became an associated state of Great Britain when the Federation was dissolved, achieving full independence in February 1979.

Anti-Obeah Laws

St. Lucia's eighteenth-century slave laws apparently lacked specific anti-obeah provisions (Grenada 1789), and we have been unable to obtain information on possible anti-obeah provisions in the island's later slave laws. However, St. Lucia's 1838 Vagrancy Act, like similar acts in other territories during the immediate post-emancipation period, contained such a provision. In clause 2, "rogues and vagabonds" included "every person pretending or professing to tell fortunes, or using or pretending to use any subtle craft or device, by palmistry, obeah, or any such like superstitious means, to deceive and impose on any of Her Majesty's subjects" (this wording was identical to that in the 1840 vagrancy law of Barbados); conviction resulted in jail with hard labor for up to twenty-eight days (St. Lucia 1853:71–72). The 1838 law remained in force until 1877, when it was repealed by the Summary Procedure Ordinance 1877 (St. Lucia 1877b:277, schedule C), but for a short period it ran concurrently with two other anti-obeah laws, enacted in 1872 and 1873.

The 1872 Obeah Ordinance was enacted because, according to the preamble, "the profession of obeah as tending to deceive and intimidate the ignorant has been productive of serious evils." Obeah was defined in this case as the "practice of witchcraft, palmistry or any occult art as well as what is commonly termed *Kembois* or obeah" (this is the only West Indian law to use this French Creole term, and the only time it seems to have been used in the laws of St. Lucia).[48] The term *obeah man* was also defined in the law, rather laboriously, as a man or woman who

> professes a knowledge of "obeah" and any person who professes by means of such knowledge or by the manipulation or use of cards or by instruments of obeah . . . or by any supernatural devices to cure or impart as the case may be, disease, love, or any other good or evil affectation . . . or to tell fortunes or future or past events or discover lost or stolen property, or in any way to benefit or injure another, either in person or property.

For the purposes of the law, an "instrument of obeah" was "any philter, phial, blood, bone, image or other article . . . intended for the practice of obeah." Conviction imposed a jail sentence with hard labor for up to six months; a male could also be whipped (but not to exceed thirty-nine lashes), while a female could be placed in solitary confinement for up to one month and have "her hair cut close to her head at the beginning and towards the termination of such imprisonment" (this is the only West Indian law to specify the cutting of hair as a penalty).[49] Those who consulted obeah practitioners or encouraged people to practice obeah on their behalf could be jailed, with or without hard labor, for up to four months. As in other jurisdictions, the penalties were more severe for a second conviction (St. Lucia 1872). The 1872 Obeah Ordinance was amended in 1873 by another ordinance that revised some wording and delineated the penalties more precisely; the substance of the 1872 ordinance, however, remained the same (St. Lucia 1873).

Both the 1872 and 1873 anti-obeah ordinances were repealed in 1877 (St. Lucia 1877b:278, Schedule C, Ordinances Repealed), but their substance was included in another law passed at the same time: the 1877 Summary Conviction Ordinance. This law slightly modified the earlier definition of obeah by including the word "fraudulent": "every pretended assumption of supernatural power or knowledge whatever, for fraudulent or illicit purposes, or for gain, or for the injury of any person"; the earlier definition of "instrument of obeah" was retained. In the 1877 Summary Conviction Ordinance, which also included categories of offenders (for example, "idle and disorderly persons" and "rogues and vagabonds"), obeah was now addressed under the separate category "Superstitious Devices." The law applied to obeah practitioners, or those who by "any occult means or by any assumption of supernatural power or knowledge" should "intimidate or attempt to intimidate any person" or "obtain or endeavor to obtain" property or money, "pretend to discover any lost or stolen goods or the person who stole the same, or to inflict any disease, loss, damage or personal injury to or upon any person, or to restore any other person to health." Also included, as in the 1872 law, were those who consulted obeah practitioners or encouraged people to practice obeah on their behalf. The penalties for these offenses were essentially the same as earlier: up to six months in jail. A male could also be whipped once during his jail term, while a female could be kept in solitary confinement for up to three days at a time, but not for more than thirty days; the 1872 provision of cutting a female's hair was dropped. In addition, if an "instrument of obeah" was found on a person or that person's property, he or she was presumed to be an obeah practitioner. Similarly, if an "instrument of obeah" was discovered on a person during a judicial hearing against a person accused of obeah, the person "shall be deemed to be a person practicing obeah and shall be dealt with accordingly" (St. Lucia 1877a:281–282).[50]

The basic anti-obeah provisions (and definitions of "obeah" and "instruments of obeah") of the 1877 law remained in effect under the "Summary Offences" section of a major new criminal code passed in 1888 (or 1887). In most sections the 1888 law contained only minor wording changes (e.g., the offense was now categorized as "Practising Obeah" rather than "Superstitious Devices," as in the 1877 law), and the penalties were modified: imprisonment for six months was now mandatory, whipping for males was eliminated, and solitary confinement for females was extended to not more than six days during the six-month term (St. Lucia 1889:381–382, 430–431).

The criminal code Amendment Ordinance, 1905, refined some of the wording in the 1887 law and added a few provisions, but the substance of the law was the same. There were slight changes in the definitions of "obeah," "obeah practitioner,"[51] and "instrument of obeah." Since 1872 "instrument of obeah" had been defined as "any philter, phial, blood, bone, image or other article," but was now simply "anything used or intended to be used" in the practice of obeah; material objects were no longer specified. There were slight changes in the wording of the penalties and some procedural and substantive changes—for example, a person found with an "instrument of obeah" was presumed to be a practitioner, and it was made illegal to write, publish, or distribute "any pamphlet or matter calculated to promote the superstition of obeah," with the last offense bringing up to six months in jail (St. Lucia 1905).

In the criminal code of 1920 (which became law in 1921), anti-obeah provisions were now included among "offences affecting property," specifically fraud (along with bankruptcy, "falsification," and forgery). As a type of fraud, obeah was included under "false pretences" along with "witchcraft and the like." There were, however, no fundamental changes to the 1905 law, although it included procedural changes related to arrest, conviction, and punishments; conviction still resulted in a six-month jail sentence. One substantial modification was that the 1920 criminal code now made it illegal to consult or employ an obeah practitioner; conviction for this offense brought a ten-pound fine, and anyone who accepted money or other compensation under the "pretence of using any kind of witchcraft, sorcery, enchantment, or conjuration, or art of telling fortunes" could be jailed for three months (Salmon 1920:86–87).

Under St. Lucia's revised ordinances of 1957, chapter 250 of the new criminal code was identical, in its anti-obeah provisions and sections, to the 1920 law (Lewis 1959:532–533), and all these older provisions and sections were reproduced in subsequent amendments to the criminal code. The only variations in the laws consisted of differences in fines for consulting an obeah practitioner, which were made consistent with contemporary monetary standards (e.g., St. Lucia 1992:75–77). However, in 2004, a new code repealed the entire 1920 criminal code, including its anti-obeah provisions. Obeah was simply not mentioned in the 2004 criminal code and thus, as of January 1, 2005 (when the law went into effect), obeah as such ceased to be a criminal offense in St. Lucia (St. Lucia 2004a:754; St. Lucia 2004b).[52] With the passage of its 2004 law, St. Lucia became the most recent jurisdiction in the Caribbean to decriminalize obeah, following Anguilla (1980), Barbados (1998), and Trinidad and Tobago (2000).

St. Vincent and the Grenadines

Political and Governmental History

After being fought over by the British and French for most of the eighteenth century, St. Vincent was ceded to Britain in 1783, leading to its amalgamation with the Grenadines as a single administrative unit. However, like most of the Windward Islands, St. Vincent did not become fully established as a British possession until after the Napoleonic Wars. The old representative system, introduced in the late eighteenth century, remained in effect during much of the nineteenth century, but in 1868 governance changed, and St. Vincent and the Grenadines became a full Crown colony. The territory was administered as part of the Windward Islands government until 1958, when it became a member of the Federation of the West Indies (1958–62). In the early 1950s, as also occurred in other British West Indian territories, universal adult suffrage was granted as the first move toward internal self-government. After the dissolution of the Federation, St. Vincent and the Grenadines became an associated state of Great Britain, with full internal self-government. In October 1979 the territory gained its independence from Britain.

Anti-Obeah Laws

During the late eighteenth century, the slave laws of St. Vincent did not specifically address obeah (e.g., IUP 1816–18:26; Grenada 1789). The earliest slave law with an anti-obeah provision was enacted in August 1803. Although this law focused on runaways (fugitive slaves), it also included a provision "punishing obeah men." Clause 4 noted that "much mischief arises from the practice of a certain description of people, known by the name of obeah men or obeah doctors." The law punished any "white, coloured, or slave" convicted of "practicing obeah, conjuration, incantation or divination by any charm, ceremony, cards, sieve, bible and key, or by any means of instruments whatever" to cure disease, to offer protection or threaten to harm anyone, to recover lost or stolen goods, or to "administer any love potions or philters."[53] Whether slave, white, or free colored, the convicted offender was to be whipped in the public market "at the discretion of the court"; if a death resulted from the administration of "any potion or drug," the perpetrator (regardless of racial group) was to be executed (St. Vincent 1803:191–192).

The 1803 law (along with other St. Vincent slave laws) was repealed by a June 1821 consolidated slave act, three clauses of which specifically addressed obeah. Clause 47 referred to the "mischiefs" of "obeah men and women" (the term *doctor* was now deleted) and punished persons, "whether free or slave" (the terms *white* and *coloured* were now replaced), "who shall pretend to use any supernatural power, for any evil purpose whatsoever" or who used "such practices with an intent . . . to affect or endanger the life or health of any slave or other person." Those convicted were to "suffer death accordingly." Clause 48 similarly imposed the death penalty on any "free or slave" convicted of using poison, "pounded glass, or other deleterious matter, in the practice of obeah" to harm someone—even if death did not result. And clause 49 specified that anyone found with poison, "pounded glass, or other materials notoriously used in the practice of obeah" was to be transported from the island or receive any other punishment the court saw fit, but not "extending to life" (St. Vincent 1821:337–338).[54]

Unlike most of the other British West Indian jurisdictions, St. Vincent did not have any vagrancy acts during the post-emancipation period (see, for example, St. Vincent 1864), and the earliest law to refer to "occult" practices was enacted in 1854. The Summary Offence Act, 1854, included a clause targeting "the practice of unlawful pretences to skill in palmistry, cards, and occult sciences." Although the word *obeah* was not specifically mentioned, the law asserted that various practices of "occult science" had "become so prevalent and so productive of mischievous consequences among the more simple, illiterate and ill-informed inhabitants" that legislation was needed to "restrain and punish persons who shall be guilty of such practice." The wording of the 1854 law was similar to that found in the anti-obeah laws of other territories, being directed against those who, through pretence or "skill in occult science," palmistry, "or the cutting of cards" interpreted past events, told fortunes, claimed an ability to discover lost or stolen property, or claimed to be able to cause as well as cure "disease or sickness, pain, or any other infirmity." Conviction could bring a fine of up to fifty pounds or imprisonment, with or without hard labor, for up to one year; the sentence might also include from one to three public or private whippings during the course of the jail term.

Although the 1854 law was amended in 1860 and again in 1861, the clause treating "occult practices" was not affected (St. Vincent 1864:280–282, 528–532, 541). Another Summary Offences Act was enacted in May 1880. Its clause 28, respecting "the practice of unlawful pretences to skill in palmistry, cards, and occult sciences," retained the same wording as the 1854 law. Once again the word *obeah* was not mentioned, and the only difference of consequence between this clause and the one from 1854 was in the punishment. The fine and prison term remained the same, but now the whipping provision applied only to males, who could be "once privately whipped during the term of imprisonment" (St. Vincent 1884:72–73).

Although the word *obeah* is conspicuously absent from the 1854 and 1880 laws, it did occur in later legislation. Its first appearance was in the Summary Conviction Offences of St. Vincent's 1895 revised laws. Under the title "Police Offences," the heading "rogues and vagabonds" included several clauses, one of which addressed a number of specific offenses commonly found in vagrancy acts, such as the fraudulent collection of alms for charity, loitering on private property, or possession of implements that could be used in burglary. Another clause prohibited fortune-telling, palmistry, reading cards, and so on "to deceive or impose on any person." Obeah was not mentioned in either of these clauses. However, a third clause specifically addressed obeah practitioners: "every person who practices obeah, or by any occult means or by any assumption of supernatural power" attempts to frighten or harm someone, find lost or stolen goods and the party responsible, or "restore any person to health." Those convicted were liable to a ten-pound fine or imprisonment for three months for the first offense (St. Vincent 1912:159). The same provisions, wording, and penalties were retained in later laws—for example, the Summary Convictions Offences amended in 1912 and in force as of May 1926 (Rae 1927:159) and May 1954 (St. Vincent 1954). They remained in effect until repealed with the passage of the criminal code of 1988 (St. Vincent 1989:94; St. Vincent 1990:93).

Although the 1988 criminal code repealed earlier ordinances, it continued to include, in rephrased form, various provisions explicitly directed against obeah. Section 285, for instance, defined as "idle and disorderly persons"—liable to jail sentences of three months—certain categories of beggars along with those soliciting "for any immoral purpose in any public place," those engaged in gambling in public, and anyone who "pretends to deal in obeah ... or witchcraft, or tells fortunes by palmistry or like superstitious means, intending to deceive or impose on people." Section 290 specifically addressed obeah: a person "practising or dealing in obeah" was one who, "to effect any fraudulent or unlawful purpose or for gain, or for the purpose of frightening any person, uses or pretends to use any occult means, or pretends to possess any supernatural power of knowledge." As in several other jurisdictions (Jamaica, Bahamas, Antigua, Montserrat, Dominica, and Grenada), "instrument of obeah" was vaguely defined as "anything commonly used in or associated with the practice of obeah"; if found with such an "instrument," one was presumed to be an obeah practitioner. Those convicted of practicing obeah under section 290 were liable to a one-year prison sentence. A similar sentence awaited those convicted of writing, publishing, distributing, or otherwise promoting any literature "calculated to promote the superstition of obeah," as well as those who consulted an obeah practitioner "for any fraudulent or unlawful purpose" (St. Vincent 1988:682–683, 689–690).[55]

As of January 1, 2010, the anti-obeah provisions of the 1988 criminal code had not been repealed (e.g., St. Vincent 2009; St. Vincent 2010; St. Vincent 2010b:17). Although it appears that enforcement has been infrequent in recent years, court cases do occasionally still arise (e.g., Huggins 2006).

British Honduras/Belize

Political and Governmental History

Although the British settled this Central American territory in the early 1660s, it was not until 1786 that the Colonial Office appointed the first of a series of administrators, or "superintendants," to administer the settlement. In 1862 the Colonial Office established British Honduras as a dependency of Jamaica, with which the settlement had long-standing ties, and in 1884 it became a Crown colony. Crown colony government continued until the 1950s, when the Colonial Office granted universal adult suffrage; internal self-government was achieved in 1964. Having adopted the name Belize in 1973, the country gained full independence from Britain in 1981. Today it is a parliamentary democracy within the Commonwealth of Nations (the former British Commonwealth).

Anti-Obeah Laws

A "regulation respecting obeah" was decreed in October 1791, about five years after Britain established control of what was later to become the colony of British Honduras. The 1791 ordinance was probably based on the anti-obeah provisions of Jamaica's slave acts, with which it shared some key wording, for example, "In order to prevent the many mischiefs that may arise from the wicked art... of obeah men and women, pretending to have communication with the devil and other evil spirits whereby the weak and superstitious are deluded into a belief of their having full power to exempt them whilst under their protection from any evils that might otherwise happen." The regulation was directed against "any free person of colour or slave" who claimed "any supernatural power in order to affect the health or lives of others," extorted money or goods "under false pretences," or encouraged slaves to escape their masters, hide runaways, or rebel. The penalty for conviction was death, "or such other punishment" as the authorities saw fit to administer (Burdon 1931:195–196).[56]

The earliest anti-obeah provision of the post-emancipation period formed part of what appears to have been the colony's first vagrancy act: the 1863 "Act for the Punishment of Idle and Disorderly Persons, and Rogues and Vagabonds in British Honduras."[57] Like the vagrancy acts in other territories, the British Honduras law was closely modeled on England's 1824 Vagrancy Act, with which it shared certain key language. The word *obeah* was simply inserted into a clause devoted to the definition of "rogues and vagabonds." The latter included "any person pretending or professing to tell fortunes, or using any subtle craft or device by palmistry, obeah, or any such like superstitious means to deceive and impose upon any of Her Majesty's subjects." The penalty for initial conviction was jail for up to three months.

The 1863 vagrancy act was amended in 1865 and again in 1877 (Robinson 1985:14, 32) but was then superseded by the 1878 Summary Conviction Offences Ordinance. Among sixteen paragraphs detailing offenses classified as "petty misdemeanors"—such as spreading false rumors, creating or fostering "public alarm," lewd or obscene behavior, or fraudulent collection of alms for charities—paragraph 10 (repeating some of the wording of the 1863 vagrancy act) targeted persons "pretending or professing to tell fortunes or using any subtle craft, or devise by palmistry, obeah, or any such like superstitious means to deceive and impose upon any person whatsoever." Those convicted of a "petty misdemeanor" in this category could be jailed for up to three months, with or without hard labor, or fined up to $125 in local currency (Francis 1924:1245–1262).

The 1878 ordinance was amended several times over the years (e.g., Francis 1924:1245), with amendments continuing to be made after 1884, when British Honduras was separated from Jamaica, but the section on obeah, palmistry, and so on remained the same (e.g., British Honduras 1887:433–439). By the 1950s, however, the fine for all petty misdemeanors had been raised to $150; although the jail sentence was still up to three months, the hard labor stipulation was removed (C. J. X. Henriques 1960:604–606). As part of later changes to the laws, the penalty was increased to a fine of three hundred dollars or jail for up to six months (Dickson 1983:6, 9). Through all these revisions, obeah was never singled out for special attention among the petty misdemeanors. In the most recent edition of Belize's laws, in effect as of December 31, 2000, the Summary Jurisdiction (Offences) Act included essentially the same long list of petty misdemeanors as in the earlier legislation. Paragraph viii, dealing with obeah, was identical to the previous version, and the penalty for a first offense remained a maximum of three hundred dollars or jail for up to six months (Belize 2000:12, 16).

As of January 1, 2010, the Summary Jurisdiction (Offences) Act of 2000 had not been repealed (Belize 2010a:78; Belize 2010b), meaning that its anti-obeah provision, the gist of which dates back to 1878, was still in force. Obeah, therefore, continued to be a petty misdemeanor in Belize.

Turks and Caicos

Political and Governmental History

The British took control of the Turks and Caicos in 1799, at which time this archipelago of approximately forty islands was combined administratively with the Bahamas. In 1848 the Turks and Caicos were separated again from the Bahamas and given their own president and council. However, in 1874 Britain annexed the islands to Jamaica as a dependency, responsible to the governor of Jamaica. The Turks and Caicos remained a Jamaican dependency, with no representative institutions, until 1959, when universal adult suffrage was introduced. With Jamaica's independence in 1962, the islands became a separate British dependency and then a colony, receiving their own governor in 1972; in 1976 internal self-government was attained. Today the Turks and Caicos are a British Overseas Territory with the same status as the Cayman Islands.

Anti-Obeah Laws

During the early nineteenth century the Turks and Caicos were subject to Bahamian laws. Following emancipation, the earliest law to include an anti-obeah provision was the Vagrancy Act of June 1839 (clause 2), which was identical to the 1839 Vagrancy Act of the Bahamas in its date of passage, title, phrasing, and penalty; the category of "rogues and vagabonds" included anyone "pretending or professing to tell fortunes, or using, or pretending to use, any subtle craft or device, by palmistry, obeah, or any such like superstitious means, to deceive or impose on any of Her Majesty's subjects, or upon any other person." The 1839 Turks and Caicos Vagrancy Act was amended in February 1846, but the anti-obeah provision remained the same, and the act was still in force as of 1862 (Duncombe 1862:277–278; cf. Anderson 1850:286–288); in fact, it probably remained in force until the Turks and Caicos were annexed to Jamaica in 1874.

The history of legislation during the years following 1874 remains somewhat unclear, although we presume that Jamaican law applied during this period. In 1899 the Legislative Board of the Turks and Caicos passed a Summary Offences Ordinance that made liable for up to six months in prison "any person who pretends or professes to tell fortunes or uses any subtle craft, means, or device, by palmistry, obeah, or otherwise, or who pretends to cure injuries or diseases, or effect any purpose by means of any charm, incantations, or other pretended supernatural practice" (St. Aubyn 1908:475). The wording of this section of the ordinance was exactly the same as that of the Small Charges Act, 1891, of the Leeward Islands (Leewards 1892), and very similar to the wording of vagrancy acts in other West Indian jurisdictions, all of which represented slight modifications of the 1824 English Vagrancy Act. The six-month prison sentence was similar to penalties found elsewhere.

Another Summary Offences Ordinance went into effect on January 6, 1900, and had the same anti-obeah section as the earlier law. The 1900 ordinance was amended a number of times over the years, but the anti-obeah provision of 1900 was still in force as of the late 1970s—after the Turks and Caicos had established a new constitution—and it remained in effect, with the same wording, as of January 2001 (e.g., Cundall 1952:453; Glover 1970:361, 369; Glover 1980:90; Turks and Caicos 1998; Turks and Caicos 2001:61). Indeed, this law, with the same anti-obeah provision, appears to have been in force as of 2009 (e.g., Turks and Caicos 2009) and probably still is as of the present.

Cayman Islands

Political and Governmental History

Ceded by Spain to Britain around 1660, the three islands comprising the Cayman Islands became a dependency of Jamaica after 1734, making them subject to Jamaica's laws. Until 1962 the Caymans (along with the Turks and Caicos) remained formal dependencies of Jamaica, whose governor was responsible for them although they retained their own legislative body, which they had had since late 1831. In 1962, when Jamaica attained independence, the Caymans became a separate colony with their own governor and a considerable degree of local autonomy. Today they are a self-governing British Overseas Territory, one of Britain's few remaining dependencies in the Caribbean, along with Anguilla, the British Virgin Islands, and the Turks and Caicos.

Anti-Obeah Laws

For many years prior to 1959, the Cayman Islands were subject to Jamaica's laws, "as well as to certain laws approved by Jamaica for local application" (Donaldson 1981:1; for laws in the latter category, see Cayman Islands 1889).

The Jamaican Obeah Act of June 1898 was adopted in the Cayman Islands almost verbatim, with only a few minor changes of wording reflecting the territory's political and legal status—for example, in the Caymans version of the Obeah Act, the word *law* was substituted for *act*, and "Resident Magistrate" for "Grand Court" (Henry and Laming n.d.:1633–1635; cf. Jamaica 1898). However, while the 1898 Jamaica Obeah Act remains in force in Jamaica (as of 2011), the Obeah Law of the Caymans was repealed by the territory's penal code of 1975 (Cayman Islands 1975:69–70, part XI, section 296; cf. Cayman Islands 1989:63).

Nonetheless, obeah remained illegal in the Cayman Islands even after this, because the 1975 penal code that brought about the repeal of the older obeah law itself included anti-obeah provisions. Section 146, for example, which was aimed at "idle and disorderly persons"—including those who "indecently" exposed themselves, gambled in public, or solicited "for immoral purposes in any public place"—also applied to anyone who "pretends to deal in obeah, myalism, duppy catching or witchcraft or to tell fortunes by palmistry or like superstitious means intending to deceive or impose on people." Conviction could result in up to three months in jail or a fine of up to twenty dollars or both (Cayman Islands 1975:38). (The only other British West Indian jurisdiction whose laws include the term *duppy catching* is Montserrat. Interestingly, *myalism*, which also turns up in Cayman Islands law, has a similarly limited distribution, occurring only there and in the laws of Montserrat, Jamaica, and the British Virgin Islands.)

Section 157 of the same penal code, which deals with "offences injurious to the public in general," declares "guilty of an offence" any persons found practicing "obeah" or "myalism" for "any fraudulent or unlawful purpose, or for gain, or for the purpose of frightening any person." Reproducing the wording of the Jamaican Obeah Act, the Caymans law, like those of other territories, defines neither of these terms, nor does it clarify the meaning of "instrument of obeah or myalism," defining it vaguely as "anything commonly used in the practice of obeah or myalism." The law was also directed against those who sold, printed, or distributed anything "calculated to promote the superstition of obeah." All that was legally needed to charge a person with practicing obeah was a statement such as, "He is a person practising obeah" (Cayman Islands 1975:41).

Although the 1975 penal code was revised and amended a number of times over the years (for a list of these revisions and amendments, see Cayman Islands 2007:1), the revised penal code as of 2007 still contained essentially the same anti-obeah provisions as before. However, there were minor modifications having to do with arrest; for example, if a suspect was found in possession of "any instrument of obeah or myalism," that person was presumed by law to be a practitioner. The only significant change other than this was that penalties were made somewhat stricter, conviction now bringing a jail sentence of three months as well as a fine of five hundred dollars (Cayman Islands 2007:58, 62–63).

Conclusion

IN OUR INTRODUCTION WE DISCUSSED some of the shortcomings and flawed assumptions that we believe characterize much of the existing literature on obeah, past and present. Here we would like to raise a few final critical thoughts.

Perhaps most striking about the complex and diverse body of legislation we have surveyed in this book is the common, unshifting ideological ground that appears to underlie anti-obeah enactments from different territories and at different periods of time. When these materials are viewed together, a high degree of continuity is noticed between older and newer attempts to use the law to suppress and control ill-defined and often misunderstood expressions of a subaltern worldview that has remained at odds with that of ruling elites since the beginning years of colonization and slavery in the West Indies. Admittedly there are stark differences between the slavery and post-emancipation eras in terms of severity of punishment—gruesome executions and transportation for obeah convictions are, of course, things of the distant past. Nonetheless, it is remarkable that through the twentieth century, and in many parts of the region even today, otherwise law-abiding citizens could, theoretically at least, be imprisoned and fined (or even whipped in Jamaica) for barely defined—though culturally marked as "African" and "black"—and poorly understood beliefs and practices. Contemporary extensions of the slavery-period laws targeting obeah can be seen as part and parcel of a larger historical process of social control, cultural domination, and hegemonic reality construction, realized ultimately through the power to impose punitive sanctions from above. Even if seldom enforced today, these laws, so long as they remain on the books, continue to serve as symbolic expressions of the oppressive power that made possible the construction of slave societies and, after emancipation, the preservation of political and economic structures supporting glaring social divisions based on class and "race"/color.

Like the laws themselves, certain commonly held views of obeah today must be viewed as remnants of this process and the power upon which it depended. In fact, as we suggested in the introduction to this book, anti-obeah legislation is not only a product of oppressive power but also a major factor contributing to the construction and maintenance of cultural hierarchies through which beliefs, practices, and expressions identified as "African" and "black" have continued to be stigmatized and devalued throughout much of the West Indies. In addition, we contend that several of the problematic and flawed assumptions contained in these laws have made their way into the scholarly and broader literature, thus contributing in subtle and insidious ways to the reproduction of hegemonic values and representations that hark back to previous centuries. Let us consider just a few examples.

As shown in our discussion of the laws in individual jurisdictions (chapter 4), many laws criminalizing obeah, particularly during the period of slavery, focus on the ostensible use of witchcraft or sorcery to harm others. Few scholars have seriously questioned the fundamental premise behind this component of anti-obeah legislation—namely the assumption that fears of witchcraft accurately represent the actual practice of those thought of as witches (in this case, obeah practitioners). Like the legislators who created these laws, scholars from various fields in the social sciences and humanities who have examined the literature on obeah trials or allegations of witchcraft/sorcery against obeah practitioners have tended to accept the testimony of ostensible victims at face value, without knowing, in most cases, whether spiritual aggression or "supernatural harming" (Chireau 2003:31) actually took place. Such a presumption is hardly defensible, given what social scientists and historians have long known about the nature of witchcraft accusations as a general social phenomenon, that is, that such accusations often say much more about social tensions within a community—as well as personal anxieties and fantasies—than about real activities by spiritual practitioners.

By encoding such fears in law and treating witchcraft accusations as reliable indexes of truth, legislators and contemporary writers turned what was probably largely a fantasy of obeah (i.e., the notion that it was an inherently evil form of magic) into reality—a "reality" that has been unwittingly perpetuated by writers who have uncritically relied on the written record. This record, as we noted earlier, may at times have accurately represented common fears and certain psychogenic illnesses related to them (cf. Handler 2006:200–202), even while erroneously reducing everything labeled "obeah" by the enslaved to such negative phenomena. What we believe is a distorted reality, shaped in part by unquestioning acceptance of witchcraft fears and accusations as an accurate reflection of normal spiritual practice, has fed into and reinforced the reductive, hegemonic definition of obeah as harmful witchcraft. And it remains the case today that widespread fears about the use of obeah to cause misfortune and illness are often uncritically accepted—in the absence of any evidence one way or the other—as accurate indicators of the actual practices of obeah men and women.

Another flawed assumption contained in much anti-obeah legislation, especially during the post-emancipation era and into modern times, is the notion that the practice of obeah was and is inherently fraudulent and driven by purely pecuniary motives. Partly through the influence of vagrancy laws that transferred British cultural assumptions about "fortune-telling," palmistry, and similar divination practices to Caribbean contexts, West Indian laws reduced obeah practitioners to charlatans who knowingly exploited the superstitions of their gullible and ignorant clients for profit. However, Bilby can attest to the general inaccuracy of this characterization, having observed and discussed such matters with spiritual workers (whether self-identified as obeah practitioners or not) in Jamaica, French Guiana, and Suriname. It is a characterization based on the false assumption that material compensation is fundamentally incompatible with the rendering of genuine spiritual services. To most ethnographers who have done field research and worked with actual spiritual practitioners in the Caribbean (and, indeed, in Africa), the idea that monetary or other payment necessarily suggests lack of sincerity or genuine belief in the efficacy of the spiritual treatments being administered would appear to be entirely inappropriate. In these cultural contexts (and in many others in other parts of the world, as anthropologists have long known), material exchanges often carry symbolic meanings and cannot be reduced to mere economic motives, and this is perhaps even more the case when overtly spiritual transactions are involved. Today, as in the past, compensation for spiritual services in many parts of the Caribbean is often in the form of goods—for example, food, rum, tobacco, or any number of other items—although monetary remuneration is also common. There is little evidence, however, to support the notion that spiritual practitioners in the Caribbean in general are motivated exclusively or primarily by a desire for material gain.

These and other misconceptions about Afro-Caribbean spiritual practices, past and present, retain a good deal of their power in scholarly representations of obeah, because scholars from a variety of fields have had a tendency to rely exclusively on written depictions created across a vast cultural gulf. Indeed, this tendency continues to be noticeable among commentators on contemporary culture, ranging from journalists to literary critics, who often contribute to the negative representations of obeah. These commentators have usually had little or no contact with those whose ostensible beliefs and practices they portray. And most have had no more exposure to the specific ritual and spiritual contexts within which obeah practitioners operate than did the ruling elites who framed the laws that played such a large role in shaping public understandings of obeah over the past centuries. If what we contend is true, then it follows that hegemonic representations of obeah derive their continuing power in large part from ongoing ignorance of the phenomena they purport to represent.

The fundamentally oppressive nature of anti-obeah legislation is perhaps revealed most clearly in the laws that made it possible to punish someone for simply consulting an obeah practitioner. These laws covered all kinds of consultations, not just those ostensibly concerned with using spiritual power to harm enemies. It is difficult for most of us in the present to see how imprisonment and flogging for the mere act of seeking relief from psychic and physical ailments—to take but one example—could be deemed justifiable. But it must be re-emphasized that these laws formed part of an ongoing campaign (although not a systematically, centrally organized one) to stamp out what ruling elites—including their missionary allies and local converts—considered to be degrading forms of "superstition" associated with blackness and an "uncivilized" African past. The "civilizing" mission that provided ideological support to both colonization and slavery could not tolerate beliefs or practices that differed from those being imposed from above, even those associated with entirely benevolent goals. Viewed against this background, the laws against consultation of obeah practitioners suggest a shift of emphasis from externally enforced means of control over the bodies and actions of the enslaved to more subtle forms of mind control after slavery ended.

As has been shown, sanctions against obeah became less harsh over time; the major reductions in penalties occurred after the period of slavery as the emphasis in legislation shifted from witchcraft to fraud. West Indian lawmakers, regardless of jurisdiction, might defend the continuation of anti-obeah provisions today by arguing that contemporary legislation is really designed to protect people from deceptive and fraudulent economic practices rather than to impose restrictions on spiritual beliefs or personal faith. But in view of the realities of Afro-Caribbean spiritual practices, we believe that this distinction must be seen as false. Indeed, it is difficult to see how one could determine in an objective and non-prejudicial manner who genuinely believes what and therefore whose practices are based on fraudulent motives versus sincere intentions. By the same token, it would be equally difficult to draw a firm and non-arbitrary line between practices that could be categorized in some contexts as obeah and in others as legitimate expressions of spiritual faith, protected by statutes concerned with religious freedom—for example, faith healing or prayers (whether by an individual or a group) intended to produce specific outcomes.

One last point deserves consideration here. As we have stressed repeatedly, obeah is not now nor has it ever been a unitary phenomenon. The term has carried multiple meanings and connotations, some of them contradictory, across both time and space. West Indians who today define obeah as an inherently negative form of spiritual power used to cause harm (in short, witchcraft or sorcery) may represent the majority view. One could argue that since language, like culture more generally, is a product of historical processes and not frozen in time, this contemporary sense is no less "correct" than any other that has been attached to the term in other times and places. From this perspective, it might be seen as inappropriate to critique or challenge a usage that has come to be widely accepted in the Caribbean, even among many in the working class and in non-elite groups. However, we argue that such a view, while taking account of the dynamic nature of culture, stops short of a truly processual approach and leads paradoxically to an ahistorical perspective on the phenomenon of obeah.

Rather than arguing for anything as simple as a "correct" meaning of *obeah*, we wish to emphasize the ways in which the various meanings attached to the term have been historically constructed. Our discussion and review of anti-obeah legislation point clearly to the important role of the legal apparatus in the slave and colonial past—along with other enactments of colonial power—in the construction of the negative meanings that remain dominant today. These meanings must be understood, at least in part, as living artifacts of that historical process. The very fact that many in the former colonies of the British West Indies continue to dissent privately from these dominant meanings (or vacillate between differing and sometimes contradictory meanings) tells us that we should remain skeptical of any view of obeah that reduces it simply to something evil and harmful. To understand obeah, then, is to understand its multiplicity, and this means grappling with the contradictions and confusions the term has come to embody. One thing that remains relatively clear and stable in this often cloudy picture, as this book shows, is a body of legislation that consistently criminalizes and demonizes something called *obeah* while never really defining it.

Much is still not known about obeah now and in the past (e.g., the range and types of specific actions used by self-defined practitioners in the same and different territories and how practitioners decide to become practitioners and learn their arts), but it remains clear that the laws targeting what is labeled *obeah* have the effect of stigmatizing and making punishable both the use (or ostensible use) of spiritual power with harmful intentions and a vast array of beliefs and practices intended to help people resolve personal and social problems. Despite the negative stereotypes, beliefs and practices in the latter category, today as in the past, constitute a large portion of what contemporary West Indians think of—if only in private—as obeah. In effect, by failing to specifically define obeah in the laws (or to encode understandings of it that take account of the term's ambiguity and its full semantic range), legislation against it, today as in the past, renders all forms of African-identified (or "black") religious expression suspect, potentially unlawful, and immoral. In criminalizing varieties of religiosity deemed unacceptable largely because of their association with those at the bottom of the social hierarchy, rather than any real threat posed to society, these laws do little more than reproduce cultural hierarchies dating back to the era of slavery. In the final analysis, we are inclined to agree with Rex Nettleford (1979:20), who considered the continuing existence of anti-obeah legislation in his homeland of Jamaica during his lifetime not only as an unfortunate aspect of "an ex-colonial society doused in colonial attitudes and mores" but also a violation of the principle of "freedom of conscience."

Notes

Introduction

1. To our knowledge, no systematic studies have been done of obeah prosecutions in recent years, but our sense that such prosecutions have become relatively rare is based on general verbal reports from several West Indian lawyers and academics and a survey of online Anglophone Caribbean newspapers over the past few years (cf. Paton 2009:16).

Chapter 1

1. In the Francophone and Hispanic Caribbean, other terms are or were used for those involved in the types of activities (e.g., healing and protection) associated with obeah practitioners in the Anglophone Caribbean (Handler and Bilby 2001:89; cf. Paton and Forde 2012:passim). The Netherlands Caribbean (formerly Netherlands Antilles) Papiamento-speaking "ABC" islands (Aruba, Bonaire, and Curaçao) use the term *brua*, while in the English-speaking areas (the Windward islands of Saba, St. Eustatius, and St. Maarten), *obeah* is the common term (Jay Haviser, letter to Handler, March 6, 2012; also W. Klooster, letter to Handler, March 3, 2012). In the Danish West Indies *obeah* was "the only term . . . for magic performed by the slaves" (N. Jensen, letter to Handler, March 1, 2012; B. Higman, letter to Handler, March 7,

109

2012; also Hall 1992:passim; Jensen 2012:68–72). The term *obeah* also appears in the Chesapeake and Carolina Low Country—perhaps reflecting early contacts with the British West Indies—but may have been more common in colonial times than later. In any case, the term *conjurer* (or *hoodoo*) was more apt to be employed for a healer with supernatural powers in the British North American colonies and the antebellum U.S. South (Handler and Bilby 2001:89; cf. Morgan 1998:620; Chireau 2003; Rucker 2006; Young 2007:126). Divination is categorized as a type of *obia* among the Maroon peoples of Suriname.

2. A survey of online Anglophone Caribbean newspapers from 2008 through March 2012 yielded numerous reports from a variety of territories—many of them from Jamaica—of people who felt aggrieved in one way or another. They either accused a specific person of "working obeah" on them or more generally attributed sickness, bad luck, or some type of misfortune to the evil force of obeah. Examples of such newspaper reports include a woman in the parish of Clarendon, Jamaica, who had a skin condition that a medically prescribed remedy failed to cure. She believed her condition was a "result of obeah" and feared for her safety because "people with whom she has had disagreements may have turned to obeah" (*Jamaica Star* 2011). Another report from Jamaica concerned a man who was recently hospitalized for a nervous condition because he believed he was "being plagued by the duppy of a woman he bewitched many years ago" (*Jamaica Star* 2011b), and a Trinidadian man, having confessed to the police a variety of property thefts, blamed those acts on obeah, explaining, "My girlfriend family don't like me. They take my clothes and put them in a cemetery . . . . That is what made me do those things" (*Trinidad Express* 2011). Whether any of these accusations had any basis in truth, in terms of the intentional malevolent actions of others, is another matter entirely.

3. A simple illustration from Jamaica: in his now well-known diary, Thomas Thistlewood—who, in common with many whites in Jamaica, disapproved of obeah—briefly, almost cursorily, records an incident in 1780. One of his favored slaves was in great distress over a miscarriage and the sickness and deaths of several of her children. The diary entry makes it clear that she called in an obeah man (whom she hid in her house, although he was later found and expelled by Thistlewood) in an effort to identify the person responsible for her problems and to achieve an explanation for her misfortunes (Burnard 2004:224; cf. Hall 1989:279). Eighteenth-century primary sources for Barbados also contain negative views of obeah practitioners while inadvertently yielding evidence for the positive role they played in the life of the enslaved (for specific examples, see Handler 2000:70–72).

4. See Cassidy and Le Page (1967:326–327) and Allsopp (1996:412–413).

5. Kwasi Konadu (2010:139–140) has recently proposed a novel origin for the term. He argues that, in areas where an Akan presence was strong or dominant, the term *obia* may have derived from the concept *bayi*, which, he states, is linked to an "optimistic

utterance" meaning "it will be good or well." This utterance, according to Konadu, is typically "made to provide hope to those who need to consult" the particular kind of spiritual practitioner known as *obayifoo*. However, J. H. Nketia (verbal communication to Bilby, October 2, 2011) suggests that, while one could theoretically use such an utterance in this way, one would not normally do so in public because of the negative connotations of the terms *bayi* and *obayifoo*.

6. See, for example, Warner-Lewis (2003:190–191), Aborampah (2005:132), and Duncanson-Hales (2011:76–78). Recently published definitions of obeah from different parts of the region (in popular publications) include the following: "black magic; to put a spell on someone" (Jamaica; Henry and Harris 2002:37); "a form of black magic" (Antigua; Murphy n.d.:7); "witchcraft" (Antigua; Lawrence 2003:30); "bewitch" (Belize Kriol Project 1997:62); "witchcraft" (U.S. Virgin Islands; Ellis 1990:65); and "a kind of witchcraft or sorcery practiced in the Caribbean, a survival of African magic rites, specializing in poisons and the power of terror through charms and fetishes" (Trinidad and Tobago; Mendes 2003:132).

7. It is important to stress that not all activities identified with the term *obeah* can be reduced to the manipulation of impersonal supernatural entities or forces. For example, duppies are commonly used in Jamaica by obeah practitioners, who often know the names (or supposed names) of the deceased individuals with whose duppies they sometimes work. And in certain Afro-Jamaican religious traditions such as Kromanti Play and Kumina, ancestral spirits regularly possess mediums and interact with the living, much like the *lwa* in Haiti (Moore 1953; Bilby 1981; Bilby and Fu-Kiau 1983). Among Surinamese Maroons, different possessing deities are routinely referred to as *obia*. In Ndyuka/Aluku, for example, "A obia kon a tapu a sama" [the obeah came on top of the person] would be the normal way of saying "the god possessed the person" (Bilby n.d.).

8. Williams may have erred in representing the Asante-Twi term *obayifo* as having an entirely negative meaning and treating it as the equivalent of "malevolent sorcerer." Konadu (2010:140) defines the Akan term *obayifoo* as "the one who does or uses the neutral force of *bayi*." However, according to J. H. Nketia (verbal communication to Bilby, October 2, 2011), *bayi* would usually be glossed in English as "witchcraft" and *obayifoo* as "witch." Both terms, he states, are "mostly negative" and refer to practitioners and powers that would be consulted and used only in private. In his view, then, although it may be possible for an individual to direct *bayi* toward positive or beneficial purposes, the term usually carries the assumption that the theoretically neutral power denoted by it is used for harmful purposes. One would not normally talk in public about consulting with an *obayifoo* because that would cause other people to gossip and conjecture about what that person was up to and would likely raise suspicions of witchcraft.

9. Aside from Jamaica, where the term *myal* regularly crops up in anti-obeah laws from

the early nineteenth century to the present, the term is mentioned only in the laws of Montserrat (1983–present), the British Virgin Islands (1997–present), and the Cayman Islands (1898–present). The anomalous occurrence of the term in Montserrat and the British Virgin Islands (the Caymans are a different case, since prior to 1959 they were subject to the laws of Jamaica and adopted its 1898 anti-obeah act) appears to shed some light on the dubious logic that seems to have guided the formulation of anti-obeah provisions in many instances. Myal, as such, appears to have been essentially a Jamaican phenomenon, and, so far as we know, the term has not been documented in the historical, ethnographic, or popular literature and newspapers in the British Virgin Islands or Montserrat (or, for that matter, the Cayman Islands). That it would suddenly appear in laws intended to regulate spiritual conduct in these territories late in the twentieth century suggests that the lawyers and legislators responsible for these enactments were largely ignorant of the actual spiritual practices of those whose behavior they were attempting to control (the legislation's wording seems to have been adopted from Jamaican or Jamaican-derived texts). Indeed, it seems likely that when anti-obeah provisions were introduced in Montserrat and the British Virgin Islands, few if any residents of those islands had ever heard of "myalism," although they were now theoretically liable to arrest and prosecution should they decide to practice whatever it might be (as remains the case today).

10. Morrish (1982:40–48) is a good example of a later study of obeah that relies heavily and uncritically on Williams's ideas (sometimes without crediting them). For examples of relatively recent scholarly studies that accept versions of the obeah–myal dichotomy promoted by Williams, see Gordon (1997:146–147), Chevannes (1998:6–7), Warner-Lewis (2003:190–191), Kelleher and Leavey (2004:41), Rucker (2006:n. 91), and Hodges (2008:30). For a pointed critique of Williams's one-sided representation of obeah, see Murphy (1994:226 n. 17).

11. Gerbner's unpublished paper (2010) is cited with the author's permission. A PhD student in history at Harvard University, Gerbner is trained in reading Old German. This early reference to obeah in Jamaica was yielded by her extensive work in the Moravian archives in Herrnhut, Germany. The paper cited here draws on material from her forthcoming dissertation, "Christian Slavery: Protestant Missionaries and Slave Conversion in the Atlantic World, 1660–1760." Even the Jamaican planter Edward Long, certainly no admirer of obeah, referred to "a famous obeiah [sic] man or priest, *much respected* among his countrymen," who played a role in the 1760 revolt (Long 1774:451; emphasis added).

12. The Aluku Maroons, whose language has been influenced by both coastal Guianese Carib (Galibi/Kali'na) Indians and their own Cariban-speaking Wayana neighbors in the interior rainforest, use *obia* and *piyai*—close cognates of these Dominica Carib (Kalinago) terms—in a similar contrastive way. The former refers to positive spiritual

power while the latter, as a synonym for *wisi*, refers to sorcery meant to harm another (Bilby n.d.).

Chapter 2

1. In 1772 an enslaved woman was convicted in Jamaica for "having in her possession, cats teeth, cats claws, jaws, hair, beads, knotted cloths, and other materials relative to the practice of obeah" (Paton 2001:932).
2. The following is a list of specific "instruments of obeah" mentioned in the laws of various territories. Jamaica 1760: *cotton-tree juice* (Jamaica 1771:52–53); Jamaica 1761: *broken bottles, egg shells, feathers* (Jamaica 1771:63); Jamaica 1761, Grenada 1825: *alligator's teeth, dog's teeth, glass, grave dirt, parrots beaks, rum* (Jamaica 1771:63; Grenada 1830:332); Jamaica 1809 and 1816, St. Vincent 1821, Grenada 1825: *pounded glass* (Jamaica 1809:45; Lunan 1819:125; St. Vincent 1821:337–338; Grenada 1830:332); Jamaica 1761, Grenada 1825, Bahamas 1924, St. Lucia 1872: *blood* (Jamaica 1771:63; Grenada 1830:332; Malcolm 1929; St. Lucia 1872); St. Lucia 1872, Bahamas 1924: *bone* (St. Lucia 1872; Malcolm 1929); British Guiana 1918: *skull* (MacKenzie 1923:497–498); St. Lucia 1872, Bahamas 1924: *image* (St. Lucia 1872; Malcolm 1929); British Guiana 1893 and 1920, Grenada 1874, St. Lucia 1872, St. Vincent 1803: *cards* (British Guiana 1895:523–525; MacKenzie 1923:511–512; Grenada 1875:586–587; St. Lucia 1872; St. Vincent 1803:191–192).

   Other "instruments of obeah" were also mentioned in the laws. Barbados 1818, Dominica 1831, Jamaica 1857, Leewards 1892, St. Kitts and Nevis 1904: *charm* (Barbados 1818a; Dominica 1831; Curran 1889–90, vol. 4:44–66; Leewards 1892; Lewis 1964:531–533); Dominica 1788 and 1821, St. Vincent 1803, Barbados 1806, Jamaica 1816, Grenada 1825: *potions or drugs* (Dominica 1789; 1821; St. Vincent 1803:191–192; Barbados 1806; Lunan 1819:125; Grenada 1830:332); St. Vincent 1803, British Guiana 1918, Bahamas 1924, St. Lucia 1872: *philtre* or *philter* (on a few occasions specified as "love" philter or potion (St. Vincent 1803:191–192; MacKenzie 1923:497–498; Malcolm 1929; St. Lucia 1872); St. Vincent 1803, Barbados 1806, Jamaica 1816, Grenada 1825: *poison* (St. Vincent 1803:191–192; Barbados 1806; Lunan 1819:125; Grenada 1830:332).

   In early 1905 the commissioner of Montserrat reported on twenty obeah cases (involving forty-one people) that he had tried since 1900. The "objects produced in evidence" as alleged "instruments of obeah" included "packs of cards, small oval looking glasses, tufts of hair in small cloth parcels, coins, chains, and rosaries," as well as "powder of bones, human remains, skulls, etc." in addition to other items (Skinner 2005:147, 150). In March 1905, a district magistrate in St. John's, Antigua, wrote to the British colonial secretary and included "a return" showing the number of persons "charged with the offence of obeah" in the jurisdiction from 1900 to 1905. The letter also included a "list of the articles [so-called instruments of obeah] produced as evidence before the Magistrates." These included "packs of cards" and "bottles containing assafoetida, rum or some other nauseous liquid" (four cases each); "paper and cloth parcels containing garlic, peppers, seeds, herbs, jumby beads, coral" (four cases); and "bones and powder of bones" (two cases), while one case each involved "tinder horn"; "bottles containing rice, oatmeal, salt"; "fowl (cock)"; "pill box containing dead flies"; "doll in shape of human head"; "piece of skull"; "piece of rosary"; or "candles, sulphur, blue, tobacco, leaden ball, screws, old nails, resin, twine" (Whyham to Colonial Secretary, March 11, 1905; CO 152/287, enclosure 4). The wide array of objects allegedly used by obeah practitioners undoubtedly explains why the laws in general increasingly ceased to itemize the "instruments of obeah" and left the definition vague.

3. Poison is first mentioned in a 1788 Jamaican slave law but was not explicitly linked to obeah until 1792. "Cotton-tree juice" was included in the list of materials allegedly used by obeah practitioners in the 1788 law, but the word *poison* was not explicitly associated with it.

4. An anonymous reader of an earlier draft raised the question of how these punishments worked if the convicted individual was a free person. It is a fair question but we cannot answer it in detail. As best as we can tell, free persons are mentioned in anti-obeah provisions of the *slave* laws of five or six jurisdictions (Barbados, Dominica, Grenada, St. Vincent, British Honduras/Belize, and possibly Nevis). These references imply or explicitly refer to free people of color (i.e., freedmen), but in some cases (Barbados, Dominica, St. Vincent, and possibly Grenada) they also state or imply white persons. Where the court had the option of banishment or execution, a convicted free person could have been executed but was more probably transported abroad without being sold into slavery. We have no individual case information that would help clarify this issue. Diana Paton, however, suggests "free people were probably very rarely convicted under the obeah laws during slavery. After c. 1820, though, if they were convicted they might have been transported rather than executed, as transportation was by then a state-run system rather than selling into slavery" (letter to Handler, March 12, 2012; cf. Paton 2008).

5. Paton (2001) provides a detailed and informative examination of penalties imposed on convicted slaves in mid- to late-eighteenth-century Jamaica. Her discussion is applicable to other territories in the slave colonies of the West Indies.

6. A unique punishment in St. Lucia was cutting the hair of females, but this occurred only in an island law of 1872; the penalty was dropped in an 1877 ordinance.

7. In his richly detailed study of a Saramaka Maroon *óbiama* (obeah man), Richard Price (2008:295) reflects on the important role played by "communal divination" as a means of negotiating shared understandings among ethnically diverse Africans

during the formative years of Saramaka society some three centuries ago, as well as its continuing importance in present-day Saramaka life. For brief discussions of a variety of systems of divination among the Aluku Maroons, see Bilby 1990:214–215 and Bilby 2009:196–197. In both of these Guianese Maroon societies, divination is categorized as a type of obia.

8. Handler (2000:66–68) discusses the role of divination in African belief systems and in the healing practices of enslaved Barbadians.

9. The term *Negro doctor* was also used in Barbados in the late eighteenth century, sometimes synonymously with *obeah practitioner* but not pejoratively (Handler 2000:63–65). *Doctor* could also apply to an obeah practitioner in Berbice/British Guiana (Browne 2011:476; Moore 1995:330 n. 30), and a February 1785 advertisement in the *Cornwall Chronicle*, a Jamaican newspaper, reported on the fugitive slave "Abraham, an old Eboe Negro fellow, [who] pretends to be an Obeah-Man and Doctor" (Chambers 2010:82). The term *doctor* was probably more widely applied to obeah practitioners than in the few territories and examples cited here. It can be noted that this use contrasts with the term *doctor* that was sometimes used for enslaved men trained in rudimentary Western medical procedures; they worked in plantation sick-houses or infirmaries and in Jamaica, for example, were known as "hothouse doctors" (Sheridan 1985:89–96).

10. Barbados has changed considerably over the past several decades and obeah does not play the role that it did in earlier times, but there are a few obeah people—perhaps more than commonly acknowledged—who are still consulted. As a popular Barbadian-authored guide to local customs and beliefs notes, for a fee these practitioners are "consulted in secret" and asked "to patch lovers' quarrels, exact revenge on an enemy, counteract evil, tell fortunes, interpret omens, secure marriages or keep errant husbands at home" (Carrington et al. 2003:140). "People, it is claimed," wrote a well-known Barbadian newspaper columnist, "have gone to obeah men or women to bring misfortune on neighbors against whom they bore a grudge, but much more familiar are the cases where it is claimed women have used obeah to get men to marry them if they seemed reluctant to take the trip up the aisle" (Best 2006). Recent newspaper articles such as those cited above, reporting specific instances, illustrate how the obeah practitioner is asked to direct forces for socially beneficial purposes; however, it is still believed that practitioners have the power to harm and control people, and misfortune and bad—luck, including mental—illness, can be explained in terms of an alleged obeah spell.

Most Barbadians, like many others in the West Indies, hold a largely negative view of obeah; they regard it as fundamentally evil and consider it akin to "black magic." Yet, except for an older and less formally "educated" generation, most would probably deny believing in the powers of obeah even though they still acknowledge its existence and do not easily entirely dismiss it. A university lecturer, a Barbadian student of the island's culture, summarized the situation to Handler by saying, "It is and yet it is not, it is whispered and denied and yet feared. Many dismiss but reserve a possibility." Another person, a middle-aged university-educated Barbadian woman, related a recent experience to Handler: "A large (massive, terrifying) centipede appeared on my bed a week ago while I was sitting up and reading and I could not figure out where it came from. Of course after much panic and screaming I killed it and mentioned it to [a friend's] mother the next day. Her immediate response was that it was evil. It was an omen of evil or harm that someone wanted to do to me. I laughed it off but she was very serious and concerned for my well-being." She continued, "There is still a fear of it so people prefer not to discuss it. Some say it is foolishness. Others know somebody who believes strongly in it and of people who go to so-called obeah women . . . [but] the practice is still feared and quietly denied" (letters to Handler, February 16, 2011; April 19, 2011; cf. Fisher 1985:106–107, 132; Gmelch and Gmelch 1997:145–146; Barbados 2005).

Notes on Images of Obeah

1. The lithographs in the John Carter Brown volume are hand-colored; in other copies (e.g., the British Library), they are in black and white. Forty of Benoit's 100 lithographs, including the one shown here, are displayed on the website "The Atlantic Slave Trade and Slave Life in the Americas: A Visual Record," http://hitchcock.itc.virginia.edu/Slavery.
2. In this translation, italicized words are in the original; French words in the original are in quotation marks and enclosed in brackets.
3. Referring to the 1770s in Suriname, John Stedman was told by "several old Negroes and Indians" that "nothing was more dreaded by their wives and children than the Watra Mama, which signifies the Mother of the Watters [and by which name, strange to tell, they distinguish their *Sybils*]" (Price and Price 1988:457 [*Note*: We cite the Prices's transcription of Stedman's original 1790 manuscript because it contains his original wording; the passages we bracket here and below were inserted into the first published edition of 1796 by its editor; see Stedman 1796, vol. 2:178]). In this case, Stedman is referring to the manatee which, Price and Price (1988:655) point out, "some observers confuse . . . with the female water spirit that plays a role in Afro-Suriname religions and who has widespread antecedents in Africa."

   Elsewhere in his work, Stedman described the "superstitions" of the "common class" of the black population, who are "kept in darkness by their pretended Locomen or Prophets & who find theyr interest in their blindness, by selling them obias, or amulets . . . with other charms. . . . Nor are a kind of Sibils wanting amongst them who deal in oracles, these sage matrons dancing and whirling round in the middle of an audience, till absolutely they froath at the mouth and drop down in the middle of them matrons [the 1796 edition says "dancing and whirling round in the middle of an assembly, with amazing rapidity, until they foam at the mouth, and drop down as convulsed"]; whatever she says to be done during this fit of madness is sacredly performed by the surrounding multitude, which makes these meetings exceedingly dangerous amongst the slaves, who are often told to murder their masters or desert to the woods, & on which account the excessive piece of fanatism, is forbid in the Colony of Suriname on pain of the most rigorous punishment. Yet it is often put in execution in private places . . . this is called here Winty Play or the Dance of the Mairmaid" (Price and Price 1988:521; cf. Stedman 1796, vol. 2:262–263). Price and Price (1988:660) note that "spirit possession was (and remains) a core feature of Afro-Suriname religious behavior. Today 'Winti' has become the general name for coastal Afro-Suriname religion."

Although the scene described by Benoit appears to revolve specifically around the use of Papa snake gods and their healing powers, it also apparently references beliefs and practices that, at least today, are associated with a number of other Afro-Surinamese religious traditions, such as those focusing on other kinds of water spirits. A reading of Stedman's account alongside that of Benoit suggests something of the close relationship of these different religious systems during their formative years.

In his account, Benoit (1839:26) also refers to an incident that was related to him involving a missing gold ring belonging to a plantation manager's wife. A household slave was suspected of being the thief. To deal with the case, Benoit reports, the "The Loacouman-Quasi, that is to say the diviner, was summoned." As it turned out the ring had not been stolen at all.

4. Platte Brug (Flat Bridge), an anchorage for small vessels in Paramaribo.
5. Elsewhere, Benoit (1839:21) writes that "Sarameca-Straat is where the most and best stores and shops of the colony are located. . . . It is the general congregating place not only for foreigners, but also of all classes of locals." Saramaccastraat, as it is referred to today, is still one of the busiest shopping streets in Paramaribo.
6. Although one cannot be certain, the mention of "tatooed" parts of the body probably referred to some form of cicatrization or scarification, which was observed among some Africans in Suriname during the period of Benoit's visit and which also became common among Surinamese Maroons in later years. Until recently, cicatrization or scarification was usually applied, primarily for aesthetic reasons, to the face, neck, and (especially for women) chest area—as well as other parts of the body—among Guianese Maroons of all groups.
7. Benoit (1839:21, 54) refers to the local language as "takie-takie," today known officially as Sranan, a widely spoken creole language of Suriname which combines grammatical elements of English and West African languages with vocabulary elements mainly of English and Dutch origin (Wilner et al. 1994; Allsopp 1996:526). Today

the term *taki-taki* (which literally means "chatter, gossip, noise") is still sometimes used to refer to this language, although many native speakers reject this usage and consider it pejorative.

8. In his *De landbouw in de kolonie Suriname*, Teenstra (1835:236) writes about a "strong spirit" called "voorloop," adding "elsewhere also called kelduivel." Kelduivel is Kill-Devil or rum (thanks to Wim Klooster for this source and translation). Stedman, during the 1770s, described "Kil-devil" [*sic*] as a "species of rum which is distilled from the scum and dregs of sugar chaldrons; it is much drunk in this colony and the only spirits allowed the Negroes when they get any. Many Europeans also from a point of oeconomy make use of it to whom it proves no better than a slow and pernacious poison" (Price and Price 1988:96; cf. Stedman 1796, vol. 1:96 ["a slow and fatal poison"]; Stedman 1796, vol. 2:327). Richard Ligon (1657:92–93, following p. 122 ["The Table"]), writing of rum manufacture in Barbados in 1647–1650, gives some examples of the combustibility that arises from the "strong drink, which the planters call kill-devill [*sic*]."

9. We cannot be certain about the type of snake to which Benoit refers, although it was most likely a small or young boa constrictor. (The French "couleuvre" translates as garter snake; however, in Guyanais, the French-lexicon creole spoken in French Guiana, which neighbors Suriname, boa constrictors are known as *koulèv-ter*, or "couleuvre-terre" [Barthélémi 2011]). "These unaccountable women," Stedman wrote, "by their voice know how to charm the ammodytes, or papaw serpent, down from the trees . . . nor is the . . . snake ever kill'd or hurted by the Negroes, who on the contrary adore it as their friend and guardian, and are even happy to see it enter in their huts . . . . it is even common to see the reptile twine and wreathe about theyr arms, neck, and breast . . . while the woman stroakes and caresses it with her hand." In a footnote, Stedman describes the snake as "from 3 to 5 feet long, and being perfectly harmless it has not the smallest apprehension to be hurted, even by man while the undescribable brilliancy of its colours are perhaps another inducement for the adoration by the negroes" (Price and Price 1988:522–523; cf. Stedman 1796, vol. 2:263).

In their notes to the Stedman transcription, Richard and Sally Price (1988:660) suggest that the "papa" [Stedman's "pawpaw serpent"] is a boa constrictor, although Stedman's description seems to indicate a much smaller snake than a full-grown boa constrictor. Moreover, the online *Oxford English Dictionary* (2nd ed., 1989; accessed December 14, 2011) defines ammodyte as a "venomous snake," but clearly Stedman's (and Benoit's) reference is not to a poisonous snake. It merits considering the description given in a late-eighteenth-century natural history: "The Surinam Serpent, which some improperly called the Ammodytes, is equally harmless and desirable among the savages of that part of the world. They consider themselves as extremely happy if this animal comes into their huts. The colours of this serpent are so many and beautiful, that they surpass all description" (Goldsmith 1774:223–224). In any case, in all of today's Surinamese creole languages, the term *papa*, in reference to a snake, specifically denotes the boa constrictor.

10. The "branche" appears from the semantic associations of the term (as well as what is known of contemporary Afro-Surinamese practices) to be a natural or unmodified "branch" or tree limb; the "bâton" appears from both the semantic associations and the context to be a modified stirring stick, perhaps one that has been carved.

11. Stedman describes a 6:00 a.m. to 6:00 p.m. curfew in Paramaribo that was enforced by the colonial militia. The watch was set at 6:00 p.m. when the commanding ship in the harbor fired the "evening gun," after which "no negro whatever of either sex is allowed to appear in the streets, or on the river without a proper pass, signed by the master or mistress that he belongs to—without which he is taken up, and without further ceremony flog'd the next morning" (Price and Price 1988:237–238; cf. Stedman 1796, vol. 1:292). By the time of Benoit's visit, the curfew appears to have started later since he met with his guide at the *Platte Brug* at 7:00 p.m.

12. In modern Sranan, as well as the closely related eastern Maroon languages of Suriname, Kwasi is a "ritual name for a man born on Sunday" (Shanks et al. 1994; Wilner 2007). We could find no other translation for Quasi/Kwasi. It may be, however, that during the time of Benoit's visit, *Quasi/Kwasi* had become a generic term for a healer (or more generally, ritual specialist), having been derived from the name of Kwasimukámba. Kwasimukámba or Kwasi had been born in Africa about 1690 and was transported to Suriname as a child; he was to become famous in the colony during much of the eighteenth century when he was Suriname's leading curer and diviner (Price 1979; Price 1983:155–157). In one passage, Benoit (1839:26) uses the term "Loacouman-Quasi" to refer specifically to a diviner. (Cf. Stedman [Price and Price 1988:521; Stedman 1796, vol. 2:262], who mentions "*Loco-men* or *Prophets*" who sell "*obias*, or *amulets*" to clients.) This reference seems to support the idea that the term *Quasi/Kwasi* was once used in this more general sense to refer to practitioners of various kinds of obeah. (In both modern Sranan [Wilner et al. 1994:56] and the eastern Maroon languages of Suriname [Shanks et al. 1994:118], *lukuman* means "seer" or "diviner.")

13. The volume contains 27 plates, 13 of which are shown on the website "The Atlantic Slave Trade and Slave Life in the Americas: A Visual Record" http://hitchcock.itc.virginia.edu/Slavery.

14. Brian Austen (n.d.). Bridgens's racist perspectives on enslaved Africans and his defense of slavery are discussed in Barringer and Martinez-Ruiz (2007: 460–461).

15. We have been unable to identify either of these terms. For example, *Dadie*, or a variant spelling, in the sense of some kind of spiritual practitioner does not appear in a recent comprehensive dictionary of Trinidadian English Creole (Winer 2009:280, 307); and, although the dictionary records *Doo di Doo*, it merely quotes

Bridgens's account without giving a specific meaning for the term. The terms are also absent from Richard Allsopp's (1996) standard dictionary of Caribbean English, and queries sent to scholars knowledgeable about early Trinidad have failed to produce information that would elucidate these terms.

Chapter 3

1. Jack P. Greene read an earlier draft of this section and was of considerable assistance in improving it, but he is in no way responsible for any errors in our understanding of early West Indian governance systems. Greene (2010) provides an excellent discussion of the struggles between local assemblies and "metropolitan intrusions into colonial affairs."
2. Other offenses frequently included in West Indian vagrancy acts (sometimes worded in exactly the same way as the English law, in which perpetrators are designated "rogues and vagabonds") included lacking a fixed abode and living in unoccupied buildings, barns, and so forth; publicly displaying "obscene" or "indecent" pictorial images; "lewdly and obscenely exposing [one's] person" in public "with intent to insult any female"; publicly exposing "wounds or deformities" in order to obtain alms; fraudulently soliciting charitable contributions; abandoning a wife and children so they are left to be supported by public charity; gambling in public; and possessing a "gun, pistol, cutlass" or other "offensive weapon ... with intent to commit any felonious act" (Raithby 1824:781).

Chapter 4

1. The paragraph(s) prefacing each territorial discussion (sketching the political and administrative history of the territory in question) are based on information compiled from several secondary sources, including Wrong (1969), Burns (1954), Spurdle (n.d.), Greene (2010), and Higman (2011), as well as http://memory.loc.gov/frd/cs/cxtoc.html and http://www.foreignlawguide.com. Woodville Marshall also contributed his extensive knowledge, for which we are grateful. We accept full responsibility for whatever errors remain in our summaries of what are sometimes rather complicated and confusing governmental/administrative histories.
2. There is occasional confusion in the scholarly literature about the date of this act. Although passed in December 1760, the final paragraph/clause of the act clearly states that it "shall be and continue in force from and after the first day of January, which will be in the year of our Lord one thousand seven hundred and sixty-one" (Jamaica 1771:57).

3. Another consolidated slave act was passed in December 1787, but it never went into effect and was ultimately replaced by the 1788 law. In any case, the 1787 law basically repeated the wording of the anti-obeah provisions in the 1760 law, but "cotton-tree juice" (the only such reference in British West Indian laws) was added to the list of materials allegedly used by obeah practitioners; the provision against using poison was first mentioned in this law, but obeah was not explicitly linked to poison (Jamaica 1788:20–21; Jamaica 1789a:v). The cotton tree, or silk cotton tree (*Ceiba pentandra*), played an important role in the belief system of enslaved Jamaicans and their descendants as one of the locales where duppies, or spirits of the dead, were believed to reside. The 1787 law appears to be the only one that implies that cotton-tree sap ("juice") could be used in a poisonous concoction, although there is no evidence that the sap has any toxic qualities. The cotton tree has been of continuing importance in Afro-Jamaica religion into modern times (e.g., Warner-Lewis 1977).
4. This law may have modified an identically titled law passed two years earlier, but we could not locate the 1807 law; it may have been disallowed (Jamaica 1809:155).
5. The 1826 law was disallowed in 1827 or 1828 (Lunan 1828:214; Keane to Huskisson, January 12, 1828, CO 137/167, no. 21 [reference provided by Diana Paton, letter to Handler, September 14, 2009]; see also Goderich to Belmore, June 16, 1831 (Jamaica 1831b). For subsequent rejections by the Crown, see Ragatz 1963:419.
6. Information provided by Diana Paton (letter to Handler, September 11, 2009; the citation is Glenelg to Sligo, April 13, 1836, CO 138/59, no. 250).
7. Paton (2009:6 n. 29) errs in stating that obeah was mentioned in Jamaica's 1839 Vagrancy Act. It was, however, included in the 1840 act.
8. The 1898 act was revised in 1973. However, this revision included no substantive changes and in fact merely placed the law and others in a twenty-seven-volume set of acts in force as of December 31, 1973, which was published in 1974 (see http://moj.gov.jm/sites/default/files/laws/Obeah%20Act.pdf). The 1898 act is discussed in detail in McKenzie (1994). See also Moore and Johnson (2004:27–30) for a discussion of the 1899 and 1903 obeah amendment laws as well as other nineteenth- and early-twentieth-century Jamaican anti-obeah laws. Between 1893 and 1977, Paton (2009:8 n. 36) estimates, there were approximately 680 arrests and prosecutions for obeah in Jamaica; today, according to the deputy director of public prosecutions, "the police no longer seriously enforce the Obeah Act" (RJR News 2010; also e.g., Pragg 1999).
9. The 1688 law mentions "many heinous and grievous crimes . . . committed by Negroes, or other slaves, and many times maliciously attempted by them to be committed" (Hall 1764:116). When a British parliamentary committee queried Barbadian authorities specifically on the existence of an anti-obeah law in the colony, the Barbados Council replied: "They [obeah practitioners] have been considered too despicable to come under the notice of any public law" (Barbados 1789). Moreover,

as the governor of Barbados wrote to the Colonial Office in justifying the island's 1818 anti-obeah law, "obeah has existed time out of mind" in Barbados and "was never considered a crime which could be punished by any existing law" (Combermere 1818b; also Combermere 1818a). As noted above, the earliest Barbadian antiobeah law was enacted in 1806. The Barbadian historian Karl Watson (1979:88, 97 n. 107) errs in saying this law replaced one enacted in the eighteenth century; in any case, there is no evidence for this earlier law, and Watson's source citation is inadequate for corroboration.

10. Psychogenic death or illness caused by beliefs in witchcraft or sorcery in Barbados (with implications for other West Indian territories) is discussed in Handler (2006:200–202).

11. An earlier version of the bill passed by the House of Assembly referred only to *slave*, but the Barbados Council altered the bill to refer to *person*, a change agreed to by the Assembly; no reason was given for this change (Barbados 1818b).

12. The major deficiency of the 1806 law, Governor Combermere (1818b) wrote to the colonial secretary, was that it "did not extend to cases where obeah men and women might use the influence of their art for the promotion of insurrection and rebellion. Indeed, the salutary effects of such a law among the ignorant slaves, and even free coloured people, has been extensively experienced, both in this, and the other West Indian islands, and colonies, where similar practices prevail. It is a fact . . . that when the obeah people fail in affecting the imagination of the deluded and ignorant slaves, they do not hesitate in having recourse to poisonous drugs."

The island's one major slave revolt took place in 1816. None of the many documents relating to this revolt mention (or allege participation by) obeah practitioners, though such practitioners had previously been accused of having prominent roles in slave insurrections or conspiracies in other British West Indian colonies—most notably Antigua in 1736 (Gaspar 1985:246–247), Jamaica in 1760 (Craton 1982:131), and Berbice in 1763–64 (Schuler 1966:230). Lazarus-Black (1994:42) claims that "obeah and its practitioners played a pivotal role" in several slave conspiracies and revolts, including the one in Barbados; however, she misuses the secondary source (Beckles 1987:96–97) on which she relies for Barbados, which in fact says quite the opposite.

13. Paton (2009:5 n. 17) confuses the 1818 and 1819 laws. The former was expanded to include non-slaves; the latter merely repeated the wording of the former.

14. In 1825 the Barbados legislature passed a version of this bill but for some reason it was not signed by the governor and did not go into effect. This bill also contained the three anti-obeah clauses of the 1826 law, with identical wording except for one case: persons claiming the "power of divination" and so forth could be "worked in the said chain gang" instead of "worked in the public service" (Barbados 1825, clauses 39–41). In 1829 two slaves were transported from Barbados after having been "convicted of obeah" (Barbados 1829).

15. We have not seen the 1838 act, but C. G. Hall (1997:355–362) discusses it in detail and compares it to the 1840 law. The 1840 act can be found in Barbados 1855 (256–257) and Bovell and Greaves (1893:16–18). The 1818 and 1819 laws continued on the books until they were belatedly repealed in 1842; the 1826 Slave Consolidation Act was also repealed at this time (Barbados 1842). Thus, during the approximately two-year period between 1840 and 1842, obeah was considered both a capital and a minor offense.
16. The reason for this omission was that when the attorney general of Barbados and his staff were discussing the draft of the 1998 law, they decided to leave out all references to obeah, viewing it as a relic of colonial times and no longer relevant to Barbadian society. This information was told to Handler by Professor Velma Newton, dean of the Law School at the University of the West Indies, Cave Hill, Barbados. She had received her information from the Hon. David Simmons, chief justice of Barbados, who was attorney general when the 1998 act was drafted and enacted. For another comment on this legislation, see Hall 1997:362–365.
17. Apparently none of Tobago's slave laws enacted between 1788 and 1816 and 1823–24 mentioned obeah (IUP 1816–18:27; IUP 1823–24:286). We have no information on later laws during the period of slavery.
18. A vagrancy ordinance of 1836 expired because the Crown had not confirmed it (Trinidad 1852:33).
19. The Crown may never have confirmed the September 10 ordinance, because only three days before the Trinidad council approved it, on September 7, 1838, the Crown issued a proclamation in England as an "order for the suppression of Vagrancy, and for the punishment of idle and disorderly person, rogues and vagabonds." The order first listed the offenses of "idle and disorderly persons" (e.g., failing to provide for one's family, begging in public, solicitation by prostitutes in public) and then defined "rogues and vagabonds" as those previously convicted of being "an idle and disorderly person" as well as having committed other offenses. Topping the list of other offenses was "pretending or professing to tell fortunes, or using or pretending to use any subtle craft or device, by palmistry, obeah, or any such like superstitious means, to deceive and impose on any of her Majesty's subjects." Conviction could bring up to twenty-eight days of hard labor (Trinidad 1852:81–87). This order was still in effect as late as 1848 (Trinidad 1852:8) and probably remained in force until even later; in any event, the 1868 Summary Convictions Ordinance supplanted it.
20. This definition remained in later editions of the laws (e.g., Trinidad 1925, Trinidad 1941, Trinidad 1951, Trinidad 1980) until removed in the Miscellaneous Laws Act of 2000 (Trinidad 2000, section 2). See Trotman (1986:223–229 and passim) for anti-obeah cases in nineteenth-century Trinidad.
21. We are still unclear about possible anti-obeah legislation during this period. A British commission investigating criminal and civil justice in the West Indian colonies

reported on its visit to British Guiana in 1824, noting "there are certain Ordinances ... having the effect of law, which have from time to time been framed in the mother country (Holland) or in the Colony, for the government and protection of the slaves" (IUP 1825–29b:509). The commission, however, gave no information on these slave laws.

Randy Browne (2011:456 n. 9) suggests that there was a law (or "proclamation") against obeah in 1801, but he provides no details. Several laws affecting slaves were enacted in the second and third pre-emancipation decades of the nineteenth century (Shahabuddeen 1973:70–71; Thompson 2002:passim), but we have little information on those laws, and obeah does not seem to have been mentioned. The lengthy Berbice Slave Code of 1826 established the office of "Protector of Slaves" and introduced a number of ameliorative measures in slave governance, working conditions, manumission procedures, and so forth; it also required slave masters with more than six working slaves to keep a "punishment record book" to record all disciplinary measures. The law, however, does not mention obeah (document reproduced in Thompson 2002:206–228).

22. Randy Browne speculates that the 1810 proclamation was in force for the remainder of the slave period, because obeah continued to be a punishable crime on Berbice plantations until the end of slavery. He reached this conclusion by examining the plantation punishment record books mandated by the 1826 slave code (Browne, letter to Handler, September 8, 2011). But the crime seems to have been infrequently punished. For example, for the six-month period July 1 to December 31, 1828, a total of 5,633 punishments were given in Berbice, but only one person, a male, was flogged for "practicing obeah" (Thompson 2002:115–117).

23. In late 1821 and early 1822, a slave was placed on trial for the "crime of obeah and murder." Willem, a reputed obeah man, was accused of being responsible for the death of an alleged obeah woman (identified as a "witch") who had been suspected of inflicting harm and causing the death of a number of slaves, including children. Willem was found guilty of "willful and atrocious murder" and sentenced to be hung, after which he was to be decapitated and his severed head placed on a pole (Thompson 2002:150–157; also British Guiana 1823). Although the punishment record books of individual plantations up to emancipation in 1834 show that "practising obeah" was one of several "offences" that were regularly punished, it is unclear from Willem's trial record whether he was executed under laws making murder a capital offense or executed for practicing obeah. Although no specific law against either is mentioned in the trial record, it may be that the severe sentence was imposed because of the alleged role of obeah in the murder (Thompson, letter to Handler, September 6, 2011; Browne, letter to Handler, September 2, 2011). The case of Willem is discussed in detail in Browne 2011; cf. Mullin 1992:180–181, 354 n. 28).

24. Moore (1995:146) discusses the contemporary social effects of this law in British Guiana.

25. For revisions to the 1893/1894 Obeah Act after 1920, see Major (1930:197–198) and Kingdon (1954:435–436).
26. As in other Caribbean territories today, the Guyanese law is rarely enforced. Moreover, if obeah practitioners are taken to court for not delivering the services or promises for which they have been paid, the practitioners are charged with fraud, not with practicing obeah (Kean Gibson, letter to Handler, February 3, 2012).
27. The Vagrancy Act of 1939 did not mention obeah, although, among other offenses, "a person who pretends or professes to tell fortunes" was liable to a fine or imprisonment for two months. This act, with its amendments up to 1987, was still in force as of April 2002 and may be on the books up to the present day (Bryce 1988:1223–1225; Bahamas 2000:chapter 89).
28. Another section of the penal code dealt with "False Pretences and Frauds." It stipulated a four-month jail sentence for accepting or offering "to accept any money or other property for or on pretence of using any kind of witchcraft, sorcery, enchantment or conjuration, or art of telling fortunes"; however, obeah was not specifically mentioned (Malcolm 1929:663). Hedrick and Stephens (1977) provide useful information on obeah beliefs and practices in the Bahamas during the 1970s, although they are not always reliable when discussing beliefs and practices in the wider West Indies.
29. The 1904 act was apparently derived from Jamaica's 1898 Obeah Act. Its clauses contained similar, sometimes identical, wording, but singularly missing was any reference to myal; the penalties were essentially the same.

    Reporting to the Colonial Office in May 1905, Governor Knollys opined, "There is no doubt that the Act of 1904 has done much to destroy the practice of obeah. The exposure in the courts and the inability of the professors of obeah to protect themselves [against whippings, by using their alleged supernatural powers] have to a great extent destroyed the belief in its power." (The administrator of St. Lucia had made a similar comment in 1878; see note 50.) Knollys enclosed a photograph "of all the obeah people now in gaol in Antigua"—all apparently having been convicted under the 1904 act—and points out that of the eleven people shown (two women and nine men), five are from Nevis, three from Dominica, and one each from Antigua, Montserrat, and St. Kitts (Knollys to Lyttelton, May 12, 1905; CO 152/287, enclosure 5); this and related photos are shown and discussed in Forde and Paton (2012:1–3). From 1900 to 1905, seven persons were charged with "the offence of obeah" in Antigua. The case against three was dismissed, while two defendants received three-month sentences and the other two six and twelve months, respectively (Whyham to Colonial Secretary, March 11, 1905; CO 152/287, enclosure 4).
30. For example, the whipping sanctions imposed in the 1904 act were slightly modified by the Obeah Amendment Act, 1905, but the latter was disallowed by the Crown (Leewards 1905; Trusted 1930:15). For other minor amendments and revisions, see Leewards 1929:11, Trusted 1930:14, and Leewards 1957.

31. A published compilation of Antigua's laws from 1865 (Snagg 1865:178–183) includes the second clause of the 1834 law, but for unknown reasons it omits the phrase referring to obeah found in the manuscript original.
32. Diana Paton brought Handler's attention to the 1851 and 1857 laws; Guy Grannum provided photographic copies of these laws (CO 8/28, ff. 110–112; CO 8/29, ff. 62–67).
33. In recent years the law has been enforced only occasionally (see, for example, Obeah in Town, *Antigua Sun*, September 5, 2002).
34. Although there is no explicit anti-obeah provision in Anguilla's laws, as in other West Indian territories, people accused of being practitioners can be prosecuted for engaging in fraudulent practices involving the supernatural. Thanks to Don Mitchell, QC, for his help with this section on Anguilla.
35. There is an exception, however. A British commission sent by the Colonial Office to investigate the legal systems of the West Indian colonies arrived at Nevis in October 1823. The commission discovered that the island's laws enacted from May 1818 to the time of its arrival were only in manuscript form. One of these laws—referred to as number 246 (date of passage unspecified)—was "An Act for Punishing, with Death, All Negroes and Coloured Persons Whatsoever, Who Shall Practise What Is Called Confu, or Obeah Doctor, or Who Shall Take Away, or Attempt to Take Away, the Life, or Injure the Health, of Any Person or Persons Whatsoever." We have not seen this law, and it does not appear in published editions of Nevis's slave laws. The commission learned that this act, "so disgraceful to Nevis," was "generally reprobated." The act extended, in the commission's words, to "all negroes or coloured persons (but not to whites) who, practising or pretending to practise obeah, possessing, keeping, preparing, advising or willfully administering drugs, etc. in the practice of obeah, or otherwise; or injuring, or attempting to injure, the health or life of any person thereby; or in such practice, or otherwise, are declared felons, and shall suffer death for the same, and may be tried for those offences" (IUP 1825–29a:209). This act contains the only mention of the term *confu* of which we are aware in all West Indian anti-obeah laws. It is a puzzle why it should crop up only in an early Nevis law, but in the law it is clearly associated with obeah. The Guyanese linguist Kean Gibson (2001:1) has suggested that this spelling is a variant of what is commonly referred to as *comfa* in Guyana, where the term "is the generic term for the manifestation of spirits." The word *confu*, Gibson also writes, "is probably related to the Twi word 'O'komfo,' and Guyana 'Comfa.' 'M' and 'n' are related in that both are nasals. Also the 'a' in 'Comfa' is pronounced like the 'oo' in 'foot.'" Despite the variation in spelling there is at least "a fundamental meaning similarity" (letter to Handler, February 2, 2012; cf. Allsopp 1996: 165). In the Kromanti language of Jamaica's Windward Maroons, the term "kumfu-man," referring to a ritual specialist, is very likely a cognate of both the Nevisian and Guyanese terms, likewise being derived from an Akan etymon (Bilby 1981: 58, 93 n. 18).

36. The Customs Act was amended in 2001 with a list of "prohibited imports" that included "all publications, articles, or other matter associated with black magic, secret magic, obeah, witchcraft or other magical arts and occultism" (St. Kitts 2001).
37. Because the Obeah Act of 1904 was repealed in 1997, Paton (2009:5 n. 19) assumed that anti-obeah provisions were removed from the laws of the British Virgin Islands; she seems to have been unaware of the 1997 criminal code.
38. In February 2004, the comptroller of customs reported on attempts by a female airline passenger to smuggle into the Virgin Islands "items suspected to be related to obeah practice." The woman reportedly had hidden in her luggage "a miniature wooden coffin . . . inside [of which] was a red rag doll pierced in the centre with a two-inch needle" (*Island Sun* 2004).
39. Although Paton (2009:5 n. 19) correctly observes that the Obeah Act of 1904 was repealed in 1983, she incorrectly assumed that because of this, all anti-obeah provisions were removed from the laws of Montserrat; she was apparently unaware of the 1983 penal code.
40. Duppies are spirits of the dead. There is a widespread fear of such spirits in the Anglophone Caribbean, although most available ethnographic and historical information appears to relate specifically to Jamaica. In Jamaica, duppies reside in certain locales, including graves and the roots of cottonwood trees, which may help explain why late eighteenth-century Jamaican slave laws mention "cotton-tree juice" as one of the materials allegedly used by obeah practitioners. Duppies are believed to wander at night and can inflict harm on living human beings. For a fee, an obeah practitioner—sometimes known as a "duppy catcher"—could be retained to find the troublesome duppy and "catch" it, thereby removing the evil spirit and curing the afflicted. It is puzzling why the term "duppy catching," which is still used in Jamaica, was not included in early Jamaican laws (Robinson 1893:211; Cassidy and Le Page 1967:164–165; Mcleod 2007; cf. F. Henriques 1960:180; Leach 1961; Carley 1963:137; Beckwith 1969:145–148; Allsopp 1996:207–208; Carrington et al. 2003:68; Paton 2001:941–942). For the related concept of "shadow-catching," which does not appear in the laws either, see Barclay 1826:190–191; Leach 1961; and Cassidy and Le Page 1967:403 (and sources cited therein).

    It is important to note that in Jamaica, and perhaps elsewhere as well, there is also a positive side to duppies, although this has received much less attention in the literature. In Jamaica, obeah practitioners, for example, can employ duppies to help with healing, provide protection from wandering spirits, fight off spiritual attacks by other practitioners, or assist with a wide variety of other problems. Certain kinds of duppies, such as those of ancestors or other close relatives, may be revered, regularly consulted in dreams, and given offerings from time to time in exchange for blessings and protection. In religious traditions such as Kumina or Kromanti Play among the Maroons, ancestor spirits form part of the community of the living and are regularly invoked to come and take possession of mediums, so that those who knew them while they were alive can maintain contact and request favors of them (Bilby 1981; Bilby and Fu-Kiau 1983). The tendency in the literature to emphasize fear of duppies while neglecting their positive dimension is no doubt closely related to hegemonic constructions that reduce obeah to harmful witchcraft. Complicating this picture is the widespread belief that obeah practitioners will readily oblige paying clients who ask them to harm their enemies by setting duppies on them. This aspect of duppy belief, though it represents only part of the picture, is easily assimilated to such hegemonic constructions of obeah if framed in a one-sided way (see also figure 4).

41. We are uncertain about the relationship between the 1840 law and the 1891 Small Charges Act; the 1840 law may have remained in force until the 1904 Obeah Ordinance was passed.

42. Information verbally given to Handler by Reginald Winston, registrar general, Supreme Court of Dominica (July 23, 2011), and cited with his permission. As in other areas of the Caribbean, obeah is still very much part of the belief system of many Dominicans. However, it is not discussed freely and openly and is considered "witchcraft" by some segments of the population, particularly those influenced by the Catholic Church (e.g., Caribbean Media Corporation 2005). The anthropologist Jeffrey Mantz (2007:24), who conducted his primary field research in Dominica between December 1999 and January 2001, found that "obeah is a taboo subject in Dominica. Very few individuals will discuss it and even then only very privately."

During a brief stay on the island in July 2011, Handler had a similar experience. He conducted informal interviews with several persons of different socioeconomic levels and found a reluctance to discuss the subject or freely offer opinions on it. Granted, Handler had established only a superficial rapport with these people, but the general reluctance to engage in conversation on the topic, well documented by Mantz, was very noticeable. For example, a fisherman in a small coastal village in southern Dominica, although initially reluctant to talk about obeah (while at the same time proclaiming his disbelief in it), finally opined that there was "good obeah" and "bad obeah," the former being directed toward healing, the latter toward harming others or "witchcraft." "Bad obeah," he reported, "is when something is put on you, then you have to go to an obeah person to make things right." (The good obeah–bad obeah distinction is common in Dominica, according to Mantz [letter to Handler, August 11, 2011].) Another person, from a different socioeconomic level—a middle-class professional, part owner of a tour company in the capital of Roseau—was initially unwilling to discuss the subject (the atmosphere in an otherwise jovial conversation suddenly changed when Handler brought up the subject) and almost stridently proclaimed her disbelief in obeah, emphatically denying that there was such a thing as "good" obeah and insisting that it was entirely evil. Her responses probably reflect a more widespread view in Dominica, particularly among her socioeconomic peers and those who identify themselves as Catholics.

Although the term *obeah* is used in official documents and the laws, the Dominican anthropologist Lennox Honychurch suggested in a conversation with Handler that for the "man on the street" the common term is *pyai*, a word of Carib origin meaning "to make magic." On a website containing excerpts from his forthcoming book, *A to Z of Dominica Heritage*, under the entry "obeah" Honychurch (2011) writes that *pidy* comes from the "Carib for shaman" and is also used as it relates to the "casting of spells." It can be noted that Douglas Taylor (1945:510–511, 527), a leading authority on the Caribs of Dominica, presented a somewhat different interpretation of *pidy* [sic], which he translated as the making and working of black magic," while the term *obeah* was used in the sense of positive or beneficial magic.

43. The 1825 law's preamble lists the earlier slave laws that it repealed; judging by their titles alone, it does not appear that any of these laws related to obeah, but it is not certain (Grenada 1830:323–324). A slave convicted of attempting to poison his plantation manager in 1806 was sentenced to be executed; the court reported he had "practiced what is termed obye [sic]." However, he was convicted of attempting to murder a white man, not for his alleged obeah activities (Grenada 1806).

44. Pierre, a free black, was convicted under this law for having exerted "dangerous influences" on certain plantation slaves. He was sentenced to be transported to, among other places, Australia. In 1834 Pierre petitioned the Colonial Office for a reprieve. The administrator of Grenada, in forwarding the petition to Governor Smith, found the sentence too harsh: "the imputed offence is obeah. The real crime is nothing more or less than that of having practiced as a quack doctor" (Grenada 1834).

45. Paton (2009:17) refers to the 1897 criminal code as the "Summary Conviction Ordinance 1897" (citing CO 103/22, no. 2), but the edition of the Grenada laws in which the ordinance was published is very clear that "This Ordinance may be cited as the criminal code" (Grenada 1897:709).

46. Another modification was that in 1958 "obeah" and "instrument of obeah" were defined for the first time. The definitions were the same as in the 1927 penal code of the Bahamas: the former was "any pretended assumption of supernatural power or knowledge, whatever, for fraudulent or illicit purposes, or for gain, or for the injury of any person," and the latter "any philtre, vial, blood, bone, image, or other article or thing . . . used or intended to be used in the practice of obeah" (Malone 1962:694).

47. In November 2003 a woman was arrested in Grenada "for practicing the obeah religion." According to an account by an Associated Press writer, her arrest was "the only such case in recent memory on the Caribbean island" (D. Brown 2003). The 1994 Family Court Act was repealed in 1996 (Grenada 2010a:87).

48. "This popular infatuation, known in St. Lucia by the name of Kembois," wrote a longtime resident of the island in the early 1840s, "still prevails to an incredible extent amongst the uneducated classes. 'Kembois' is another name for obeah" (Breen

1970:249). A variant of the term *kembois* (conventionally spelled *quimbois*) is also found in the French-based creoles of Martinique and Guadeloupe, where its meaning is essentially the same as *obeah* and where it similarly often carries negative connotations of sorcery. In St. Lucia today the term is spelled *tjenbwa* (pronounced *chen-bwa*, with *-en* representing a nasal vowel, as in French), and "'Fè tjenbwa' means to practice obeah" (thanks to Paul Garrett and Hazel Simmons-McDonald for their help; letters to Handler, October 1 and November 8, 2009).

49. In 1876 the governor of the Windward Islands notified St. Lucia's administrator, G. William Des Voeux, that the practice of "cropping hair of female prisoners" should be forbidden. Des Voeux responded that during his tenure of office, starting in 1869, he had not permitted the practice; moreover, he stated, "no woman has, as yet, been convicted of obeah" (St. Lucia 1876).

50. The acting administrator of St. Lucia reported in April 1878 that as of that date there had been only one "public flogging" over the preceding five years for the "offence of obeah"; the convicted person received twenty strokes. Until the ordinance of 1872 was enacted, he wrote, "the practice of Obeah, to which the Negro is much addicted, was largely on the increase in the island ... the Negro labourer ... believe implicitly in the power of the 'Obeah Man,' and he [the Obeah practitioner] is himself so confident of his power to control events, that he laughs at the idea that any punishment can be inflicted upon him." Publicly whipping the convicted obeah practitioner, the administrator opined, "has therefore the effect of disabusing the minds of his dupes as to the power to which he pretends, while at the same time of punishing him in a manner not easily to be forgotten" (St. Lucia 1878). A similar observation was made several decades later by the governor of Antigua (see n. 29).

51. The 1887 law defined obeah as "any pretended assumption of supernatural power or knowledge whatever, for fraudulent or illicit purposes, or for gain, or for the injury of any person." In the 1905 law "a person practicing obeah" was defined as one "who, to effect any fraudulent or unlawful purpose, or for gain, or for the purposes of frightening any person, uses or pretends to use any occult means, mesmeric or otherwise, or pretends to possess any supernatural power or knowledge" (St. Lucia 1889:430–431; St. Lucia 1905).

52. In his throne speech on March 28, 2000, St. Lucia's governor general, in reviewing the island's criminal code and reflecting wider sentiments in the St. Lucia government, raised several issues of "critical importance," including "Should obeah continue as an offence"? (St. Lucia 2000). As in other jurisdictions, the 2004 St. Lucia criminal code contained provisions against fraud. Section 432 of the code very broadly states that "any person who defrauds or deceives any other person by any false claim" could be imprisoned for five years (St. Lucia 2004a:470). Theoretically, obeah practitioners could be prosecuted under this section.

53. The "sieve and shears" and the "bible and key" were ancient methods of divination

used in England and elsewhere, and they were usually employed to find lost or stolen objects or to identify a thief. The special magistrate John Anderson, based in St. Vincent during the apprenticeship period in 1836–38, reported in his journal: "The negroes have recourse also to divination to discover crime. 'The Shifter,' is the most ordinary. A bible and key, or pair of scissors are the instruments. The latter are so turned as to point to the supposed culprit, who is instantly seized; confession is occasionally extorted; but as may be credited, these ordeals are commonly used on innocent parties agt. [sic] whom the complainant has a grudge" (McDonald 2001:157). Although obeah practitioners throughout the West Indies were commonly consulted to find lost or stolen objects and to identify alleged thieves, Anderson's observation is the only direct reference to the bible and key of which we are aware. *Conjuration*, while not a common term in the laws, also appears in laws of Antigua, British Guiana, the Bahamas, Grenada, and St. Lucia; aside from an 1826 Barbados law, the 1803 St. Vincent law is the only one to use the term *divination*.

54. St. Vincent passed another consolidated slave act in 1825, but the Crown may have disallowed it. The 1825 act was probably an earlier version of the Consolidated Slave Act passed in 1830 (see Ragatz 1963:419). Both of these acts probably contained anti-obeah provisions, but they could not be located. St. Vincent special magistrate John Anderson reported that "the practice of 'Obeah' . . . is rare & punishable with death, but still this species of sorcery lingers in the isle" (McDonald 2001:156). Although obeah was a capital offense under various Vincentian slave laws, we are unclear whether these laws were operative during the apprenticeship period.

55. The sentences imposed for conviction seem ambiguous. Clause 285 clearly imposes a three-month jail term, while clause 290 specifies "liable to imprisonment for one year"; the distinction seems to be that the former applied to those who pretended to practice obeah, while the latter to those convicted of actually practicing it.

56. This regulation was transcribed verbatim from an original source identified by Burdon (1931:195, 290), the transcriber, as "Laws [of Honduras], 1765–1810." Paton (2009:4–5 n. 13) cites the same secondary source but erroneously refers to the "Laws of Honduras, *1806–1810*" (emphasis added) as the primary source. The "Laws" appear to have been one of several compilations done by William Hunt, clerk of the British Honduras court (Burdon 1934:8, 117), but apparently these early laws were never published.

57. Cited by title in Paton (2009:17). The act is 26 Victoria, chapter 5, in *British Honduras Laws, 1862/63* (held by the library of the Institute of Advanced Legal Research, University of London). We have not seen this act but Paton willingly shared her notes (letter to Handler, September 10, 2009). A list of British Honduras laws passed between 1855 and 1901 does not show any vagrancy acts prior to 1863; see Robinson 1985.

Note on Sources

This work's primary goal—to identify and trace obeah laws through time—presents considerable challenges. There is no general legislation covering the entire Anglophone/British Caribbean; each jurisdiction developed its own laws, although these often borrowed from earlier legislation in other territories. Some laws focus exclusively on obeah (and include the word in their titles, making it easier to locate them in indexes to published volumes of laws), while others subsume obeah provisions under other offenses. Still others do not mention obeah at all but target various phenomena or characteristics usually associated with obeah in other laws, for example, "fortune-telling." In brief, anti-obeah enactments are scattered throughout various kinds of documents and can be found in different forms at different times. Even in the same jurisdiction, such enactments may be found, depending on the period, in laws solely concerned with obeah—the so-called obeah acts or obeah ordinances—or in sections of vagrancy acts, summary jurisdiction acts or ordinances, criminal codes, or penal codes—or in both.

Records of West Indian laws relating to obeah are not easily obtainable, and the ones discussed in this work are scattered among a number of libraries and archival repositories. Although we have not exhausted every last possibility, we are confident that we have located the vast majority of these laws and all of the more important ones. Manuscript copies of British West Indian laws during the colonial period exist in the National Archives in London (formerly the Public Record Office), but circumstances did not permit an exhaustive search of those for every jurisdiction we discuss; hence we have relied heavily on printed or published copies of the laws. Many of these laws were published in the Official or Royal Gazettes, which were colonial government newspapers sent to the Colonial

Office twice yearly. These periodic gazettes, including their supplements, typically reproduced the texts of new laws as they were enacted. It was not possible to examine copies of all the gazettes (also located in the National Archives), so we have had to depend to a great extent on printed versions of the laws compiled in volumes that were periodically published for West Indian jurisdictions. These irregular publications are dispersed across different libraries, and, as far as can be ascertained, no single library in the United Kingdom, United States, or West Indies (such as the law library at Cave Hill) holds all of the volumes of laws that are relevant to this study.

Research for the present study was conducted in the United Kingdom (the National Archives, British Library, and Institute of Advanced Legal Studies, University of London), the United States (law libraries of the Library of Congress, the University of Virginia, and the College of William and Mary, as well as the Library Company of Philadelphia), and the law library of the University of the West Indies, Cave Hill, Barbados. The last has been particularly valuable, especially for gathering information on contemporary laws.

References

Abbreviations

CO   Colonial Office Papers, Public Record Office (National Archives), London

IUP   Irish University Press Series of British Parliamentary Papers, Shannon, Ireland

Aborampah, Osei-Mensah
    2005 Out of the Same Bowl: Religious Beliefs and Practices in the Akan Communities in Ghana and Jamaica. *In* Fragments of Bone: Neo-African Religions in a New World. Patrick Bellegarde Smith, ed. Pp. 124–142. Urbana: University of Illinois Press.

Alleyne, Keith H. C., ed.
    1963 Obeah Ordinance (chapter 43). August 2, 1904. The Laws of Dominica in Force on the 31st day of December, 1961, vol. 1. London: Eyre and Spottiswoode.

Allsopp, Richard
    1996 Dictionary of Caribbean English Usage. Oxford: Oxford University Press.

Anderson, G. C., ed.
    1850 An Act for the Better Suppression of Vagrancy, and for the Punishment of Idle and Disorderly Persons, and Rogues, Vagabonds, and other Vagrants (no. 8). June 21, 1839. The Statute Law of the Bahamas, vol. 1. London.

1862 An Act for the Better Suppression of Vagrancy, and for the Punishment of Idle and Disorderly Persons, and Rogues, Vagabonds, and other Vagrants (no. 4). June 21, 1839. The Statute Law of the Bahamas, Comprising all Acts of the General Assembly of the Bahama Islands in Force to . . . 1861, Inclusive. London.

Anguilla
1985 Law Revision (Miscellaneous Repeals and Amendments) (no. 4) Ordinance, 1980 (no. 15). November 3, 1980. Laws of Anguilla, 1980–1981. Barbados: Coles Printery.
1988 Anguilla Consolidated Index of Statutes and Subsidiary Legislation to 1st January 1988. Compiled at the Faculty of the Law and Law Library, University of the West Indies, Barbados. Holmes Beach, FL: Gaunt and Sons.

Antigua
1789 Hutchinson, Answer to Query 26 [concerning anti-obeah laws]. *In* Great Britain, Parliament, Report of the Lords of the Committee of Council Appointed for Consideration of All Matters Relating to Trade and Foreign Plantations . . . Concerning the Present State of the Trade to Africa, and Particularly the Trade in Slaves . . . Part III, Antigua. London.
1818 An Act for Punishing Persons Pretending to Exercise Witchcraft, Fortune-Telling, or by Crafty Science to Discover Stolen Goods (no. 611). August 9, 1809. The Laws of the Island of Antigua: Consisting of the Acts Passed by the Captain-General, Council, and Assembly from 26th May, 1804, to 13th June, 1817, vol. 3. London.
1834 An Act for the Punishment of Idle and Disorderly Persons, Rogues and Vagabonds, Incorrigible Rogues and Other Vagrants in this Island. July 3, 1834. Act 381. CO 8/24, ff. 400–408.
1851 An Act to Repeal a Part of the Second Clause of an Act Entitled An Act for the Punishment of Idle and Disorderly Persons. March 27, 1851. Act 651. CO8/28, ff. 110–112.
1857 An Act for Further Improving the Administration of Criminal Justice, September 8, 1857. Act 1099. CO 8/29, ff. 62–67.
2010a Antigua and Barbuda Consolidated Index of Statutes and Subsidiary Legislation to 1st January 2010. Compiled at the Faculty of Law Library, University of the West Indies, Barbados. Faculty of Law Library: University of the West Indies, Barbados.
2010b Legislation Antigua and Barbuda. World Law Guide. Updated March 2, 2010. http://www.lexadin.nl/wlg/legis/nofr/oeur/lxweeaab.htm (accessed February 14, 2011).

Antoine, Rose-Marie Belle
2008 Commonwealth Caribbean Law and Legal Systems. 2nd edition. London: Cavendish.

Archer, C. V. H., and W. K. Fergusson, eds.
1944 An Act for the Suppression and Punishment of Vagrancy. August 30, 1897. Laws of Barbados . . . Revised and Consolidated 1894–96–1906–5, vol. 2. Barbados.

Austen, Brian
  N.d. Richard Hicks Bridgens. Oxford Art Online/Grove Art Online, http://www.oxfordartonline.com:80/subscriber/article/grove/art/T0 11315.

Bahamas
  1789 Earl of Danmore, Answer to Query 21 [concerning anti-obeah laws]. *In* Great Britain, Parliament, Report of the Lords of the Committee of Council Appointed for Consideration of All Matters Relating to Trade and Foreign plantations . . . Concerning the Present State of the Trade to Africa, and Particularly the Trade in Slaves . . . Part III, Bahamas. London.
  1796 An Act to Consolidate and Bring into One Act, the Several Laws Relating to Slaves, and for Giving Them Further Protection and Security. 1796. Returns and Papers Relating to the Slave Trade, 1816–18. Slave Trade 62. Pp. 35–46. IUP, Shannon, Ireland, 1971.
  1824 An Act to Amend, Consolidate, and Bring into One Act, the Several Laws Relating to Slaves, and for Giving them Further Protection and Security. January 28, 1824. Papers Relating to the Conditions of Slaves in British Possessions and other Papers Relating to Slavery and the Slave Trade, 1826–27. Slave Trade 73. Pp. 260–274. IUP, Shannon, Ireland, 1969.
  1965 penal code (chapter 48). The Statute Law of the Bahama Islands . . . in force on the 1st April 1965, vol. 2. Nassau: Government of the Colony of the Bahama Islands.
  2000 penal code (chapter 84), and An Act to Control Vagrants and for Purposes Related Thereto (chapter 89). The Statute Law of the Bahamas . . . in Force on the 2nd April, 2002. Rev. edition of 2000 [*sic*], vol. 2. Capetown, South Africa: Juta.
  2007 penal code (chapter 84). Government of the Bahamas website. Updated January 17, 2007. http://laws.bahamas.gov.bs/cms/images/LEGISLATION/PRINCIPAL/1873/1873-0015/PenalCode_1.pdf (accessed September 12, 2012).
  2010a The Commonwealth of the Bahamas Consolidated Index of Statutes and Subsidiary Legislation to 1st January 2009. Compiled at the Faculty of Law Library, University of the West Indies, Barbados. Faculty of Law Library: University of the West Indies, Barbados.
  2010b Legislation Bahamas. Lexadin. Updated March 2, 2010. http://www.lexadin.nl/wlg/legis/nofr/oeur/lxwebhs.htm (accessed February 14, 2011).

Barbados
  1789 Barbados Council, Answer to Query 26 [concerning anti-obeah laws]. *In* Report of the Lords of the Committee of Council Appointed for Consideration of All Matters Relating to Trade and Foreign Plantations . . . Concerning the Present State of the Trade to Africa, and Particularly the Trade in Slaves . . . Part III, Barbados. London: Parliament of Great Britain.

1806 An Act for the Punishment of Such Slaves as Shall Be Found Practising Obeah. November 4, 1806. CO 30/18, no. 262. Returns and Papers Relating to the Slave Trade, 1816–18. Slave Trade 62. Pp. 56–57. IUP, Shannon, Ireland, 1971.

1818a An Act for the Better Prevention of the Practise of Obeah. July 28, 1818. CO 30/20, no. 367. Correspondence and Papers Relating to Slavery and the Abolition of the Slave Trade, 1823–24. Slave Trade 66. Pp. 294–295. IUP, Shannon, Ireland, 1969.

1818b Barbados House of Assembly. Journal, June 30 and July 28, 1818. CO 31/47.

1819 An Act for the Better Prevention of the Practise of Obeah. May 26, 1819. CO 30/20, no. 383. Papers Relating to the Conditions of Slaves in British Possessions and other Papers Relating to Slavery and the Slave Trade, 1826–27. Slave Trade 73. Pp. 350–351. IUP, Shannon, Ireland, 1969.

1825 An Act to Repeal Several Acts and Clauses of Acts Respecting Slaves and for Consolidating and Bringing into One Act, the Several Laws Relating Thereto. March 25, 1825. Act 446. CO 30/20.

1826 An Act to Repeal Several Acts and Clauses of Acts Respecting Slaves and for Consolidating and Bringing into one Act, the Several Laws Relating thereto. October 23, 1826. Papers Relating to the Conditions of Slaves in British Possessions and other Papers Relating to Slavery and the Slave Trade, 1826–27. Slave Trade 73. Pp. 285–310. IUP, Shannon, Ireland, 1969.

1829 J. B. Skeete, President of Barbados House of Assembly, January 11, 1829 [forwards message from the House of Assembly to Governor Combermere concerning transportation of two slaves, Castello and Bynoe, convicted of obeah]. CO 28/103, no. 2, fos. 8–11.

1842 Governor Edward Grey to Colonial Office, August 4, 1842 [forwarding copies of Act 776, An Act to Repeal Two Certain Acts of This Island, one entitled "An Act for the Better Prevention of Obeah," and the other "An Act to Repeal Several Acts and Clauses of Acts Respecting Slaves, and for Consolidating and Bringing into One Act the Several Laws Relating Thereto"]. CO 28/144.

1855 An Act for the Suppression and Punishment of Vagrancy (no. 166). January 7, 1840. Laws of Barbados [1646–1854]. London.

1971 An Act for the Suppression and Punishment of Vagrancy (chapter 156). August 30, 1897. Laws of Barbados, 1971. Rev. edition. Barbados.

1997 An Act for the Suppression and Punishment of Vagrancy (chapter 156). August 30, 1897. The Laws of Barbados in Force on the 31st Day of December, 1996, vol. 6. Barbados: Government Printer.

1998 An Act to Revise the Law in Relation to Certain Minor Offences. February 5, 1998. Act 1998-1. Barbados Acts 1998. Bridgetown: Government Printing Office.

2005 Barbados Court of Appeal, April 20. Citation BB 2005 CA 5. http://carilaw.cave hill.uwi.edu (accessed January 21, 2009).

Barclay, Alexander
  1826 A Practical View of the Present State of Slavery in the West Indies. London: Smith, Elder.

Barringer, T., G. Forrester, and B. Martinez-Ruiz, eds.
  2007 Art and Emancipation in Jamaica: Isaac Mendes Belisario and His Worlds. New Haven, CT: Yale University Press.

Barthélémi, Georges
  2011 Dictionnaire Créole Guyanais-Français. Matoury, French Guiana: Ibis Rouge.

Beck, Jane C.
  1976 The Implied Obeah Man. Western Folklore 36:23–33.

Beckles, Hilary
  1987 Black Rebellion in Barbados: The Struggle against Slavery. Bridgetown, Barbados: Carib Research.

Beckwith, Martha
  1969 [1929] Black Roadways: A Study of Jamaican Folk Life. New York: Negro Universities Press.

Belize
  2000 Summary Jurisdication (Offences) Act, Chapter 98. Rev. edition. Showing the Law as at 31st December, 2000. Belmopan, Belize: Government Printer.
  2010a Belize Consolidated Index of Statutes and Subsidiary Legislation to 1st January 2010. Compiled at the Faculty of Law Library, University of the West Indies, Barbados. Faculty of Law Library: University of the West Indies, Barbados.
  2010b Legislation Belize. Lexadin. Updated March 2, 2010. http://www.lexadin.nl/wlg/legis/nofr/oeur/lxweblz.htm (accessed March 10, 2010).

Belize Kriol Project
  1997 Belize Kriol Glossary and Spelling Guide. Belize City: Belize Kriol Project.

Bell, Hesketh J.
  1889 Obeah: Witchcraft in the West Indies. London: S. Low, Marston, Searle and Rivington.

Benoit, Pierre Jacques
  1839 Voyage à Surinam. Bruxelles, Belgium.

Besson, Jean
  2002 Martha Brae's Two Histories: European Expansion and Caribbean Culture-Building in Jamaica. Chapel Hill: University of North Carolina Press.

Best, Tony
  2006 Best on Tuesday: Obeah Still with Us. Nation News (Barbados), June 27. http://bararchive.bits.baseview.com/archive_detail.php?archiveFile=2006/June/27/Editorial/21990.xml (accessed September 12, 2012).

Bilby, Kenneth M.
    N.d. Dictionary of Aluku, a Guianese Maroon Radical Creole (with Comparative Data from other Creole Languages). Unpublished MS.
    1981 The Kromanti Dance of the Windward Maroons of Jamaica. New West Indian Guide/Nieuwe West-Indische Gids 55:52–101.
    1997 Swearing by the Past, Swearing to the Future: Sacred Oaths, Alliances, and Treaties among the Guianese and Jamaican Maroons. Ethnohistory 44:655–689.
    2009 African American Memory at the Crossroads: Grounding the Miraculous with Tooy. Small Axe 13:185–199.
    2012 An (Un)natural Mystic in the Air: Images of Obeah in Caribbean Song. *In* Obeah and Other Powers: The Politics of Caribbean Religion and Healing. Diana Paton and Maarit Forde, eds. Pp. 45–79. Durham, NC: Duke University Press.

Bilby, Kenneth M., and Fu-Kiau kia Bunseki
    1983 Kumina: A Kongo-Based Tradition in the New World. Brussels: Centre d'Étude et de Documentation Africaines.

Bilby, Kenneth M., and Jerome S. Handler
    2004 Obeah: Healing and Protection in West Indian Slave Life. Journal of Caribbean History 38:153–183.

Bliss, B. H., ed.
    1957 penal code (chapter 69). The Statute Law of the Bahama Islands . . . in Force on the 1st January 1957, vol. 2. Toronto: Garden City Press.

Bovell, Henry A., and W. Herbert Greaves, eds.
    1893 An Act for the Suppression and Punishment of Vagrancy. January 7, 1840. Laws of Barbados, vol. 1. Barbados.

Bradshaw, Maria
    2005 Obeah Man Casts Final Spell. Nation News (Barbados), July 23. http://bararchive.bits.baseview.com/archive_detail.php?archiveFile=2005/July/23/LocalNews/5848.xml (accessed September 12, 2012).

Brathwaite, Edward Kamau
    1974 The African Presence in Caribbean Literature. *In* Slavery, Colonialism, and Racism. Sidney W. Mintz, ed. Pp. 73–109. New York: W. W. Norton.

Breen, Henry H.
    1970 [1844] St. Lucia: Historical, Statistical, and Descriptive. London: Frank Cass and Company.

Bridgens, Richard
    1836 West India Scenery, with Illustrations of Negro Character . . . from Sketches Taken During a Voyage to, and Residence of Seven Years in, the Island of Trinidad. London.

British Guiana
  1823 Trial of a Slave in Berbice, for the Crime of Obeah and Murder. [May 1823]. Papers Relating to the Slave Population of the West India Colonies and the Abolition of the Slave Trade, 1823. Slave Trade 65. N.p. IUP, Shannon, Ireland, 1969.
  1855 Ordinance to Repress the Commission of Obeah Practices (no. 1), January 8. Printed at the Royal Gazette Office. CO 111/304.
  1873 The Laws of British Guiana Chronologically Arranged from the Year 1773 to 1873, vol. 2. Georgetown, Demerara: L. M'Dermott, at "The Colonist" Office.
  1895 An Ordinance to Consolidate and Amend the Laws Relating to Offences Punishable on Summary Conviction (no. 17). March 1, 1894. The Laws of British Guiana, a New and Revised Edition, vol. 5. Oxford: Printed at the University Press for the Government of British Guiana.
  1918 An Ordinance to Amend the Summary Convictions (Offences) Ordinance, 1893, in Regard to the Practice of Obeah (no. 26). July 26, 1918. CO 113/14.
  1920 An Ordinance to Amend the Summary Convictions (Offences) Ordinance, 1893, in Regard to the Practice of Obeah (no. 11). March 19, 1920. CO 113/15.

British Honduras
  1887 Consolidated Laws of the Colony of British Honduras. London: Stevens and Sons.

Brown, Desmond
  2003 Woman Charged with Practicing Obeah Religion in Grenada: Police Cite Law Forbidding What Some Call Witchcraft. Associated Press Worldstream, November 9. LexisNexis. http://www.lexisnexis.com/us/lnacademic/frame.do?tokenKey=rsh 20.131384.47770694 (accessed December 15, 2008).

Brown, Henry Isaac Close, comp.
  1938 The Obeah Law (chapter 421). The Laws of Jamaica, in Force on the 1st Day of August, 1938. Rev. edition, vol. 5. Kingston: Government Printer.

Brown, Vincent
  2008 The Reaper's Garden: Death and Power in the World of Atlantic Slavery. Cambridge, MA: Harvard University Press.

Browne, Randall
  2011 The "Bad Business" of Obeah: Power, Authority, and the Politics of Slave Culture in the British Caribbean. William and Mary Quarterly 68:451–480.

Bryce, Gordon, ed.
  1988 An Act to Control Vagrants and for Purposes Related Thereto (chapter 82). February 27, 1939. The Statute Law of the Bahamas, 1799–1987; in Force on the 30th June, 1987, vol. 2. Nassau, Bahamas.

Burdon, John A., ed.
  1931 Archives of British Honduras, vol. 1: From the Earliest Date to A.D. 1800. London.
  1934 Archives of British Honduras, vol. 2: From 1801 to 1840. London.

Burnard, Trevor
- 2004 Mastery, Tyranny, and Desire: Thistlewood and His Slaves in the Anglo-Jamaican World. Chapel Hill: University of North Carolina Press.

Burns, Alan
- 1954 History of the British West Indies. London: George Allen and Unwin.

BVI (British Virgin Islands)
- 1997 Virgin Islands criminal code (no. 1). August 11, 1997. Statutory Instrument 1997, No. 35. Virgin Islands Gazette, August 21, 1997. N.p. Faculty of Law Library, University of the West Indies, Cave Hill, Barbados.
- 2003 British Virgin Islands Consolidated Index of Statutes and Subsidiary Legislation to 1st January 2002. Compiled at the Faculty of Law and Law Library, University of the West Indies, Barbados. Cave Hill, Barbados: Faculty of Law Library, University of the West Indies.
- 2010a British Virgin Islands Consolidated Index of Statutes and Subsidiary Legislation to 1st January 2010. Compiled at the Faculty of Law and Law Library, University of the West Indies, Barbados. Cave Hill, Barbados: Faculty of Law Library, University of the West Indies.
- 2010b Legislation British Virgin Islands. Lexadin. Updated September 13, 2010. http://www.lexadin.nl/wlg/legis/nofr/oeur/lxwebvi.htm (accessed February 15, 2011).

Caribbean Media Corporation (Bridgetown, Barbados)
- 2005 Priest Says Dominicans Engaging in Witchcraft in Bid to Sway May 5 [2006] Vote. April 26. BBC Monitoring Latin America. http://www.accessmylibrary.com/article-1G1-137084011/priest-says-dominicans-engaging.html (accessed December 13, 2008).

Carmichael, Gertrude
- 1961 The History of the West Indian Islands of Trinidad and Tobago, 1498–1900. London: Alvin Redman.

Carley, Mary Manning
- 1963 Jamaica: The Old and the New. London: George Allen and Unwin.

Carrington, Sean, Henry Fraser, John Gilmore, and Addinton Forde
- 2003 A–Z of Barbados Heritage. 2nd ed. Oxford: Macmillan Education.

Cassidy, F. G., and R. B. Le Page, eds.
- 1967 Dictionary of Jamaican English. Cambridge: Cambridge University Press.

Cayman Islands
- 1889 Laws of the Cayman Islands, up to No. 12 of 1889. Kingston: Government Printing Establishment.
- 1975 The penal code (no. 12). Laws and Regulations, Cayman Islands, supplement No. 2, published with Gazette No. 24 of 1975. Georgetown.

1989 Cayman Islands Consolidated Index of Statutes and Subsidiary Legislation to 1st January 1989. Compiled at the Faculty of Law Library, University of the West Indies, Barbados. Cave Hill, Barbados: Faculty of Law Library, University of the West Indies.

2007 penal code (2007 Revision), supplement No. 9. Published with Gazette 16 of August 6, 2007. http://www.gazettes.gov.ky/gazette-supplements/2007/06/08/gazette-16-supplement-9 (accessed September 12, 2012).

Chambers, Douglas B., ed.
2010 Jamaican Runaways, 1718–1817: A Compilation of Fugitive Slaves, vol. 1. Unpublished MS, Department of History, University of Southern Mississippi.

ChatyChaty (Jamaica)
2010 Jamaica Should Get Rid of the Obeah Act, Says Public Prosecutor. November 14. http://chatychaty.com/index.php/en/latest-news/46news/444-jamaica-should-get-rid-if-the-obeah-act-says-public-prosecutor (accessed June 3, 2011).

Chevannes, Barry
1971 Revival and Black Struggle. Savacou 5:27–39.
1998 Rastafari and Other African-Caribbean World Views. New Brunswick, NJ: Rutgers University Press.

Chireau, Yvonne
2003 Black Magic: Religion and the African American Conjuring Tradition. Berkeley: University of California Press.

Combermere, Lord [Stapleton Cotton, 1st Viscount Combermere]
1818a A Case for the Opinion of His Majesty's Crown Lawyers [concerning the obeah trial of Jack, an enslaved person]. December 21. CO 28/87.
1818b Letter to Secretary Bathurst, December 28. CO 28/87.

Craton, Michael
1982 Testing the Chains: Resistance to Slavery in the British West Indies. Ithaca, NY: Cornell University Press.

Cundall, Joseph L., comp.
1952 The Summary Offences Ordinance (chapter 48). January 6, 1900. The Laws of the Turks and Caicos Islands in Force on the 1st of January, 1951, vol. 1. London: Government Printer.

Curran, C. R., ed.
1889–90 The Statutes and Laws of the Island of Jamaica, revised ed. 12 vols. Kingston: Government Printing Establishment.

Curtin, Philip
1955 Two Jamaicas: The Role of Ideas in a Tropical Colony. Cambridge, MA: Harvard University Press.

De Groot, Silvia W.
- 1968 Naar aanleiding van het herdrukken van Benoit's Voyage à Surinam. Nieuwe West-Indische Gids/New West Indian Guide 46:292–296.

Devaux, Justin Louis, and Elliot Frances Maingot, eds.
- 1941 An Ordinance Relating to Offences Punishable on Summary Conviction (chapter 4). May 19. Trinidad and Tobago Revised Ordinances, 1940, Prepared under the Authority of the Law Revision Ordinance, vol. 1. London.

Dickson, Arthur R. F., ed.
- 1983 Summary Jurisdication (Offences) Ordinance (chapter 99). May 9, 1953. The Laws of Belize in Force on the 31st Day of December, 1980, vol. 3. Belmopan, Belize: Government of Belize.

Dobbin, Jay D.
- 1986 The Jombee Dance of Montserrat: A Study of Trance Ritual in the West Indies. Columbus: Ohio State University Press.

Dominica
- 1789 An Act, Respecting Negroes, December 23, 1788. In Report of the Lords of the Committee of Council Appointed for Consideration of All Matters Relating to Trade and Foreign plantations . . . Concerning the Present State of the Trade to Africa, and Particularly the Trade in Slaves . . . Part III, Dominica. London: Parliament of Great Britain.
- 1793 An Act to Revive and Make Perpetual an Act of This Island, Intitled, "An Act for the Encouragement, Protection and Better Government of Slaves." March 15, 1793. Returns and Papers Relating to the Slave Trade, 1816–18. Slave Trade 62. P. 60. IUP, Shannon, Ireland, 1971.
- 1818 An Act for Regulating the Government and Conduct of Slaves, and for Their More Effectual Protection, Encouragement, and the General Melioration of their Condition. April 22, 1818. Papers Relating to the Suppression of the Slave Trade, 1818–21. Slave Trade 63. Pp. 112–115. IUP, Shannon, Ireland, 1971.
- 1821 An Act for Regulating the Government and Conduct of Slaves, and For Their More Effectual Protection, Encouragement, and the General Melioration of their Condition. June 2, 1821. Correspondence and Papers Relating to Slavery and the Abolition of the Slave Trade, 1823–24. Slave Trade 66. Pp. 304–311. IUP, Shannon, Ireland, 1969.
- 1826 An Act for the Further Encouragement and Protection and Better Government of Slaves, and for the General Amelioration of Their Condition. January 21, 1826. Correspondence and Papers Relating to Slavery and the Abolition of the Slave Trade, 1823–24. Slave Trade 66. Pp. 535–556. IUP, Shannon, Ireland, 1969.
- 1831 An Act to Consolidate and Amend the Laws Relating to Slaves. June 28, 1831. Papers Relating to the Measures Adopted for the Melioration of the Conditions of Slaves in British Possessions, 1831–32. Slave Trade 79. Pp. 117–127. IUP, Shannon, Ireland, 1969.

1858 An Act for the Punishment of Idle and Disorderly Persons, Rogues and Vagabonds, Incorrigible Rogues and Other Vagrants in this Island (no. 58). May 9, 1840. Laws of the Island of Dominica from 1763 to 1841, vol. 1. London.

2008 Obeah Act, Chapter 10:38. Revised Laws of Dominica 1990, Acts and Statutory Rules and Orders 1991–2008. Government of the Commonwealth of Dominica. http://www.dominica.gov.dm/laws/index.php (accessed March 11, 2010).

2009 The Commonwealth of Dominica Consolidated Index of Statutes and Subsidiary Legislation to 1st January 2009. Compiled at the Faculty of the Law and Law Library, University of the West Indies, Barbados. Cave Hill, Barbados: Faculty of Law Library, University of the West Indies.

2011 Legislation Dominica. Lexadin. Updated January 1, 2011. http://www.lexadin.nl/wlg/legis/nofr/oeur/lxwedma.htm (accessed February 15, 2011).

Donaldson, Roderick
1981 A Guide to the Laws of the Cayman Islands. Hialeah, FL: Peninsular Promotions.

Duncanson-Hales, Christopher
2011 The Full Has Never Been Told: Theology and the Encounter with Globalization. PhD dissertation, Faculty of Theology, Saint Paul University, Ottawa.

Duncombe, Alfred John, comp.
1862 An Act for the Better Suppression of Vagrancy, and for the Punishment of Idle and Disorderly Persons, and Rogues, Vagabonds, and Other Vagrants (no. 8). June 21, 1862. Laws of the Turks and Caicos Islands . . . in Force at the Date of the Publication of This Work. London.

Edwards, Bryan
1793 The History, Civil and Commercial, of the British Colonies in the West Indies, vol. 2. Dublin: Luke White.

Ellis, Karen
1990 Domino: Traditional Children's Songs, Proverbs and Culture from the American Virgin Islands. Gulph Mills, PA: Guavaberry Books.

Evans-Pritchard, E. E.
1937 Witchcraft, Oracles and Magic among the Azande. Oxford: Clarendon Press.

Firth, H. A., comp.
1864 The Laws of British Guiana [1811–69], vol. 1. Georgetown, Demerara: L. M'Dermott, at "The Colonist" Office.

Fisher, Lawrence E.
1985 Colonial Madness: Mental Health in the Barbadian Social Order. New Brunswick, NJ: Rutgers University Press.

Flannigan, Mrs.
  1844 Antigua and the Antiguans, vol. 2. London: Saunders and Ottley.

Forde, Maarit, and Diana Paton
  2012 Introduction. *In* Obeah and Other Powers: The Politics of Caribbean Religion and Healing. Diana Paton and Maarit Forde, eds. Pp. 1–31. Durham, NC: Duke University Press.

Francis, Cyril B., ed.
  1924 Summary Conviction Offences Ordinance (chapter 180). October 1, 1878. The New Edition of the Consolidated Laws of British Honduras 1924, Containing the Ordinances of the Colony in Force on the 21st Day of July, 1924, vol. 2. London: Waterlow and Sons.

Garcia, George Lewis, ed.
  1883–86 An Ordinance for Rendering Certain Offences Punishable on Summary Conviction (no. 6). April 7. Laws of Trinidad. Rev. edition, vol. 3. London.

Gaspar, David Barry
  1985 Bondmen and Rebels: A Study of Master–Slave Relations in Antigua. Baltimore: Johns Hopkins University Press.

Gerbner, Katharine
  2010 "They Call Me Obea": The Rise, Fall and Resurrection of the Moravian Mission on Jamaica, 1754–1770. Paper presented at the Moravian History and Music Conference, Bethlehem, PA, October 14–16.

Geschiere, Peter
  1997 The Modernity of Witchcraft: Politics and the Occult in Post-Colonial Africa. Charlottesville: University Press of Virginia.

Gibson, Kean
  2001 Comfa Religion and Creole Language in a Caribbean Community. Albany: State University of New York Press.

Glover, J. N., comp.
  1970 Summary Offences Ordinance (chapter 25). January 6, 1900. The Laws of the Turks and Caicos Islands; Containing the Ordinances in Force on the 8th Day of April 1969, vol. 1. Dobbs Ferry, NY: Government of the Turks and Caicos Islands; Oceana.
  1980 Summary Offences Ordinance (chapter 25). January 6, 1900. The Laws of the Turks and Caicos Islands, Continuation Volume 1977, Containing Ordinances Enacted during 1977. Cockburn Town: Government of the Turks and Caicos Islands.

Gluckman, Max
  1955 Custom and Conflict in Africa. Glencoe, IL: Free Press.

Gmelch, George, and Sharon Bohn Gmelch
  1997 The Parish behind God's Back: The Changing Culture of Rural Barbados. Ann Arbor: University of Michigan Press.

Goldsmith, Oliver
  1774 An History of the Earth, vol. 7. London.

Goodman, G. Aubrey, and C. P. Clarke, eds.
  1912 An Act for the Suppression and Punishment of Vagrancy (Act 1897-3). August 30, 1897. Laws of Barbados [1667–1912], vol. 2. Barbados.

Gordon, Shirley
  1997 God Is Dumb until the Drum Speaks: Religious Life in Jamaica before Emancipation. Comparative Studies of South Asia, Africa and the Middle East 17:145–156.

Greene, Jack P.
  2010 Liberty and Slavery: The Transfer of British Liberty to the West Indies, 1627–1865. *In* Exclusionary Empire: English Liberty Overseas, 1600–1900. Jack P. Greene, ed. Pp. 50–76. Cambridge: Cambridge University Press.

Grenada
  1789 Spooner, Answer to Query 26 [concerning anti-obeah laws in Grenada, St. Christopher and other West Indian islands]. *In* Report of the Lords of the Committee of Council Appointed for Consideration of All Matters Relating to Trade and Foreign plantations... Concerning the Present State of the Trade to Africa, and Particularly the Trade in Slaves.... Part III, Grenada and St. Christopher. London: Parliament of Great Britain.
  1806 Frederick Maitland to Secretary of State [concerning case of slave convicted of attempting to poison his plantation manager], December 7, 1806. CO 101/44, fos. 177–178.
  1808 The Laws of Grenada, from the Year 1763, to the Year 1805. London.
  1830 An Act to Consolidate All the Laws Now in Force Relating to the Slave Population, for Making More Effectual Provision for their Maintenance and Protection, and for the Admissibility of their Testimony in Certain Cases (no. 164). April 26, 1825. The Laws of Grenada, and the Grenadines, from the Year 1766. Grenada: Alexander M'Combie.
  1834 Governor Lionel Smith to Secretary of State [forwarding the petition of Pierre, a free black man], March 6, 1834. CO 101/78, fos. 15–16, 19–20.
  1852 The Laws of Grenada and the Grenadines; From the Year 1766 to the Year 1852. Surrey, England.
  1875 An Act to Consolidate the Laws Relative to Offences Punishable on Summary Convictions, and to Define the Duties of Constables in Certain Cases (no. 138). September 25, 1874. The Laws of Grenada and the Grenadines, from ... 1766 to 1875

[with a supplement containing acts passed between April 1875 and June 1876]. London.

1897 An Ordinance to Establish a Code of Offences Punishable on Summary Conviction and on Indictment (no. 2), 1897 [criminal code]. Laws of Grenada. London: Waterlow and Sons.

1995 Family Court Act (no. 34 of 1994; enacted November 11, 1994). Grenada Laws 1994, Part 1. St. George's, Grenada: Government Printer.

2010a Grenada Consolidated Index of Statutes and Subsidiary Legislation to 1st January 2010. Compiled at the Faculty of the Law and Law Library, University of the West Indies, Barbados. Cave Hill, Barbados: Faculty of Law Library, University of the West Indies.

2010b Legislation Grenada. Lexadin. Updated March 2, 2010. http://www.lexadin.nl /wlg/legis/nofr/oeur/lxwegrn.htm (accessed February 15, 2011).

Guyana

1997 Summary Jurisdiction (Offences) (Amendment) Act 1997 (no. 8). August 13. Official Gazette Legal Supplement A, 14th August. Georgetown, Guyana.

1998 Summary Jurisdiction (Offences) (Amendment) Act 1998 (no. 10). December 31. Official Gazette Legal Supplement A, 31st December. Georgetown, Guyana.

2007 Summary Jurisdiction (Offences) (Amendment) Act 2007 (no. 19). May 24. Laws of Guyana. Georgetown, Guyana.

2009 Guyana Consolidated Index of Statutes and Subsidiary Legislation to 1st January 2008. Compiled at the Faculty of the Law and Law Library, University of the West Indies, Barbados. Cave Hill, Barbados: Faculty of Law Library, University of the West Indies.

2010 Legislation Guyana. Lexadin. Updated March 2. http://www.lexadin.nl/wlg/legis/ nofr/oeur/lxweguy.htm (accessed February 14, 2011).

Hall, Clifford G.

1997 A Legislative History of Vagrancy in England and Barbados. Caribbean Law Review 7:350–353.

Hall, Douglas

1989 In Miserable Slavery: Thomas Thistlewood in Jamaica, 1750–86. Warwick University Caribbean Studies. London: Macmillan.

Hall, Neville A. T.

1992 Slave Society in the Danish West Indies, St. Thomas, St. John and St. Croix. B. W. Higman, ed. Kingston: University of the West Indies Press.

Hall, Richard, ed.

1764 An Act for the Governing of Negroes [act 82, clause 12]. In Acts, Passed in the Island of Barbados, from 1643, to 1762, Inclusive. London.

Handler, Jerome S.
  1974 The Unappropriated People: Freedmen in the Slave Society of Barbados. Baltimore: Johns Hopkins University Press.
  1982 Slave Revolts and Conspiracies in Seventeenth Century Barbados. New West Indian Guide/Nieuwe West-Indische Gids 56:5–43.
  1997 Escaping Slavery in a Caribbean Plantation Society: Marronage in Barbados, 1650s–1830s. New West Indian Guide/Nieuwe West-Indische Gids 71:183–225.
  2000 Slave Medicine and Obeah in Barbados, ca. 1650–1834. New West Indian Guide/Nieuwe West-Indische Gids 74:57–60.
  2006 Diseases and Medical Disabilities of Enslaved Barbadians from the Seventeenth Century to around 1838, Part 2. Journal of Caribbean History 40:177–214.

Handler, Jerome S., and Kenneth M. Bilby
  2001 On the Early Use and Origin of the Term Obeah in Barbados and the Anglophone Caribbean. Slavery and Abolition 22:87–100.

Harris, Francis O. C., D. Bhagowtee, and Ray C. M. Harris, eds.
  1991 An Act for Preventing and Punishing Persons who Pretend to Exercise or Use Any Kind of Witchcraft, Sorcery or Other Supernatural Practices [Obeah Act] (chapter10:38). August 2, 1904. Laws of Dominica. Rev. edition, vol. 3. Roseau: Government of the Commonwealth of Dominica.

Hedrick, Basil, and Jeanette Stephens
  1977 It's a Natural Fact: Obeah in the Bahamas. Museum of Anthropology Miscellaneous Series no. 39. Greeley: University of Northern Colorado, Museum of Anthropology.

Henriques, Cyril G. X., ed.
  1960 Summary Jurisdiction [Offences] Act (chapter 23). May 9, 1953. The Laws of British Honduras, in Force on the 15th Day of September 1958, vol. 1. London: Waterlow.

Henriques, Fernando
  1960 Jamaica: Land of Wood and Water. London: MacGibbon and Kee.

Henry, K. C. St. L., and R. C. Laming, comps.
  N.d. [1964?] The Obeah Law (chapter 113). June 2, 1898. The Laws of the Cayman Islands in Force on the 31st Day of December, 1963, vol. 3. London: Eyre and Spottiswoode.

Henry, L. Mike, and Kevin S. Harris
  2002 LMH Official Dictionary of Jamaican Words and Proverbs. Kingston: LMH Publishing.

Herskovits, Melville J.
  1930 Review of Black Roadways, by Martha Warren Beckwith. Journal of American Folklore 43:332–338.

Herskovits, Melville J., and Frances S. Herskovits
 1934 Rebel Destiny: Among the Bush Negroes of Dutch Guiana. New York: McGraw-Hill.

Higman, B.W.
 2011 A Concise History of the Caribbean. New York: Cambridge University Press.

Hodges, Hugh
 2008 Soon Come: Jamaican Spirituality, Jamaican Poetics. Charlottesville: University of Virginia Press.

Hogg, Donald W.
 1964 Jamaican Religions: A Study in Variations. PhD dissertation, Department of Anthropology, Yale University.

Honychurch, Lennox
 2011 A to Z of Dominica Heritage by Lennox Honychurch. http://www.avirtualdominica.com/heritage2.htm (accessed August 11, 2011).

Huggard, Walter Clarence, ed.
 1925 An Ordinance Relating to Offences Punishable on Summary Conviction (chapter 25). May 19, 1921. The Laws of Trinidad and Tobago Containing the Ordinances of the Colony in Force on the 30th Day of June, 1925. Rev. edition, vol. 1. London.

Huggins, Haydn
 2006 Lawyer on Obeah Charges. June 23. Nation News (Barbados), June 23. http://bararchive.bits.baseview.com/archive_detail.php?archiveFile=2006/June/23/Regional/21814.xml (accessed September 15, 2012).

Hurault, Jean
 1961 Les noirs réfugiés Boni de la Guyane française. Dakar: IFAN.

Island Sun (British Virgin Islands)
 2004 Attempted "Obeah" Smuggling Investigated. February 21. http://islandsun.com/2004-february/21022004/locall-v12i16.html (accessed December 16, 2008).

IUP [Irish University Press]
 1816–18 Copies of, or Extracts from, All Such Laws as Have Been Enacted . . . in America or the West Indies, Relative . . . . to the Protection or Good Government of Slaves . . . Since the Year 1788 [to 1816]. Returns and Papers Relating to the Slave Trade, 1816–18. Slave Trade 62. Pp. 21–27. IUP, Shannon, Ireland, 1971.
 1823–24 Papers Relating to the Treatment of Slaves in the Colonies; viz, Acts of Colonial Legislatures; 1818–1823. Correspondence and Papers Relating to Slavery and the Abolition of the Slave Trade, 1823–24. Slave Trade 66. Pp. 283–286. IUP, Shannon, Ireland, 1969.
 1825–29a Third Report of the Commissioner [sic] of Inquiry into the Administration

of Criminal and Civil Justice in the West Indies and South American Colonies [October 1826]. Reports from the Commissioners of Inquiry on the Administration of Civil and Criminal Justice in the West Indies and South American Colonies, 1825–29. Colonies: West Indies 3. Pp. 167–284. IUP, Shannon, Ireland, 1971.

1825–29b Second Report (Second Series) of the Commissioners of Enquiry into the Administration of Criminal and Civil Justice in the West Indies and South American Colonies [April 1828]. Reports from the Commissioners of Inquiry on the Administration of Civil and Criminal Justice in the West Indies and South American Colonies, 1825–29. Colonies: West Indies 3. Pp. 473–607. IUP, Shannon, Ireland, 1971.

Jacobs, Wilfred, ed.

1992 The Obeah Act (chapter 298). August 2, 1904. Laws of Antigua and Barbuda. Rev. edition, vol. 6. London: Eyre and Spottiswoode.

Jamaica

1771 An Act to Remedy the Evils Arising from Irregular Assemblies of Slaves, and to Prevent their Possessing Arms and Ammunition, and Going from Place to Place Without Tickets; and for Preventing the Practice of Obeah; and to Restrain Overseers from Leaving the Estates under their Care on Certain Days (act 24). Acts of Assembly Passed in the Island of Jamaica: from the Year 1681 to the Year 1768. Saint Jago de la Vega, Jamaica.

1786 Acts of Assembly, Passed in the Island of Jamaica; from 1770, to 1783, Inclusive. Kingston, Jamaica.

1788 The Act of Assembly of the Island of Jamaica, to Repeal Several Acts, and Clauses of Acts, Respecting Slaves, and for the Better Order and Government of Slaves, and for other Purposes, Commonly called the Consolidated Act. London.

1789a The New Act of Assembly of the Island of Jamaica, Intitled, An Act to Repeal an Act, Intitled, "An Act to Repeal Several Acts, and Clauses of Acts, Respecting Slaves . . . Commonly Called, the New Consolidated Act, which was Passed . . . on the 6th Day of December, 1788; Being the Present Code Noir of that Island. London.

1789b Paper Relating to the Obeah-Men in Jamaica, . . . by Mr. Rheder. *In* Report of the Lords of the Committee of Council Appointed for Consideration of All Matters Relating to Trade and Foreign Plantations . . . Concerning the Present State of the Trade to Africa, and Particularly the Trade in Slaves . . . Part III, Jamaica. London: Parliament of Great Britain.

1792 The Laws of Jamaica: Comprehending All the Acts in Force, Passed Between the Thirty-Second Year of the Reign of King Charles the Second, and the Thirty-Third Year of the Reign of King George the Third, vol. 2. St. Jago de la Vega, Jamaica.

1793 An Abridgement of the Laws of Jamaica; Being an Alphabetical Digest of All the Public Acts of Assembly now in Force . . . [1681–1792] Inclusive, vol. 2. St. Jago de la Vega, Jamaica.

1809 Act for the Protection, Subsisting, Clothing, and for the Better Order, Regulation, and Government of Slaves; and for Other Purposes. December 14. Returns and Papers Relating to the Slave Trade, 1816–18. Slave Trade 62. Pp. 137–155. IUP, Shannon, Ireland, 1971.

1826 An Act to Alter and Amend the Slave Laws of this Island. December 22, 1826. Papers Relating to the Conditions of Slaves in British Possessions and Other Papers Relating to Slavery and the Slave Trade, 1826–27. Slave Trade 73. Pp. 149–182. IUP, Shannon, Ireland, 1969.

1831a An Act for the Government of Slaves. February 19, 1831. Papers Relating to Measures Adopted for the Melioration of the Conditions of Slaves in British Possessions,1831–32. Slave Trade 79. Pp. 3–54. IUP, Shannon, Ireland, 1969.

1831b Viscount Goderich to Earl of Belmore, Downing Street, June 16, 1831. Papers Relating to Measures Adopted for the Melioration of the Conditions of Slaves in British Possessions, 1831–32. Slave Trade 79. Pp. 54–58. IUP, Shannon, Ireland, 1969.

1833 An Act to Restrain and Punish Vagrancy. December 12, 1833. Papers Relating to the Abolition of the Slave Trade in the British Colonies, 1836. Slave Trade 82. Pp. 244–247. IUP, Shannon, Ireland, 1969.

1892 The Obeah and Myalism Acts Amendment Law, 1892 (no. 28). May 18, 1892. CO 139/106.

1893 The Obeah and Myalism Acts Further Amendment Law, 1893. April 28, 1893. CO 139/106.

1898 The Obeah Law, 1898 (no. 5). June 2, 1898. CO 139/108. Pp. 128–129.

1899 The Obeah Law, 1898, Amendment Law, 1899 (no. 18). July 8, 1899. CO 139/108.

1903 A Law to Amend the Obeah Laws, 1898 and 1899 (no.8). March 21, 1903. CO 139/109.

Jamaica Gleaner

2007 Joseph the Obeah Man. June 28. http://jamaica-gleaner.com/gleaner/20070628/news/news1.html (accessed December 19, 2008).

2011 Protecting Our Duppies. January 30. http://jamaica-gleaner.com/gleaner/20110130/focus/focus6.html (accessed February 21, 2011).

Jamaica Star

2010 Shottas Turn to Obeah: Seek Protection from Cops. August 27. http://jamaica-star.com/thestar/20100827/news/news2.html (accessed June 6, 2011).

2011a Obeah or Skin Disease. June 10. http://jamaica-star.com/thestar/20110610/news/news1.html (accessed March 21, 2012).

2011b Woman's Duppy Follows Lover. May 29. http://jamaica-star.com/thestar/20110729/news/news1.html (accessed March 21, 2012).

Jensen, Niklas T.

2012 For the Health of the Enslaved: Slaves, Medicine and Power in the Danish West Indies, 1803–1848. Copenhagen: Museum Tusculanum Press.

Kapferer, Bruce
  2002 Introduction. *In* Beyond Rationalism: Rethinking Magic, Witchcraft and Sorcery. Bruce Kapferer, ed. Pp. 1–30. New York: Berghahn Books.

Kelleher, David, and Gerard Leavey, eds.
  2004 Identity and Health. New York: Routledge.

Kingdon, Donald, ed.
  1954 Summary Jurisdiction (Offences) (chapter 14). March 1, 1894. The Laws of British Guiana in Force on the 1st day of July, 1953. Rev. edition, vol. 1. London.

Konadu, Kwasi
  2010 The Akan Diaspora in the Americas. Oxford: Oxford University Press.

Lawrence, Joy
  2003 The Way We Talk and Other Antiguan Folkways. St. John's, Antigua: Joy Lawrence.

Lazarus-Black, Mindie
  1994 Legitimate Acts and Illegal Encounters: Law and Society in Antigua and Barbuda. Washington, DC: Smithsonian Institution Press.

Leach, MacEdward
  1961 Jamaican Duppy Lore. Journal of the American Folklore Society 74:207–215.

Leewards (Leeward Islands Federation)
  1892 An Act to Consolidate the Laws in Force in the Presidencies of the Colony Relating to Certain Offences Punishable on Summary Conviction (no. 11). March 1, 1892. CO 154/10.
  1928–30 An Act to Prohibit the Practice of Certain Vulgar Frauds Commonly Known as Obeah and Other Pretended Supernatural or Occult Practices in this Colony (chapter 64). August 2, 1904. The Federal Acts of the Leeward Islands, Containing the Acts of the General Legislative Council in Force on the 31st Day of December, 1927, vol. 1. Antigua: Government Printing Office, Leeward Islands.
  1905 An Act to Amend the Obeah Act, 1904 (no. 10). March 21, 1905. CO 154/12.
  1929 The Obeah Act, 1904. 1928. The Acts and Ordinances of the Colony of the Leeward Islands and of the Several Presidencies in the Colony . . . Passed in the Year 1928. Antigua: Government Printing Office.
  1933 The Obeah (Amendment) Act, 1932 (no. 12). February 18, 1932. The Acts and Ordinances of the Colony of the Leeward Islands and of the Several Presidencies in the Colony . . . Passed in the Year 1932. Antigua: Government Printing Office.
  1957 The Obeah (Amendment) Act, 1932 (no. 12). February 19, 1932. The Acts and Ordinances of the Colony of the Leeward Islands and of the Several Presidencies in the Colony . . . Passed in the Year 1956. Antigua: Government Printing Office.

Lewis, A. M., ed.
 1959 The criminal code: A Code of Criminal Offences and Procedure . . . Printed with Amendments to 30th June, 1957 (chapter 250). December 11, 1920. Saint Lucia Revised Ordinances, 1957, vol. 5. [Castries], St. Lucia: Voice Publishing.

Lewis, M. G.
 1969 [1834] Journal of a West India Proprietor, Kept during a Residence in the Island of Jamaica [1815–16, 1817]. New York: Negro Universities Press.

Lewis, P. C., ed.
 1964 The Obeah Act (chapter 55). August 2, 1904. The Revised Laws of St. Christopher, Nevis and Anguilla . . . Revised Edition of the Laws Ordinance, 1959, vol. 1. London: Waterlow and Sons.
 1965 The Obeah Act (chapter 55). August 2, 1904. The Revised Laws of Montserrat, vol. 1. London: Waterlow and Sons.

Ligon, Richard
 1657 A True and Exact History of the Island of Barbados. London.

Long, Edward
 1774 History of Jamaica, vol. 2. London.

Lowenthal, David
 1972 West Indian Societies. New York: Oxford University Press.

Lunan, John
 1819 An Abstract of the Laws of Jamaica Relating to Slaves (From 33 Charles II [1681] to 59 George III Inclusive [1818]). With the Slave Law at Length, also, An Appendix, Containing an Abstract of the Acts of Parliament Relating to the Abolition of the Slave-Trade. Jamaica: Printed at the Office of the Saint Jago de la Vega Gazette.

Lunan, John, Jr.
 1828 The Jamaica Magistrate's and Vestryman's Assistant, Containing a Digest of all the Laws of the Island . . . From 33 Charles II [1681] to 8 George IV [1827]. Jamaica: Printed at the Office of the Saint Jago de la Vega Gazette.

MacKenzie, V. St. Clair, ed.
 1923 An Ordinance to Amend the Summary Conviction (Offences) Ordinance, 1893, in Regard to the Practise of Obeah (no. 26). July 27, 1918. An Ordinance to Amend the Summary Conviction (Offences) Ordinance, 1893, in Regard to the Practise of Obeah (no. 11). March 20, 1920. The Laws of British Guiana (1803 to 1921). Rev. edition, vol. 2. London.

Maingot, Elliot Francis, ed.
 1951 An Ordinance Relating to Offences Punishable on Summary Conviction (chapter 4). May 19, 1921. Trinidad and Tobago Revised Ordinances, 1950, vol. 1. London.

Mair, Lucy
    1969 Witchcraft. New York: McGraw-Hill.

Major, Charles, ed.
    1930 Summary Jurisdiction (Offences) Ordinance (chapter 13). March 1, 1894. The Laws of British Guiana. Rev. edition, vol. 1. London.

Malcolm, O. D., ed.
    1901 An Act to Consolidate the Laws Relating to Police Regulations (no. 1). April 19, 1873. The Statute Law of the Bahamas. London.
    1929 penal code (chapter 60). May 15, 1924. The Statute Law of the Bahama Islands . . . in Force on the 1st January 1929, vol. 2. London.

Malone, Clement, ed.
    1962 criminal code: An Ordinance to Establish a Code of Offences Punishable on Summary Conviction and on Indictment (chapter 76). January 20, 1897. The Revised Laws of Grenada in Force on the 31st Day of December, 1958, vol. 1. St. Georges, Grenada.

Mantz, Jeffrey
    2007 Enchanting Panics and Obeah Anxieties: Concealing and Disclosing Eastern Caribbean Witchcraft. Anthropology and Humanism 32:18–29.

McDonald, Roderick, ed.
    2001 Between Slavery and Freedom: Special Magistrate John Anderson's Journal of St. Vincent During the Apprenticeship. Philadelphia: University of Pennsylvania Press.

McKenzie, Herbert C.
    1994 The Obeah Act 1898: An Antithesis of Fundamental Rights in Jamaica. LLB thesis, Faculty of Law, University of the West Indies, Cave Hill, Barbados.

Mcleod, Dwayne
    2007 Big Money to Catch Duppy. June 29. http://jamaica-star.com/thestar/20070702/cleisure/cleisure2.html (accessed February 21, 2011).

Mendes, John
    2003 Cote Ce Cote La: Trinidad and Tobago Dictionary. Port of Spain: New Millennium.

Michelin, William P., ed.
    1922 The New Edition of the Statutes of the Presidency of St. Christopher and Nevis (Leeward Islands). London: Waterloo.

Middleton, John, and Edward Winter
    1963 Introduction. *In* Witchcraft and Sorcery in East Africa. John Middleton and Edward Winter, eds. Pp. 1–26. London: Routledge and Kegan Paul.

Montserrat
>   1983 An Ordinance to Amend and Codify the Penal Laws of the Colony and for Matters Connected Therewith [The penal code], (no. 12 of 1983). Montserrat Ordinances and Statutory Rules and Orders for the Year 1983. [Montserrat Gazette?] Law Library of the University of the West Indies, Cave Hill, Barbados.
>   2002 The penal code and Subsidiary Legislation, Revised Edition, Showing the Law as of January 1, 2002 (chapter 4.02). Legislation of Montserrat. Lexadin. Updated October 22, 2009. http://www.mapsmontserrat.ms/Legislation/Penal%20Code.pdf (accessed March 12, 2010).
>   2006 Montserrat Consolidated Index of Statutes and Subsidiary Legislation to 1st January 2001. Compiled at the Faculty of the Law and Law Library, University of the West Indies, Barbados. Cave Hill, Barbados: Faculty of Law Library, University of the West Indies.

Moore, Brian
>   1995 Cultural Power, Resistance and Pluralism: Colonial Guyana 1838–1900. Montreal: McGill-Queen's University Press.

Moore, Brian, and Michele Johnson
>   2004 Neither Led nor Driven: Contesting British Cultural Imperialism in Jamaica, 1865–1920. Kingston: University of the West Indies Press.

Moore, Joseph G.
>   1953 Religion of Jamaican Negroes: A Study of Afro-Jamaican Acculturation. PhD dissertation, Department of Anthropology, Northwestern University.

Morgan, Philip
>   1998 Slave Counterpoint: Black Culture in the Eighteenth-Century Chesapeake and Lowcountry. Chapel Hill: University of North Carolina Press.

Morrish, Ivor
>   1982 Obeah, Christ and Rastaman: Jamaica and Its Religion. Cambridge: James Clarke.

Mullin, Michael
>   1992 Africa in America: Slave Acculturation and Resistance in the American South and the British Caribbean, 1736–1831. Urbana: University of Illinois Press.

Murphy, Elaine
>   N.d. Antiguan Dialect. St. John's, Antigua: Benjie's Printery.

Murphy, Joseph M.
>   1994 Working the Spirit: Ceremonies of the African Diaspora. Boston: Beacon Press.

Murray, Deryck
>   2007 Three Worships, an Old Warlock and Many Lawless Forces: The Court Trial of an African Doctor Who Practised "Obeah to Cure" in Early Nineteenth Century Jamaica. Journal of Southern African Studies 33:811–828.

Murrell, Nathaniel S.
   2010   Afro-Caribbean Religions: An Introduction to Their Historical, Cultural, and Sacred Traditions. Philadelphia: Temple University Press.

Nation News (Barbados)
   2006   Pudding & Souse: Player's Just a Payer. November 11. http://bararchive.bits.baseview.com/archive_detail.php?archiveFile=2006/November/11/LocalNews/28659.xml (accessed September 12, 2012).
   2009   Pudding & Souse: Bad Blood over Obeah. May 16. http://bararchive.bits.baseview.com/archive_detail.php?archiveFile=2009/May/16/Commentary/2485514.xml (accessed February 17, 2011).

Nettleford, Rex
   1979   Caribbean Cultural Identity: The Case of Jamaica. Los Angeles: Center for Afro-American Studies and UCLA Latin American Center.

Nevis
   1862   An Act to Make Provision for the Punishment of Persons Who May Use Delusive and Superstitious Devices, or Other Frauds, for Purposes of Deception (no. 94). January 14. The Laws of Nevis, from 1681 to 1861, Inclusive. London.

Olmos, Margarite Fernandez, and Lizabeth Paravisini-Gebert
   2011   Creole Religions of the Caribbean. 2nd edition. New York: New York University Press.

Patchett, Keith
   1970   Criminal Law in the West Indies. Mimeograph, 37 pp. Law Library, University of the West Indies, Cave Hill, Barbados.

Paton, Diana
   2001   Punishment, Crime, and the Bodies of Slaves in Eighteenth-Century Jamaica. Journal of Social History 34:923–954.
   2008   An "Injurious" Population: Caribbean–Australian Penal Transportation and Imperial Racial Politics. Cultural and Social History 5:449–464.
   2009   Obeah Acts: Producing and Policing the Boundaries of Religion in the Caribbean. Small Axe 13:1–18.

Paton, Diana, and Maarit Forde, eds.
   2012   Obeah and Other Powers: The Politics of Caribbean Religion and Healing. Durham, NC: Duke University Press.

Patterson, Orlando
   1967   The Sociology of Slavery. London: MacGibbon and Kee.

Pragg, Sam
   1999   Culture—Jamaica: Rastafarians Object to "Anti-Witchcraft Laws." Kingston, January 21, 1999. Lexis Nexis.

Price, Richard

1979 Kwasimukámba's Gambit. Bijdragen tot de Taal-, Land- en Volkenkunde 135:151–169.

1983 First-Time: The Historical Vision of an Afro-American People. Baltimore: Johns Hopkins University Press.

2008 Travels with Tooy: History, Memory, and the African American Imagination. Chicago: University of Chicago Press.

Price, Richard, and Sally Price, eds.

1988 John Gabriel Stedman: Narrative of a Five Years Expedition against the Revolted Negroes of Surinam. Baltimore: Johns Hopkins University Press.

Raboteau, Albert

1978 Slave Religion: The "Invisible Institution" in the Antebellum South. New York: Oxford University Press.

Rae, James Stanley, ed.

1927 Summary Conviction Offences Ordinance (chapter 14). March 1, 1912. The Laws of St. Vincent Containing the Ordinances of the Colony in Force on the 4th Day of May, 1926, vol. 1. London: Waterlow and Sons.

Ragatz, Lowell J.

1963[1928] The Fall of the Planter Class in the British Caribbean, 1763–1833. New York: Octagon Books.

Raithby, John, ed.

1824 An Act for the Punishment of idle and disorderly Persons, and Rogues and Vagabonds, in that Part of Great Britain called England (chapter 83). June 21. The Statutes of the United Kingdom of Great Britain and Ireland [1823–24], vol. 9. London.

Ramphal, S. S., B. T. I. Pollard, and F. O. C. Harris, comps.

1973 Summary Jurisdiction (Offences) Act (chapter 8:02). The Laws of Guyana. Rev. edition, vol. 2. Georgetown: Government of Guyana.

Rayner, Thomas Crossley, ed.

1905 An Ordinance to Consolidate and Amend the Laws Relating to Offences Punishable on Summary Conviction (no. 17). March 1, 1894. The Laws of British Guiana. Rev. edition, vol. 3. London.

Reece, Clifford M., comp.

1935 criminal code: An Ordinance to Establish a Code of Offences Punishable on Summary Conviction and on Indictment (chapter 55). January 20, 1897. The Revised Laws of Grenada in Force on the 31st Day of December, 1934, vol. 1. London: Waterlow and Sons.

RJR News (Jamaica)
  2010 Deputy DPP calls for an end to the Obeah Act. November 2010. http://rjrnews
    online.com/local/deputy-dpp-calls-for-an-end-to-the-obeah-act (accessed February 24,
    2012).

Robinson, Joyce Hope
  1985 Belize, Formerly British Honduras, Laws 1855–1901: A List of Laws on Microfilm
    Held by the Law Library of University of the West Indies (Cave Hill). Cave Hill, Bar-
    bados: Faculty of Law Library, University of the West Indies.

Robinson, May
  1893 Obeah Worship in the East and West Indies. Folk-Lore: A Quarterly Review of
    Myth, Tradition, Institution, and Custom 32:207–213.

Rucker, Walter C.
  2006 The River Flows On: Black Resistance, Culture, and Identity Formation in Early
    America. Baton Rouge: Louisiana State University Press.

St. Aubyn, Geoffrey P., ed.
  1908 Summary Offences Ordinance, 1899 (no. 5). The Laws of the Turks and Caicos
    Islands. London: Waterlow and Sons.

St. Kitts (St. Christopher)
  1828 An Act for Further Improving the Condition of the Slave Population in the Island
    of St. Christopher. January 7. Reports from Protectors of Slaves and from Commis-
    sioners of Inquiry and Other Papers Relating to the Conditions of Slaves in British
    Possessions and to the Slave Trade, 1828–29. Slave Trade 76. Pp. 69–78. IUP, Shan-
    non, Ireland, 1969.
  1857 An Act for the Punishment of Idle and Disorderly Persons, and Rogues and
    Vagabonds in the Island of Saint Christopher (no. 73). October 21, 1847. The Statutes
    of the Islands of Saint Christopher and Anguilla. London.
  1961–76 Laws of St. Christopher, Nevis & Anguilla. Barbados: Cole's Printery.
  1987 An Act to Amend the Provisions of Certain Enactments and to Repeal other Enact-
    ments in Order to Facilitate the Revision of the Laws of the State (no. 7). July 28,
    1976. Laws of St. Christopher, Nevis, & Anguilla. Barbados: Cole's Printery.
  2001 Customs (Control and Management) (Amendment) Act 2001 (no. 7). March 14.
    St. Kitts: Government Printery.
  2009 Saint Christopher and Nevis Consolidated Index of Statutes and Subsidiary Leg-
    islation to 1st January 2009. Compiled at the Faculty of the Law and Law Library,
    University of the West Indies, Barbados. Cave Hill, Barbados: Faculty of Law Library,
    University of the West Indies.
  2010 Legislation St Kitts and Nevis. Lexadin. Updated March 2, 2010. http://www
    .lexadin.nl/wlg/legis/nofr/oeur/lxweskn.htm (accessed February 14, 2011).

St. Lucia

1853 Order in Council for the Suppression of Vagrancy. September 7, 1838. Laws at Present in Force in the Island of St. Lucia. London: William Clowes and Sons.

1872 For the Repression of Obeah and other Kindred Practices [Obeah Ordinance 1872] (no. 2). April 24. CO 255/11, fos. 81–82.

1873 Obeah Ordinance Amendment 1873 (no. 4). February 12. CO 225/11, fo. 113.

1876 Administrator G. William Des Voeux to Governor Pope Hennessy [reporting on cropping hair of females and obeah convictions], July 1. CO 321/12, fos. 292–295.

1877a Summary Conviction Ordinance 1877 (no. 10). December 14. CO 255/11, fos. 279–287.

1877b Summary Procedure Ordinance 1877 (no. 9). December 14. CO 255/11, fos. 266–278.

1878 Acting Administrator Dix to Governor George Strahan [reporting on public flogging of males and obeah convictions], April 13. CO 321/22, fos. 157–162.

1889 An Ordinance to Establish a Code of Offenses Punishable on Summary Conviction and on Indictment [criminal code] (no. 101). 1888. The Laws of St. Lucia. Oxford: Clarendon Press.

1905 The criminal code Amendment Ordinance, 1905 (no. 2). April 29. CO 255/14, fos. 287–288.

1992 The criminal code: A Code of Criminal Offences and Procedure . . . April, 1992. Castries, St. Lucia: Government Printing Office.

2000 Governor General's Throne Speech, March 28. St. Lucia Online. http://www.slucia.com/budget2000/gg_throne.html (accessed March 23, 2012).

2004a criminal code (no. 9). December 2. Saint Lucia Acts and Statutory Instruments for the Year 2004. St. Lucia Gazette. Castries, St. Lucia: Government Printing Office.

2004b New criminal code Comes into Force on New Year's Day. St. Lucia Government Information Service. Press release, December 16. http://www.lexadin.nl/wlg/legis/nofr/oeur/lxwetci.htm (accessed March 13, 2010).

St. Vincent

1803 An Act to oblige Proprietors and Possessors of Slaves in their own Right or Rights of others, Managers and Conductors of Estates, to Give in Returns of Runaways, and Punishing Obeah Men. August 10. Returns and Papers Relating to the Slave Trade, 1816–18. Slave Trade 62. Pp. 328–344. IUP, Shannon, Ireland, 1971.

1821 Act to Repeal an Act, Intitled "An Act for Making Slaves Real Estate, and to Ameliorate the Condition of Slaves, and for other Purposes" (no. 16). September 11. Correspondence and Papers Relating to Slavery and the Abolition of the Slave Trade, 1823–24. Slave Trade 66. Pp. 328–344. IUP, Shannon, Ireland, 1969.

1864 An Act to Classify and Consolidate Many of those Petty Misdemeanors . . . in which Justices of the Peace Exercise and may in Future Exercise Summary Jurisdiction (no. 104). August 22, 1854. Laws of St. Vincent. London: Edward Stanford.

1884 Offences Cognizable by Justices of the Peace (no. 5). May 7, 1880. Laws of St. Vincent, vol. 2. London: Waterlow and Sons.

1912 Summary Conviction Offences [Police Offences] (chapter 14). March 1, 1912. The Laws of Saint Vincent. Rev. edition, vol. 2. Bridgetown, Barbados: Advocate Company.

1954 An Ordinance Further to Amend the Summary Conviction Offences Ordinance, Cap. 14 (no. 16). May 7. The Laws of St. Vincent. Kingstown, St. Vincent: Government Printing Office.

1988 An Act to Amend and Codify the Criminal Laws of St. Vincent and the Grenadines and for Matters Incidental Thereto (no. 23). October 6. St. Vincent and the Grenadines Acts for the year 1988, vol. 2. Kingstown, Saint Vincent: Government Printing Office.

1989 Saint Vincent and the Grenadines Consolidated Index of Statutes and Subsidiary Legislation to 1st January 1989. Compiled at the Faculty of the Law and Law Library, University of the West Indies, Barbados. Cave Hill, Barbados: Faculty of Law Library, University of the West Indies.

1990 Saint Vincent and the Grenadines Consolidated Index of Statutes and Subsidiary Legislation to 1st January 1990. Compiled at the Faculty of the Law and Law Library, University of the West Indies, Barbados. Cave Hill, Barbados: Faculty of Law Library, University of the West Indies.

2009 Legislation St. Vincent and the Grenadines. Lexadin. Updated March 2, 2009. http://www.lexadin.nl/wlg/legis/nofr/oeur/lxwestv.htm (accessed March 12, 2010).

2010a Legislation St. Vincent and the Grenadines. Lexadin. Updated March 2, 2010. http://www.lexadin.nl/wlg/legis/nofr/oeur/lxwestv.htm (accessed February 15, 2011).

2010b Saint Vincent and the Grenadines Consolidated Index of Statutes and Subsidiary Legislation to 1st January 2010. Compiled at the Faculty of the Law and Law Library, University of the West Indies, Barbados. Cave Hill, Barbados: Faculty of Law Library, University of the West Indies.

Salmon, J. E. M., ed.
1920 Fraud (title 33). criminal code of Saint Lucia. Castries, St. Lucia: Government Printing Office.

Sanders, Todd
2003 Reconsidering Witchcraft: Postcolonial Africa and Analytic (Un)Certainties. American Anthropologist 105:338–353.

Schuler, Monica
1966 Slave Resistance and Rebellion in the Caribbean during the Eighteenth Century. Unpublished MS, Department of History, University of the West Indies, Jamaica.

1979 Myalism and the African Religious Tradition in Jamaica. *In* Africa and the Caribbean: The Legacies of a Link. Margaret E. Crahan and Franklin W. Knight, eds. Pp. 65–79. Baltimore: Johns Hopkins University Press.

1980 Alas, Alas, Kongo: A Social History of Indentured African Immigration into Jamaica, 1841–1865. Baltimore: Johns Hopkins University Press.

Semper, D. S., and A. C. Burns
1911 Index of the Laws of the Federated Colony of the Leeward Islands and of the Several Presidencies Comprising the Same. London: Sweet and Maxwell.

Shahabuddeen, M.
1973 The Legal System of Guyana. Georgetown: Guyana Printers.

Shanks, Louis, Evert D. Koanting, and Carlo T. Velanti
1994 A buku fu Okanisi anga Ingiisi wowtu/Aukan-English Dictionary. Paramaribo: Summer Institute of Linguistics.

Sheridan, Richard B.
1985 Doctors and Slaves. Cambridge: Cambridge University Press.

Skinner, J.
2005 Interning the Serpent: Witchcraft, Religion and the Law on Montserrat in the 20th Century. History and Anthropology 16:143–165.

Snagg, W., comp.
1865 An Act for the Punishment of Idle and Disorderly Persons, Rogues and Vagabonds, Incorrigible Rogues, or Other Vagrants in this Island (no. 62). July 5, 1834 [amended October 1, 1863]. The Laws of Antigua: Consisting of the Acts of the Leeward Islands in Force in Antigua, and the Acts of Antigua from . . . 1668, to 1864, etc. London.

Spurdle, F. G.
N.d. Early West Indian Government. Palmerston, NZ: F. G. Spurdle [1963].

Stedman, John Gabriel
1796 Narrative, of a Five Years' Expedition, Against the Revolted Negroes of Surinam, in Guiana . . . from the Year 1772, to 1777. London.

Stephen, Henri J. M.
1986 De macht van de fodoe-winti. Amsterdam: Karnak.

Stewart, Dianne M.
2005 Three Eyes for the Journey: African Dimensions of the Jamaican Religious Experience. Oxford: Oxford University Press.

Stewart, Robert
1992 Religion and Society in Post-Emancipation Jamaica. Knoxville: University of Tennessee Press.

Taylor, Douglas
1945 Carib Folk-Beliefs and Customs from Dominica, BWI. Southwestern Journal of Anthropology 1:507–530.

Teenstra, Marten Douwes
  1835 De landbouw in de kolonie Suriname. Groningen: H. Eekhoff.

Thompson, Alvin O., ed.
  2002 A Documentary History of Slavery in Berbice, 1796–1834. Georgetown, Guyana: Free Press.

Trinidad
  1838 An Ordinance . . . to Consolidate and Amend the Laws Relative to Vagrants, Rogues, and Vagabonds, and Incorrigible Rogues; and to Assimilate the Same, So Far as may be, to the Laws of England in Like Cases (no. 12). September 10, 1838. CO 297/2. Pp. 300–301.
  1852 Laws of Trinidad, 1831 to 1848. London: J. Bain.
  1868 An Ordinance . . . for Rendering Certain Offences Punishable on Summary Conviction (no. 6). April 7, 1868. CO 297/8. Pp. 58–61.
  1902–05 An Ordinance for Rendering Certain Offences Punishable on Summary Conviction (no. 5). [date of passage unknown]. Laws of Trinidad and Tobago. Port-of-Spain, Trinidad.
  1980 An Act Relating to Offences Punishable on Summary Conviction (chapter 11:02). May 19, 1921. The Laws of Trinidad and Tobago, Prepared by the Law Revision Commission. Port-of-Spain, Trinidad.
  2000 An Act to Amend Certain Provisions of the Summary Courts Act, the Summary Offences Act and the Offences Against the Person Act to Remove Certain Discriminatory Religious References (no. 85). November 2, 2000. Legal Supplement, Part A, to Trinidad and Tobago Gazette 39(224), November 10. Port-of-Spain, Trinidad.

Trinidad Express
  2011 Man Blames Obeah for Criminal Acts. June 18, 2011. http://www.trinidadexpress.com/news/Man_blames_obeah_for_criminal_acts-124143469.html (accessed March 21, 2012).

Trotman, David
  1986 Crime in Trinidad: Conflict and Control in a Plantation Society, 1838–1900. Knoxville: University of Tennessee Press.

Trotman, Donald, Elton Georges, and McWelling Todman, eds.
  1991 The Obeah Act (chapter 52). August 2, 1834. The Revised Laws of the Virgin Islands, vol. 1. Portsmouth, UK: Grosvenor Press.

Trusted, H. H., ed.
  1930 The Obeah Act, 1904 (chapter 64). The Federal Acts of the Leeward Islands, Containing the Acts of the General Legislative Council in Force on the 31st Day of December 1927. Rev. edition, vol. 3. Antigua: Government Printing Office.

Tudor, Daniel T., comp.
  1911 criminal code (chapter 176). January 20, 1897. The Revised Laws of Grenada, vol. 2. London.

Turks and Caicos
  1998 Summary Offences Ordinance (chapter 32). Rev. edition, Showing the Law as of May 15, 1998. Legislation Turks and Caicos Islands. Lexadin. Updated September 12, 2010. http://www.lexadin.nl/wlg/legis/nofr/oeur/lxwetci.htm (accessed December 12, 2010).
  2001 Turks and Caicos Islands Consolidated Index of Statutes and Subsidiary Legislation to 1st January 2001. Compiled at the Faculty of Law Library, University of the West Indies, Barbados. Cave Hill, Barbados: Faculty of Law Library, University of the West Indies.
  2009 Legislation Turks and Caicos Islands. Lexadin. Updated October 19, 2009. http://www.lexadin.nl/wlg/legis/nofr/oeur/lxwetci.htm (accessed March 11, 2010).

Turner, Victor
  1964 Witchcraft and Sorcery: Taxonomy versus Dynamics. Africa: Journal of the International African Institute 34:314–325.

Waddell, Hope Masterson
  1863 Twenty-Nine Years in the West Indies and Central Africa. London: Nelson.

Walker, David M.
  1980 The Oxford Companion to Law. Oxford: Clarendon Press.

Warner-Lewis, Maureen
  1977 The Nkuyu: Spirit Messengers of the Kumina. Savacou 13:61–66.
  2003 Central Africa in the Caribbean. Kingston: University of the West Indies Press.

Watson, Karl
  1979 The Civilized Island, Barbados: A Social History, 1750–1816. Ellerton, Barbados: Karl Watson.

Watts, David
  1987 The West Indies: Patterns of Development, Culture and Environmental Change since 1492. Cambridge: Cambridge University Press.

Williams, Joseph J.
  1932 Voodoos and Obeahs: Phases of West India Witchcraft. New York: Dial Press.
  1934 Psychic Phenomena of Jamaica. New York: Dial Press.

Wilner, John, ed.
  2007 Wortubuku fu Sranan Tongo / Sranan Tongo–English Dictionary. 5th edition. Summer Institute of Linguistics International. http://www.ethnologue.com/show _work.asp?id=928474510633 (accessed December 7, 2012).

Wilner, John, Ronald Pinas, Hertoch Linger, Arnie Lo-Ning Hing, Tieneke MacBean, and Celita Zebeda-Bent
  1994 Wortubuku fu Sranan Tongo/Sranan Tongo–English Dictionary. Paramaribo: Summer Institute of Linguistics.

Winer, Lise
  2009 Dictionary of the English/Creole of Trinidad and Tobago. Montreal: McGill-Queen's University Press.

Wooding, Charles J.
  1981 Evolving Culture: A Cross-Cultural Study of Suriname, West Africa and the Caribbean. Washington, DC: University Press of America.

Wrong, Hume
  1969[1923] Government of the West Indies. New York: Negro Universities Press.

Young, Jason
  2007 Rituals of Resistance: African Atlantic Religion in Kongo and the Lowcountry South in the Era of Slavery. Baton Rouge: Louisiana State University Press.

Zips, Werner
  2011 Nanny's Asafo Warriors: The Jamaican Maroons' African Experience. Kingston: Ian Randle.

Index

adult suffrage, 53, 42, 60
African beliefs and practices, denigrated, 2, 103
Afro-Caribbean spiritual practices, 14, 105
Akan, 110n5, 111n8
alligator teeth. *See* instruments of obeah
Aluku. *See* Maroon tribes
Ampuku, 31
amulet, 20, 58, 83, 116, 120n12. *See also* instruments of obeah
Anderson, John (special magistrate), 131nn53–54
Anguilla, 19, 73–74, 75; obeah decriminalized, xiii
Antigua, laws, 18, 20, 21, 23, 46
Antoine, Rose-Marie Belle, 43
Asante, 5, 111n8. *See also* Ashanti
Ashanti, 9, 10

Bahamas: laws, 18, 19, 20, 21, 23, 66; obeah beliefs in, 126n28; Police Regulations Act, 67. *See also* penal code
balm yard, 38
banishment. *See* transportation

Barbados: laws, xiii, 18, 19, 21, 22, 25; Minor Offences Act, 56, 57; current obeah beliefs, 115n10; newspaper reports on obeah, 28, 115n10
Barbuda, 70
bayi, 110n5, 111n8
Beckwith, Martha, 12, 38
Belize, 19, 23, 25, 95. *See also* British Honduras
Bell, Hesketh, 9
Benoit, Pierre Jacques, 31
Berbice, 60, 61, 115n9, 122n12, 124n21.
Bible and key. *See* instruments of obeah
black magic. *See* magic
blood. *See* instruments of obeah
boa constrictor. *See* snakes
body, human, 64
Bogue plantation (Jamaica), 13
bones, 113n2, 114n2. *See also* instruments of obeah
bottles. *See* instruments of obeah
Brathwaite, Kamau, 28
Bridgens, Richard, 35

167

British Guiana, 18, 23, 24, 60, 61;
  Willem, reputed obeah man, 124n23.
  See also Guyana
British Honduras: laws, 18, 22, 46; influence of Jamaica slave act, 96. *See also* Belize
Browne, Randy, 124n21
brua, 109n1
Bush-Negroes. *See* Maroons, Suriname

Cayman Islands, laws, 20, 100
Carib: in Dominica (Kalinago), 14, 112n12, 129n42; in Guyana, 112n12
Caries, Zacharias George (Moravian missionary), 13
Chireau, Yvonne, 5
Christianity, syncretic forms of, 11–12
Colony of the Leeward Islands. *See* Leeward Islands Federation
Combermere, Governor (of Barbados), 53
comfa, 126n35
confu, 27, 126n35
conjuration, term used in laws, 86, 131n53
conjurer, 110n1
Consolidated Slave Act: Bahamas, 66; Barbados, 55; Dominica, 84; Grenada, 85; Jamaica, 46–49; St. Vincent, 93
cotton tree, 113n2, 114n3, 121n3, 127n40
council, legislative, composition of, 41
Crown colony, 41, 42, 57, 66
Curtin, Philip, 4

dadie, 35, 119n15
decapitation, 22
Demerara, 60
devil, mentioned in laws, 18, 46, 47, 48, 85, 96
disease: caused by obeah, 26–27; cured by obeah, 26–27, 28, 31, 32–33, 38; diagnosed by obeah, 26, 28; mentioned in laws, 59, 64, 67, 69, 70, 76, 77, 84, 89, 90, 92, 93, 98
divination, 26, 36, 55: communal, 114n7; term used in laws, 131n53. *See also* fortune telling; palmistry
doctor: term for obeah practitioners, 5, 27, 58, 81, 82, 92, 93, 115n9, 125n35; West African, 5, 13
dog teeth. *See* instruments of obeah
doll. *See* instruments of obeah
Dominica: current beliefs about obeah, 128n42; laws, 19, 20, 21, 23, 25, 27. *See also* Carib
Doo di Doo bush, 35, 119n15
duppy, 38, 110n2, 111n7, 127n40
duppy catching, 80, 100, 127n40. *See also* shadow catching
Dutch Guiana. *See* Suriname

egg shells. *See* instruments of obeah
Essequibo, 60
ethnographic research, 3
Evans-Pritchard, E. E., 8
execution, 22, 46, 47, 54, 83, 102, 114n4. *See also* punishment

feathers. *See* instruments of obeah
Federation of the West Indies, 57, 70
flogging. *See* whipping
fortune-telling, mentioned in the laws, 19, 26, 27, 50, 55, 56, 65, 72, 75, 84, 86, 87, 104 *See also* divination; palmistry
franchise, 41
fraud, 18, 19, 52, 60, 63, 75, 104
freedmen. *See* free people of color
free people of color, 54, 55, 114n4

Gerbner, Katharine, 13, 112n11
Gibson, Kean, 126n35
glass. *See* instruments of obeah

grave dirt. *See* instruments of obeah
Greene, Jack P., 120n1
Grenada: laws, 18, 20, 21, 22, 46, 87;
  Pierre (free black), 129n44
Guyana, laws, 23, 25, 65, 125n26. *See also*
  British Guiana

hair, female, cutting of, 89, 114n6, 130n49
Hall, C. G., 43
Hans (slave in Berbice), 61
healing. *See* disease
Herskovits, Melville, 12
Higman, B. W., 41
Honychurch, Lennox, 129n42
hoodoo, 110n1
House of Assembly, composition of, 41

Ibibio, 6
Igbo, 6
illness. *See* disease
instruments of obeah, 19, 20, 21, 45, 67,
  69, 91, 95, 113n1; blood, 20, 46, 67, 86,
  89; bones, 20, 38, 67; grave dirt, 20, 46,
  86, 113n2; egg shells, 20, 46; feathers, 20,
  46; glass, 20, 47, 48, 49, 93; bible and
  key, 20, 92, 130n53; bottles, 20, 46; doll
  (image), 20; parrot beaks, 20, 46, 47, 48,
  86, 113n2; rum, 20, 46; skull, 20, 38, 64,
  113n2, 114n2. *See also* amulet; teeth
jail. *See* punishment
Jamaica, 13, 16, 19: Christianity, syncretic
  forms of, 10; Crown Colony status, 45;
  laws, 18, 20, 21, 22, 24, 25, 52; newspaper reports of obeah, 28, 110n2

Kalinago. *See* Carib, Dominica
Kembois (Quimbois), 18, 89, 129n48
kill-devil, 118n8
Konadu, Kwasi, 110n5
Kromanti (Kumanti), 31, 126n35

Kromanti language, 126n35
Kromanti Play, 111n7, 127n40
kumfu-man, 126n35
Kumina, 111n7, 127n40
Kwasi (Quasi), 33, 119n12
Kwasimukamba, 119n12

Leeward Islands Federation, 23, 68, 70
Loa (Lwa), 7, 111n7
Locomen, 116n3, 117n3, 119n12
Lowenthal, David, 7

magic: black, 7, 14, 38; definitions of, 7–8
Mama Snekie, 32
Mantz, Jeffrey, 128n42
Maroons, 25: in Guianas, 36; in Jamaica,
  126n35, 127n40; in Suriname, 12, 14,
  110n1, 111n7, 117n6, 119n12. *See also*
  Maroon tribes
Maroon tribes: Aluku, 12, 36, 111n7,
  112n12, 115n7; Boni, 12; Ndyuka, 111n7;
  Saramaka, 13, 114–15n7
Marshall, Woodville, 120n1
Middleton, John, 8
missionaries, 3, 10–11, 13
Montserrat, laws, 20, 23, 25, 50, 79. *See
  also* penal code
Moravians, 13
Morgan, Philip, 7
Mutilation of corpse, 22
myal, 9, 11, 24, 49, 78, 80, 100, 112n9;
  contrasted with obeah, 10, 11, 50, 51, 52
myalism. *See* myal

Negro doctor, 115n9. *See also* doctor
Nettleford, Rex, 108
Nevis, laws, 19, 23, 25, 75. *See also* St.
  Kitts
Newton, Velma, 123n16
Nketia, J. H., 111n5, 111n8

oath, 35–36, 86
Obayifo (Obayifoo), 111n5, 111n8
obeah doctor. *See* doctor
obeah: as explanation for evil or bad luck, 27; decriminalized, xiii, 91; definition of term, 1–2, 4, 7, 17, 18, 20, 106, 107; ethnographic research on, 3, 11, 104, 128n42; negative views of, 6, 14, 17, 18, 26; origin and early use of term, 4–5, 6, 9, 12, 13, 16; positive views and meanings of, 5, 6, 12, 13, 14, 27–28, 31, 38, 112n12, 129n42; practitioners, payment for service, 104, 105; printed (or written) materials promoting or used in, prohibitions against, 24–25, 52, 64, 70, 73, 77, 80, 83–84, 91, 95, 100; scholarship on, xiii, 3, 5, 6, 9, 10, 11, 12, 14 17, 28, 103, 105, 112n10; terms in non-Anglophone Caribbean, 109n1. *See also* disease; doctor; instruments of obeah; myal; punishment; slave community
obeah laws, xiii; format of, 17; enforcement of, infrequent, 23, 85, 103, 125n26; similarity throughout Caribbean, 102
obia. *see* obeah
obiama, 114n7
Old Representative System (ORS), defined, 40–41

palmistry: in 1824 English vagrancy act, 19, 43, 104; in vagrancy laws of Antigua, 72; Bahamas, 66; Barbados, 56; British Guiana, 63, 65; British Honduras, 96, 97; Caymans, 100; Dominica, 83, 84; Grenada, 86; Jamaica, 19, 49, 50; Leeward Islands, 69, 70; Montserrat, 80; St. Kitts and Nevis, 76, 77; St. Lucia, 18, 89, 88; St. Vincent, 93, 94, 95; Trinidad, 58, 123n19; Turks and Caicos, 98; in West

Indian vagrancy laws, 19, 43
Papa (Afro-Surinamese religion), 31, 117n3
papa gadu, 31
papa obia, 31
papa sineki, 31
Paramaribo, 31, 119n11
parrot beaks. *See* instruments of obeah
Patchett, Keith, 21
Paton, Diana, 4, 18, 19, 114n4
Patterson, Orlando, 6, 12
penal code: Bahamas, 20, 67, 68; Montserrat, 78, 80, 81
penalties. *See* punishment
piáy (pyai, piyai), 14, 112n12, 129nn42–43
pillory, 71
poison, 20–21, 47, 48, 49, 54, 55, 72, 82, 93, 114n3
potion, love, 28
presidential legislatures, 68
Price, Richard, 114n7; and Sally, 116n3
property, stolen, discovery of, 27, 71, 89, 90, 93. *See also* thief (and theft)
prostitute, 49, 56, 123n19
protector of slaves, Berbice, 124n21
psychogenic illness, 104, 122n10
punishment, for conviction under obeah laws in: Antigua, 71; Bahamas, 67; Barbados, 54, 55; Berbice, 124nn21–23; British Guiana, 24, 61, 62; British Honduras, 96; Dominica, 82, 83; Grenada, 86; Jamaica, 47–52; St. Kitts, 76; St. Lucia, 91, 114n6, 130n50; St. Vincent, 93, 94; Trinidad, 58, 59, 60, 123n19; for consulting obeah practitioner, 105; for practicing obeah, 21–23; reduction of harshness and severity of, in the laws, 40, 102. *See also* execution; solitary confinement; transportation; whipping

punishment record book, Berbice, 124nn21–23

Quasi. *See* Kwasi
Quimbois. *See* Kembois

Raboteau, Albert, 7
rebellion. *See* revolt, slave
revolt, slave, 46, 54, 72; 1816 in Barbados, 122n12
rogue and vagabond: mentioned in vagrancy laws, 59, 62, 63, 64, 67, 90; offenses included with, 19, 43, 50, 56, 58, 63, 66, 72, 76, 83, 88, 94, 96, 98, 120n2, 123n19
rum. *See* instruments of obeah

St. Christopher. *See* St. Kitts
St. Kitts, laws, 19, 23, 25, 75. *See also* Nevis
St. Lucia, laws, 23, 24, 25, 41; obeah decriminalized, xiii
St. Vincent, laws, 19, 21, 22, 23, 24, 25, 27
sanctions. *See* punishment
Saramaka. *See* Maroon tribes
shadow catching, 127n40. *See also* duppy catching
sibá, 13
sickness. *See* disease
sieve. *See* sieve and shears
sieve and shears, 20, 92, 130n53
silk cotton tree. *See* cotton tree
skeleton, 38
skull. *See* instruments of obeah
slave community: influence of obeah practitioners, 25–26; positive role of obeah, 13, 110n3
Small Charges Act, 69, 73, 78
snakes: in Afro-Surinamese religion, 31, 33, 118n9; boa constrictor, 31, 118n9

snake gods, 117n3
solitary confinement, 59, 62, 64, 70, 73, 89, 90
sorcery. *See* witchcraft
Spanish law, 57
spell doctor, 58. *See also* doctor
Sranan, 117n7
Stedman, John, 116n3, 118n9
Stewart, Dianne, 11
Stewart, Robert, 12
stolen property. *See* property, stolen
Summary Convictions Ordinance, Trinidad, 1868, 59
Summary Procedure Ordinance, St. Lucia, 88
supernatural harming, 103
Suriname (Dutch Guiana), 31, 32; obeah in, 12, 31

Tacky's Rebellion, 46
taki-taki, 117–18n7
Taylor, Douglas, 14
Taylor, Jeremy, 53
teeth, as instruments of obeah: alligator, 20, 46, 48, 20, 86; cat, 113n1; dog, 20, 46, 47, 48, 86
thief (and theft), 110n2: discovery of, 35, 71, 87, 117n3, 131n53; identification of, 33, 35; protection against, 14. *See also* property, stolen
Thistlewood, Thomas, 110n2
Tobago, 57. *See also* Trinidad
transportation (banishment), 22, 46, 47, 48, 49, 54, 55, 66, 102, 114n4
Trinidad, 35, 41: laws, 17, 20, 22, 23, 25, 27; newspaper reports of obeah, 110n2; obeah decriminalized, xiii
Trinidad and Tobago, laws, 25
Twi, 5

Vagrancy Act, England (1824), 39, 49, 56, 96; influence on West Indies, 19, 43, 104, 120n2

vagrancy acts. *See* vagrancy laws

vagrancy laws, 16–17, 42–44: of Antigua, 72; Bahamas, 66–67, 98, 125n27; Barbados, 56–57; British Guiana, 61–62; British Honduras, 96–97; Dominica, 83; Grenada, 86; Jamaica, 19, 49, 56; Leeward Islands, 69; St. Kitts, 76; St. Lucia, 88; St. Vincent, 93, 94; Trinidad, 58, 59; Turks and Caicos, 99; offenses included, 19, 120n2, 123n19. *See also* Vagrancy Act, England (1824)

Virgin Islands, British, laws, 23, 25, 50

Vodu (Afro-Surinamese religion), 31

Water Mama (Watra Mama), 32, 33, 116n3

Watson, Karl, 122n9

Watts, David, 7

Wayana (Suriname), 112n112

West Indies Federation. *See* Federation of the West Indies

whipping, 22, 50, 51, 55, 58, 63, 64, 72, 75, 82, 83, 90; obeah protection against, 125n29

Williams, Joseph J., 9, 10, 11, 12

Winter, Edward, 8

Winti, 117n3

Winty Play, 117n3

Wisi, 13, 113n12

witchcraft, 5, 6, 8, 9, 18, 20, 54, 62, 80, 83, 106: accusations of, 103, 104; contrasted with sorcery, 8; defined, 8, 18

Woods, Sylvester, 38

www.ingramcontent.com/pod-product-compliance
Lightning Source LLC
Chambersburg PA
CBHW021810220426
43662CB00006B/260